Code with Java 21

A practical approach for building
robust and efficient applications

Aaron Ploetz

www.bpbonline.com

First published: 2024

Published by BPB Online
WeWork
119 Marylebone Road
London NW1 5PU

UK | UAE | INDIA | SINGAPORE

ISBN 978-93-55519-993

www.bpbonline.com

Dedicated to

My children:
Khadiya, **Avery**, **Emily**, *and* **Victoria**
&
My godson:
Tim

The road to success
is paved with the footsteps of those who did not give up
and the regrets of those who did.

About the Author

Aaron Ploetz is a developer advocate at *DataStax*. He has been a professional software developer since 1997 and has a successful history of leading DBA and DevOps teams for both startups and Fortune 50 enterprises. He has been named an MVP for Apache Cassandra® three times, and has presented at multiple events; including the Fintech keynote at *Data Day Mexico City 2023*. Aaron frequently answers StackOverflow questions from other developers, and has previously authored books on distributed databases. He earned a B.S. in Management/Computer Systems from the *University of Wisconsin-Whitewater*, and an M.S. in Software Engineering (Database Technology emphasis) from *Regis University*. When not writing or coding, Aaron enjoys fishing, retro video gaming, and skijoring. Aaron and his wife, Coriene, live with their four children in the Twin Cities area.

About the Reviewer

Otavio Santana is a passionate architect and software engineer focused on cloud and Java technologies. He has deep expertise in polyglot persistence and high-performance applications in finance, social media, and e-commerce.

He has contributed to the Java and the open source ecosystem in several ways. Otavio has helped in the direction and objectives of the Java platform since Java 8 as a JCP executive member, besides being a committer and leader in several open-source products and specifications.

He is recognized for his open source contributions and has received many awards, including all JCP Awards categories and the Duke's Choice Award, to name a few. Otávio is also a distinguished Java Champions and Oracle ACE program member.

Acknowledgement

I would like to recognize my co-workers, Cédrick Lunven and Mary Grygleski, who were extremely helpful and central in influencing me to get back into Java. I would also like to recognize Otavio Santana, Sharat Chander, and countless others who made the Java community so welcoming and encouraging.

I would also like to thank Ursula Kellmann, who was taken from us too soon. She was an amazing mentor who taught me much about Java and was a brilliant example of what a true expert in their craft should aspire to be.

Finally, I would love to acknowledge my wife, Coriene, who continually inspires me to take on new challenges and to be a better version of myself.

Preface

Learning software development has always been a treacherous path. When I began my journey, books were the only medium available. When I started learning to program BASIC on my Tandy 1000, I was first introduced to Java during my final year at the *University of Wisconsin–Whitewater (1998)*. I loved the *code once, execute everywhere* message that Java trumpeted. In the 1990s, that aspect was a really big deal.

In the early 2010s, I wrote a lot of Java code while working on the *Mid-Tier Cassandra* team at *W.W. Grainger*. This was my first introduction to enterprise-level Java. The database behind our service layer (Apache Cassandra®) was also written in Java, so I was quite literally *thrown into the deep end* of troubleshooting the exceptions and nuances of Java 7.

After spending the better part of the next decade as a Cassandra DBA, I finally returned to (near) full-time Java coding in 2021. It was a breath of fresh air. I loved how much Java had evolved up through version 17. By that time, I had written two books about NoSQL databases. The more I worked with Java, the more I wanted to write a book about it.

There is so much Java code running in the world today. It runs across billions of devices and powers everything from video games to e-commerce websites that generate billions of dollars. There is no denying that knowing how to code in Java has become a valuable skill.

Today, one of the biggest obstacles for aspiring developers (aside from choosing a language) is getting a development environment installed and configured. By contrast, many of the computers that were common in the 1980s made it very easy to get started programming. Users were often only a few key presses away from getting into a software development environment.

Some early home computers (like the Tandy Color Computers and Apple II series) put the user at a BASIC programming prompt immediately after booting. These early machines were asking to be programmed by default! On the other hand, modern computers (especially phones and tablets) do not. Building a suitable programming environment on modern computers is often a struggle. This is why the first chapter of this book spends time on installing and configuring the Eclipse IDE.

However, making computers programmable again is more than just navigating technical obstacles. It is a culture shift. It is about looking at your device, and instead of asking, *What can it do for me*, it is asking, *What can I build with it?* It is this mindset that leads to a lifetime of learning.

Ultimately, my motivation for writing this book is to help flatten the learning curve for software developers. I believe that Java is the right language to do just that.

This book is structured to gradually introduce different aspects of writing code in Java, with each chapter building on lessons previously covered.

Chapter 1: Getting to Know Java – This chapter provides a simple introduction to Java. It also walks through configuring a development environment, including installing tools such as a dependency manager and an IDE. This chapter also discusses **object-oriented programming (OOP)** and introduces new features of Java 21.

Chapter 2: Fundamental Programming Structures – This chapter discusses some basic building blocks of Java's syntax. It starts with the obligatory hello world program and progresses to reading input, error handling, and controlling the flow of program logic. After covering the basics, it moves on to working with files and Java-specific ways of building methods and constructors.

Chapter 3: Strings, Characters, and Regular Expressions – This chapter covers different ways to work with and process text data. While starting with a simple example using ASCII character art, it progresses into showing how to use some of the more advanced methods included with the Java String class. It finishes by introducing regular expressions and showing how to use them in practical, real-world examples.

Chapter 4: Arrays, Collections, and Records – This chapter introduces the reader to different structures that can be used to store data in memory. While focusing on different concepts and use cases with arrays, lists, sets, and maps, this chapter also discusses records and introduces sequenced collections (new with Java 21).

Chapter 5: Arithmetic Operations – This chapter offers insight into how computers handle arithmetic at primitive levels, including the difference between integer and floating point operations. It also uses the deterministic nature of arithmetic to make a small introduction to unit testing.

Chapter 6: Common Data Structures – This chapter takes the reader through the process of using Java to build data structures like stacks, queues, and different kinds of linked lists. It also walks through building a binary tree and executing simple data searches.

Chapter 7: Working with Databases – This chapter shows how to build Java applications that store data in databases. It also introduces the PostgreSQL and Apache Cassandra® databases, showing how to build simple data models and execute common CQL and SQL commands.

Chapter 8: Web Applications – This chapter discusses building restful web services and full-stack web applications in Java. It also introduces the Spring and Vaadin frameworks, showing how to leverage them to build fully-featured web applications.

Chapter 9: Graphics in Java – This chapter uses an example-led approach to display graphics and animation. It also walks through building a classic arcade game in Java.

Chapter 10: Final Java Project – This chapter is a culmination of many topics covered in the previous chapters and shows how to use them to build a Movie data application. Vector search is introduced as a final new topic, giving the readers a simple way to build out a movie recommendation service.

Code Bundle and Coloured Images

Please follow the link to download the
Code Bundle and the *Coloured Images* of the book:

https://rebrand.ly/nkskce0

The code bundle for the book is also hosted on GitHub at
https://github.com/bpbpublications/Code-with-Java-21
In case there's an update to the code, it will be updated on the existing GitHub repository.

We have code bundles from our rich catalogue of books and videos available at
https://github.com/bpbpublications. Check them out!

Errata

We take immense pride in our work at BPB Publications and follow best practices to ensure the accuracy of our content to provide with an indulging reading experience to our subscribers. Our readers are our mirrors, and we use their inputs to reflect and improve upon human errors, if any, that may have occurred during the publishing processes involved. To let us maintain the quality and help us reach out to any readers who might be having difficulties due to any unforeseen errors, please write to us at :

errata@bpbonline.com

Your support, suggestions and feedbacks are highly appreciated by the BPB Publications' Family.

Did you know that BPB offers eBook versions of every book published, with PDF and ePub files available? You can upgrade to the eBook version at www.bpbonline. com and as a print book customer, you are entitled to a discount on the eBook copy. Get in touch with us at :

business@bpbonline.com for more details.

At **www.bpbonline.com**, you can also read a collection of free technical articles, sign up for a range of free newsletters, and receive exclusive discounts and offers on BPB books and eBooks.

Piracy

If you come across any illegal copies of our works in any form on the internet, we would be grateful if you would provide us with the location address or website name. Please contact us at **business@bpbonline.com** with a link to the material.

If you are interested in becoming an author

If there is a topic that you have expertise in, and you are interested in either writing or contributing to a book, please visit **www.bpbonline.com**. We have worked with thousands of developers and tech professionals, just like you, to help them share their insights with the global tech community. You can make a general application, apply for a specific hot topic that we are recruiting an author for, or submit your own idea.

Reviews

Please leave a review. Once you have read and used this book, why not leave a review on the site that you purchased it from? Potential readers can then see and use your unbiased opinion to make purchase decisions. We at BPB can understand what you think about our products, and our authors can see your feedback on their book. Thank you!

For more information about BPB, please visit **www.bpbonline.com**.

Join our book's Discord space

Join the book's Discord Workspace for Latest updates, Offers, Tech happenings around the world, New Release and Sessions with the Authors:

https://discord.bpbonline.com

Table of Contents

CHAPTER 1
Getting to Know Java

Introduction

Welcome to **Code with Java 21**! Whether you are a new or experienced programmer, this book will help you to understand and effectively wield one of the most widely used programming languages in the world. In addition to covering the fundamental aspects of Java, we will also discuss the new features delivered in Java version 21 and show you how to use them effectively.

Java 21 is a **Long-Term Support** (**LTS**) release with support through 2031. This book is designed not only to help you learn, but also to be a reference for the long term. It contains code designed to guide you through each example and help you become a successful programmer.

> **Note:** The terms programmer, software developer, and coder are often used interchangeably.

Structure

In this chapter, we will discuss the following topics:

- Advantages of building applications with Java.
- Examine the different components of a Java development environment

- Discuss common tools used to compliment the Java development process
- Introduce the principles of object-oriented programming
- Preview the new features in Java 21

Objectives

The goal of this book is to inspire you to build the next generation of Java applications. In this chapter, we will examine the Java language at a high level, aiming to provide enough detail to get started. By the end of the chapter, we will understand what makes Java different from other languages and how to leverage it to write powerful applications.

Why code with Java?

Java is everywhere; it is running on billions of devices around the world. It is also used by Fortune 500 enterprises to build services and applications that help them make billions of dollars each year. Needless to say, there is a high demand for Java developers, and it is likely to continue for a long time.

There are also several types of machines capable of running Java, including (but not limited to) the following:

- **Personal Computers** (**PCs**) for both home and business use
- Mobile devices
- Gaming consoles
- Embedded devices

Java's core properties of platform independence, versatility, and security have made it one of the most popular programming languages in the world. They also make it easy to get help with, as learning material for Java can be quickly found on *YouTube, LinkedIn,* and many other websites.

Whether you are interested in learning to program as a hobby or as a skill that can lead to a successful career, Java is a great skill to have.

Configuring your environment

Before we can begin writing Java programs, we need to ensure that our environment is properly built and configured. Here are the things we will need to be successful:

- A computer running Windows, Linux, or MacOS
- A **Java Runtime Environment** (**JRE**)
- An **Integrated Development Environment** (**IDE**)
- A Java dependency manager

- A source control platform

While this book makes some accommodations for developers new to Java, it is intended for those who have at least an intermediate level of overall programming experience. While an overview of configuring a development environment will be provided, exhaustive detail on every possible configuration is beyond the scope of this book. It is assumed that the reader will install and configure the necessary tools that are most familiar to them.

Operating System

One of the main advantages of Java is that it is easily portable. That means the same Java code can run on Windows, Linux, or MacOS without any changes. Likewise, it does not matter which **Operating System (OS)** platform the Java code is written on. As a programmer, it is important for you to know your OS well and to understand its nuances and differences from other OSs when appropriate.

For example, it is important to remember that Windows does not care about uppercase characters in filenames, while Linux and MacOS do. Windows also has different file line endings than Linux and MacOS. These things can pose challenges when building applications that work with files and other OS-level aspects.

Java Runtime Environment

Another part of the development environment that is required for Java is the Java Runtime Environment. This package provides all the available libraries required for your Java code to run. This book is written to focus on Java 21, which is the version of Java that should be installed to get the examples in this book to run properly.

Java Development Kit

It is also important to remember that downloads are available for both the JRE and the **Java Development Kit (JDK)**. While the JRE provides a complete environment for Java programs to run, the JDK provides *both* a JRE and additional tools for developers to build and configure Java programs. As we will need the extra development tools, a JDK is required to follow the examples put forth in this book.

JDK vendors and editions

There are several software companies that build their JDKs, including *Microsoft*, *Oracle*, and *IBM*. Their builds of the JDK are usually intended for corporate use, and most require a paid license or contract to use.

Many vendors also produce different editions based on the intended uses and underlying infrastructures:

- **Micro Edition:** A smaller build of the JDK, intended for embedded systems and other devices with a smaller amount of compute resources.
- **Standard Edition:** A middle-tiered build focusing on developer machines and workstation-grade hardware.
- **Enterprise Edition:** A full-fledged build targeting enterprises and high-throughput systems.

For this book, we will use the OpenJDK, a free and open-source version of the Java Development Kit- Standard Edition. The latest versions of the OpenJDK (version 21) for various Operating Systems and architectures can be found at **https://jdk.java.net/21/.**

Installation

You can skip this step if your IDE installation comes with a JDK. Otherwise, OpenJDK downloads come as a compressed file; usually a tarball or a ZIP file. The location that the download needs to be uncompressed to differs by operating system. However, it needs to be put into a location *pathed-in* to the environment.

> **Note: You will likely need administrator or super user permissions to install a JDK.**

You can run this command to verify your JDK installation or to see the version you have installed:

```
java -version
```

If there is already a JRE or JDK installed, you should see an output similar to this:

```
openjdk version "21-ea" 2023-09-19

OpenJDK Runtime Environment (build 21-ea+16-1326)

OpenJDK 64-Bit Server VM (build 21-ea+16-1326, mixed mode, sharing)
```

As the focus of this book is Java 21, the major version listed will need to be **21**.

Windows

The standard location for the JDK to reside is in the **Program Files** directory. Set the `JAVA_HOME` environment variable to that location. Additionally, you may need to add it to the `PATH` environment variable.

MacOS

The same approach can certainly be taken on a Mac. After uncompressing the tarball, add its location to the `PATH` environment variable (in the `.bashrc` file).

Additionally, there is a Homebrew formula available for the OpenJDK, which takes care of the install and environment variable config. It can be installed from the terminal as follows:

```
brew install openjdk@21
```

Linux

Likewise, the Linux tarball can be uncompressed and location-referenced via the **PATH** variable in the **.bashrc** file. Additionally, the delivered Linux package managers can also access the required OpenJDK repositories. The exact command used depends on the flavor of Linux.

If you are running on a Red Hat Linux derivative (for example, *Fedora, CentOS*), the OpenJDK can be installed with the **yum** package manager:

```
sudo yum install java-21-openjdk
```

Additionally, for those of you running on a Debian Linux derivative (for example, *Ubuntu, Cinnamon*), the OpenJDK can be installed with the **apt** package manager:

```
sudo apt install openjdk-21-jdk
```

It is important to note that if you have multiple JDKs/JREs installed, you may need to change your default version. This can be done by updating the system alternatives:

```
sudo update-alternatives --config java
```

Version management

Some developers may have multiple JREs/JDKs installed on their developer workstations. It is highly recommended that you use a Java environment manager. For example, MacOS and Linux users can install a tool like **jEnv** by heading to this website: **https://www.jenv. be/**.

There is also a jEnv for Windows, available in the following GitHub repository: **https:// github.com/FelixSelter/JEnv-for-Windows**.

Integrated Development Environment

Before you can write code in any language (including Java), you will need a special tool. At the very minimum, a text editor like *Notepad*, *Sublime*, or *Vim* is required. However, most developers prefer using an Integrated Development Environment.

An IDE is more than just a code editor and gives the programmer access to tools designed to make writing code easier. Usually, this allows them to easily and quickly build and compile their code, interact with source control, select a different JDK, and set specific environment variables or libraries. Here is a short list of popular IDEs:

- Eclipse
- IntelliJ IDEA
- NetBeans
- VS Code

Most developers are very particular about the IDE they use. The examples in this book will certainly work from any IDE, so you can use whichever you choose.

> **Note: As mentioned earlier, some IDEs (like Eclipse) are bundled with a JDK installation. Not having to mess around with another installation is an attractive option to many developers.**

Java dependency management

Managing library dependencies can be tricky in any language. The Java ecosystem has tools available to help with this process. The two most popular dependency management tools are Gradle and Maven.

The examples in this book and out in the corresponding GitHub repositories were created using Maven. You are free to use whichever you choose, and attempts will be made to include code when appropriate.

Source control

Git is the most widely used source control tool in the world, and it will be used for this book as well. All the examples for this book can be found in the GitHub repository of the book.

Readers who wish to take full advantage of all the available resources for learning are encouraged to create an account at **https://github.com**. Additionally, it is recommended to install Git locally for access to various commands.

> **Note: Some IDEs have a *plugin* or other bundled integration with Git, eliminating the need to install it separately.**

Git installation

If you are working on a Mac or a Windows PC, GitHub has automated installation packages available at **https://github.com/git-guides/install-git**.

Mac users can also install Git via Homebrew by executing the following:

```
brew install git
```

Linux users can install Git using their respective flavor's package manager. If you are running on a Red Hat Linux derivative, the OpenJDK can be installed with the **dnf** package manager:

```
sudo dnf install git-all
```

Or for the **yum** package manager:

```
sudo yum install git-all
```

Additionally, for those of you running on a Debian Linux derivative (for example, *Ubuntu, Cinnamon*), the OpenJDK can be installed with the **apt** package manager:

```
sudo apt-get install git-all
```

Run the following command to verify your Git installation:

```
git --version
```

If Git is installed, the output should look something like this:

```
git version 2.32.0
```

Object-oriented programming

We cannot talk about Java without first discussing **object-oriented programming** (**OOP**). In this section, we will introduce the four main principles of OOP. Additionally, we will cover some of the advantages and disadvantages of OOP, and we will look at how these principles will guide us as we progress through the chapters.

Essentially, OOP is a paradigm in which software design is driven by data and how it is classified as objects. In contrast, coding in non-OOP languages is usually driven by (*Gillis, Lewis 2021*) functions and logic.

The basic building block of OOP is a class. A class is essentially a template for an object we want to create and use later. In Java, each class is usually in its own file.

Classes generally contain methods and properties. Methods are compartmentalized blocks of code that are usually designed to perform a specific function. Properties are variables exposed to be read and modified only by calling special methods in the class.

Here are the four main principles of OOP:

- Encapsulation
- Inheritance
- Abstraction
- Polymorphism

Let us take a quick look at each of these.

Encapsulation

Java has a concept of **scope**. All variables have one of three scope classifications:

- **Private:** A variable that can only be modified by code within its own class.
- **Protected:** A variable that can be modified by code within its own package.
- **Public:** A variable that can be modified by code from anywhere.

> **Note: If a variable is declared *without* one of the scope classifications, Java assumes that it has a package-protected scope, where access is only allowed from within its current package.**

The idea behind encapsulation is that an object's data and methods are contained in a single unit. Properties within an object are privately-scoped variables that cannot be directly modified or read from outside the object. The way they are accessed is through specifically designed, publicly-scoped methods known as **getters** and **setters**. As they sound, a getter is used when another method wants to read or **get** the value of a property. Likewise, a setter is called when another method wants to change or **set** the value of a property.

From the perspective of a programmer, this allows us complete control over how our object properties are accessed. This approach can be advantageous when troubleshooting or debugging. If we want to know how or where a property is being changed, we have to simply look at its setter method and search for that in the suspect classes.

Basically, encapsulation is a development approach that imposes access restrictions to ensure that our object properties are being accessed safely.

Inheritance

The principle of inheritance allows classes to be derived from others. This is sometimes called a **parent | child** relationship, where the child class (also called the **derived** class) inherits methods and properties from the parent class (also called **base** or **super** class).

For example, an online retailer (sometimes called an **e-tailer**) wants to sell products online. Those products could differ significantly, in that they could be movies, books, snacks, or bicycles. The properties of each of those products will be different, but for the purposes of selling them online, there are some things that they share, such as name, category, and price.

To that end, we could build a base class called **Product**, which contains the **name**, **category**, and **price** properties (along with appropriate getter/setter methods). A sample **Product** class (with public accessor methods for the **name, category**, and **price** properties) is shown here:

```
class Product {
```

```java
    private String name;

    private String category;

    private BigDecimal price;

    public String getName() {

        return this.name;

    }

    public void setName(String name) {

        this.name = name;

    }

    public String getCategory() {

        return this.category;

    }

    public void setCategory(String category) {

        this.category = category;

    }

    public BigDecimal getPrice() {

        return this.price;

    }

    public void setPrice(BigDecimal price) {

        this.price = price;

    }

}
```

Each product type could then inherit the **Product** class (using the **extends** keyword). Here, we will show an example for movies:

```java
public class Movie extends Product {

    private String title;

    private int lengthInMinutes;


    public String getTitle() {
```

```
        return this.title;

    }

    public void setTitle(String title) {

        this.title = title;

    }

    public int getLengthInMinutes() {

        return this.category;

    }

    public void setLengthInMinutes(int category) {

        this.category = category;

    }

}
```

As the **Movie** class is inheriting **Product** as its base class, all objects of type **Movie** would have properties from both classes. With multiple different types of products in our online store, this saves us from having to build those base properties into each of the individual classes.

Abstraction

Abstraction refers to the idea of hiding implementation details while exposing only the essential methods of a class. Implementing abstraction in Java is done using interfaces and abstract classes. These define methods that must be implemented by the inheriting **subclass**, while also masking the details of that implementation.

Let us go back to our online retailer example, where we previously talked about building a base **Product** class. There are additional benefits to having all our product type classes inherit a base or abstract class. One is that many different types of products can be treated as **Product** objects because they inherited the **Product** class.

It would not matter if the product in question was in fact a **Movie** or **Book** class; it would still have those **Product** class properties so that it could be sold online. The best part about that is we could turn over the **Book** class to a different development team. They could just focus on leveraging the **Book** class to do book-specific things, without having to understand how their books are added to a customer's shopping cart; that is for the **Product** class to handle.

Here is a possible example showing how abstraction helps a **Movie** object get added to a customer's shopping cart:

```java
private User user;

public void movieShopping() {

    Movie movie = getMovieByTitle("The Empire Strikes Back");

    addToCart(movie, 1);

}

public void addToCart(Product product, int qty) {

    cart.add(user.getId, product, qty);

}
```

As you can see, an object of type **Movie** can be sent to the **addToCart()** method because it inherits the **Product** class. This is meant to show the advantages of **data abstraction** and how it can be used in a simple example.

Now, let us assume that our online store is part of a large retailer, with hundreds of developers. In the preceding example, we leveraged data abstraction to provide a separation of duties between the different development teams that handle the different product types.

If we look in the code for the **addToCart()** method, we can see that it simply calls the **cart** object's **add()** method. Let us take a look at what the **add()** method does:

```java
public Cart() {

    CartDAL cartDAL;


    public void add(UUID userId, Product product, int qty) {

        CartLineItem line = new CartLineItem();

        line.userId = userId;

        line.productId = product.getId;

        line.qty = qty;


        cartDAL.save(userId, product, qty);

    }

}
```

In this scenario, the developers for our website only need to worry about calling the **cart** object's **add()** method. They do not need to worry about what that method does. However, the **Cart Team's** developers build and maintain the **Cart Service**. Inside the `Cart Service`, the `add()` method is defined to take its parameters and instantiate a `CartLineItem` object, set its properties, and then save it into the **Data Access Layer** (**DAL**). This is an example of **method abstraction**, as the **Cart Team** has abstracted the details of persisting the data in the cart away from the **Website Team**.

Polymorphism

So, the concept of polymorphism is taken from a greek translation of *one thing being many*. Essentially, this is what allows certain methods and objects to take on characteristics of others. In Java, there are two kinds of polymorphism: dynamic and static.

Static polymorphism

Static polymorphism is a compile-time concept, often seen when *overloading* a method. Now you might ask simple questions like, *What does it mean to overload a method?* and *why would we want to do that?*

This is one of the features that showcases Java's versatility. Let us assume that we are building a math library. As a part of that library, we want to be able to add two integers together, so we build a method that looks like this:

```java
public int add (int num1, int num2) {

    return num1 + num2;

}
```

Simple enough, right?

Well, what if the two numbers that we wanted to add together are **BigDecimals**? In that case, the **add** method will not work due to the types not matching. The solution is to overload the **add** method by writing another **add** method that works with **BigDecimals**:

```java
public BigDecimal add (BigDecimal num1, BigDecimal num2) {

    return num1.add(num2);

}
```

> Note: Numerics of type BigDecimal do not work with the standard plus (+) operator, so we need to use their add method. We will look at this in detail in *Chapter 5, Arithmetic Operations.*

We could create another one if we had to. Maybe our user wants to be able to add two doubles together? We could allow that by overloading **add** one more time:

```java
public double add (double num1, double num2) {
```

```
    return num1 + num2;

}
```

Following the concept of polymorphism, overloading allows us to expose simple **add** methods to our users without them having to care too much about what numeric types they are working with. They simply call the **add** method with two matching types, and our class handles the rest.

Dynamic polymorphism

Polymorphism is seen in a dynamic, runtime context when overriding an inherited method. Simply put, overriding is the act of writing a new method with the same name as an inherited method so that the new method takes precedence. Now, we will look at an example.

Let us consider a car as our base class. All cars have doors, and all doors require a means by which to open them. So, our base **Car** class will have a method for opening the doors. As all **car** objects inherit the base **Car** class, they all get the default **openDoor** method:

```
public void openDoor() {

    door.open("outward");

}
```

Now, let us assume that we are building a **McLarenP1** class. As the McLaren P1's doors open upward and not out (like most cars), we are going to need a different **openDoor** method. So, we override the **openDoor** method on the base **Car** class by writing our own, locally in the **McLarenP1** class:

```
public void openDoor() {

    door.open("upward");

}
```

Maybe we are also building a **DeLorean** class? In that case, we are also going to need to override **openDoor** again with one that is a little different:

```
public void openDoor() {

    door.open("gull-wing");

}
```

What if we build a **FordFusion** class? In that case, the default **openDoor** method will do just fine.

The bottom line is that Java's adherence to polymorphism provides the ability to both overload and override methods. Those abilities help us make *one thing be like many*.

Advantages of OOP

We have discussed some of the benefits of object-oriented programming along the way, but let us be sure to point them out here:

- **Code reuse:** Commonly used methods do not need to be rewritten in every class that they are needed in. Even classes can be reused in multiple applications.
- **Modularity:** The principles of OOP encourage modularity, enabling difficult problems to be broken down into smaller tasks.
- **Collaboration:** Separate teams can work on the same or adjacent codebases together, as different modules and classes can often be built independently of each other.

Taking an OOP approach to programming has distinct advantages over a traditional logic- or function-based approach. We will put this approach into practice in the upcoming chapters.

What is new in Java 21?

Lately, we have seen some incredible new features make their way into Java. Specifically, Java 21 has three new features that we will look at: virtual threads, sequenced collections, and string templates.

Virtual threads

Probably the most talked about new feature with Java 21 is that of virtual threads. Implemented in Java 19 as a **preview feature**, virtual threading represents a significant shift in how concurrency is handled in Java. Developers now work with virtual threads in their code instead of conventional, operating system threads.

A virtual thread interacts with the **Java virtual machine** (**JVM**), which may assign the virtual thread to its own process, or it may end up sharing a process with another virtual thread. This way, virtual threads are (*Tyson 2022*) an abstraction layer for threading, leaving the JVM to manage the available resources at the OS level.

For example, a legacy Java application class may implement the **Runnable** interface to run specific parts of the application concurrently. This class may also have a public method for starting the thread:

```
public class MyApplication implements Runnable {


    private Thread appThread;


    public void startAppThread() {
```

```
        appThread = new Thread(this);

        appThread.start();

    }

// additional code would follow below
```

With virtual threads, the same class and method would look like this:

```
public class MyApplication implements Runnable {

    public void startAppThread() {

        Thread.startVirtualThread(this);

    }

}
```

This is by design and actually makes it easy to retrofit an existing, threaded Java application to take advantage of virtual threads. Using virtual threads also leads to better-performing code due to the significant decrease in the creation of individual processes at the OS level.

It is important to note that there are some restrictions (*Tyson 2022*) concerning the effective use of virtual threads:

- A semaphore should be used to control the number of concurrent threads, not a thread pool. The JVM manages the thread pool.
- All virtual threads are considered **daemon threads**, meaning that the calling application cannot be closed while they are running.
- The priority of virtual threads cannot be adjusted.

We will put virtual threads to use in the later chapters.

Sequenced Collections

Working with Java collection types (lists, sets, and maps) just became easier. Java collections now have something called (*Parlog 2023*) **encounter order**. This is made possible through the introduction of the **SequencedCollection** interface. Essentially, collections will now track the order in which their elements were added. This allows the implementation of these new methods on all lists and some **set** collection types (assuming collection **elements** of type **E**):

- **addFirst(element)**
- **addLast(element)**
- **<E> getFirst()**
- **<E> getLast()**

- `<E> removeFirst()`
- `<E> removeLast()`
- `SequencedCollection<E> reversed()`

Map collection types also have similar, new methods (assuming a map with entries key **K** and value **V**) now:

- `V putFirst(K, V)`
- `V putLast(K, V)`
- `Entry<K, V> firstEntry()`
- `Entry<K, V> lastEntry()`
- `Entry<K, V> pollFirstEntry()`
- `Entry<K, V> pollLastEntry()`
- `SequencedMap<K, V> reversed()`
- `SequencedSet<K> sequencedKeySet()`
- `SequencedCollection<V> sequencedValues()`
- `SequencedSet<Entry<K, V>> sequencedEntrySet()`

We will discuss the Sequenced Collections in further detail in *Chapter 4, Arrays Collections and Records*.

String templates

Introduced with the intent of solving complex string concatenation, string templates have been available for some time in other languages. Essentially, string templates allow variables and expressions to be injected into pre-built strings, making it much easier to compose strings at runtime.

Consider a situation where we are processing user input, such as a user who logs in to a bank or payment account. If we wanted to welcome them and display their current balance, the code would look something like this:

```
private String welcomeUser (User user) {

    String returnVal = "Hello " + user.getFirstName() + ",

      your balance is $" + user.getBalance();

    return returnVal;

}
```

Or with the **StringBuilder** class:

```
private String welcomeUser (User user) {
```

```
String returnVal = new StringBuilder()

    .append("Hello ")

    .append(user.getFirstName())

    .append(", your balance is $")

    .append(user.getBalance())

    .toString();

return returnVal;

}
```

But this is much simpler using string templates:

```
private String welcomeUser (User user) {

    String returnVal = STR."Hello \{user.getFirstName()},

    your balance is $\{user.getBalance()}";

    return returnVal;

}
```

This greatly simplifies the approach to processing data and building strings at runtime. We will cover string templates in further detail in *Chapter 3, Strings, Characters, and Regular Expressions.*

Conclusion

In short, there is a lot to be excited about with Java 21. In the chapters that follow, experienced Java programmers will find easier ways to interact with and build powerful applications. For those of you new to Java, get ready to take your first steps into a larger world!

Points to remember

- Be sure to download the JDK, not the JRE.
- It is recommended to create a GitHub account if you do not already have one.
- The following are the four main principles of OOP:
  - o Encapsulation
  - o Inheritance

- o   Abstraction
- o   Polymorphism
- The following are the new features in Java 21:
  - o   Virtual threads
  - o   Sequenced collections
  - o   String templates

Join our book's Discord space

Join the book's Discord Workspace for Latest updates, Offers, Tech happenings around the world, New Release and Sessions with the Authors:

https://discord.bpbonline.com

CHAPTER 2

Fundamental Programming Structures

Introduction

Now that we have gone over an introduction to Java and Java 21, we will look at some simple examples. This chapter will focus on working with programming fundamentals, such as using variables, building class methods, working with files, and controlling the flow of our programs.

We will also cover some Java-specific aspects when working with objects, classes, and constructors. Likewise, we will also call out certain OOP principles as they are encountered.

Additionally, we will call out points to reinforce best practices for the Java coding style. For this book, we will be using the *Kernighan and Ritchie style*. It is also known as the **one true brace style** or **1TBS** in hacker-speak.

Structure

In this chapter, we will discuss the following topics:

- Getting started
- Maven
- Variables and formatting
- Reading input

- Error handling
- Flow control with conditional statements and loops
- Files
- Methods and constructors

Objectives

The objectives for this chapter are to do the following:

- Help you learn how to write simple Java code and run it in an IDE
- Build a solid foundation of knowledge around the core Java syntax
- Understand how Java works with the underlying operating system

Getting started

Let us create a new, empty project. The steps will differ slightly depending on your IDE and choice of dependency manager. For this book, we will show examples of the Maven dependency manager.

In case it is not already there, configure your IDE by adding Java 21 as an available JRE. In the Eclipse IDE, we can do this by clicking the following menus and dialogs: **Window** | **Preferences** | **Java** | **Installed JREs**.

Maven

In your IDE, create a new Maven project. Make sure the following group ID and artifact are set in the **pom.xml** file:

```
<groupId>com.codewithjava21</groupId>
```

```
<artifactId>chapterexercises</artifactId>
```

Also, add the following properties so that the correct version of Java is used:

```
<properties>
    <java.version>21</java.version>
    <maven.compiler.source>21</maven.compiler.source>
    <maven.compiler.target>21</maven.compiler.target>
</properties>
```

> **Note: Depending on the default version of the JDK being used by the IDE, we may also need to set Java 21 as the JRE system library in our new project's build properties.**

HelloWorld

Let us create a new Java class in our project with the following properties:

- **Name:** `HelloWorld`
- **Package:** `chapter2`
- **Checkbox for** `public static void main(String[] args)`: *Checked*

Note: Almost every programming book has an obligatory 'hello world' program. The idea is to show beginners the basics of how to build and run programs.

Depending on the IDE used, the new class will already contain a small amount of code. For example, those of us using the Eclipse IDE should see something like this:

```java
package chapter2;


public class HelloWorld {

    public static void main(String[] args) {

        // TODO Auto-generated method stub


    }

}
```

Here are a few things worth noting:

- The first thing we see here is a definition for our package. A **package** is simply a container for Java classes related to each other.
- Between the package and class definitions, we would **import** additional libraries. This class is simple, so we will not need the **import** statement at this time.
- Our class definition defines the publicly-scoped class **HelloWorld**. All the code that follows must be contained within the curly braces **{ }**.
- Next, we define our **main** method, which has a few parts of its own:
  - Like the class, it is **publicly scoped**. This means it can be called from inside and outside the class.
  - It is declared as **static**, which means it can be called from outside the class without requiring the class to be instantiated as an object.
  - It does not return a value, so the method's return type is **void**.
  - The name of the method is **main**.

- o The method accepts an array of strings as an argument. This is by design and allows the developer to ingest any passed-in parameters quickly.
- o Inside the **main** method, there is a comment. It leads with the message **TODO** to remind us *to do* something about it later. Any line in Java starting with two forward slashes "**//**" is a comment.

> **Note: We can also encapsulate multiple lines in a "block comment" using a forward slash and a star "/*" at the beginning and then closing with a star and a slash "*/."**

Let us start by removing the comment and replacing it with a line of code that does something. We want to print the words **Hello world** to the screen, and we can do that with a simple line of code:

```
System.out.print("Hello world!");
```

This invokes the **print** method from within Java's **System.out** library. The idea is that the quoted text in the method's parameter list is printed to the terminal or console.

Our **main** method should now look like this:

```
public static void main(String[] args) {

    System.out.print("Hello world!");

}
```

Your IDE should have a button or other means to trigger your program to run. Running this program from within our IDE produces the following output:

```
Hello world!
```

> **Note: If that does not run, look at the error messages reported in the console. The error messages are descriptive and usually indicate the nature and location of the problem.**

Anonymous main classes

Java 21 also introduces a new preview feature known as **anonymous main classes**. The idea is to make this exercise easier for Java beginners to follow. This means our **main** method could look like this instead:

```
public main() {

    System.out.print("Hello world!");

}
```

This is much easier for beginners to understand!

If you want to enable preview features in your JDK, there are a few ways (for example, *Baeldung 2022*) to do that. While disabled by default, they can be activated in your IDE's project or Java compiler settings. Maven users can also enable JDK preview features using the Maven compiler plugin in the **pom.xml** file:

```xml
<plugins>

    <plugin>

        <groupId>org.apache.maven.plugins</groupId>

        <artifactId>maven-compiler-plugin</artifactId>

        <configuration>

            <source>21</source>

            <target>21</target>

            <compilerArgs>

                --enable-preview

            </compilerArgs>

        </configuration>

    </plugin>

</plugins>
```

You can also use the **enable-preview** flag when running Java from a terminal:

```
java --enable-preview HelloWorld.class
```

Note: Preview features are often not complete and may produce unpredictable results. They should only be enabled by advanced users.

Variables and formatting

Now let us take a look at variables. Variables are similar to bookmarks; they point to specific data stored in a computer's **random-access memory** (**RAM**). We can access the data stored in a Java variable as long as the following two conditions are met:

- We know the variable's name.
- The variable's scope allows us to access it.

As mentioned in *Chapter 1, Getting to Know Java*, all variables have one of three scopes: private, protected, and public. By following the rules defined for each scope, we can access the variable's data. We will get more details on scope later on.

All variables will have a type. The type of a variable tells Java (and the programmer) what kind of data is being stored. For now, we will focus on the **String** type. Strings let us store ASCII and UTF-based text data. We will cover this in detail in *Chapter 3, Strings, Characters, and Regular Expressions*. The main thing to remember is that string lets us work with text data.

> **Note: ASCII stands for American Standard Code for Information Interchange, which was the character encoding standard for early computers. It has since been included in the much larger, more extensible UTF standard, which stands for Uniform Transformation Format. UTF has been extended to encode more than 1 million characters from multiple written languages. An ASCII/UTF character conversion chart is included in the appendices of this book.**

It is important to understand that while there are several variable types in Java, they are always either a **reference type** or a **primitive type**. Primitive types are stored in memory as their literal values, while reference types are essentially *bookmarks* to another location in memory. Reference types are usually objects, but they can also be other static classes. A list of the primitive types in Java can be seen in *Table 2.1*:

Name	Description
boolean	A one-bit type that only has the value of either 'true' or 'false'
Byte	An 8-bit type used for working with binary data
Char	A 16-bit type used for storing a single ASCII/UTF character
double	A 64-bit floating point type
Float	A 32-bit floating point type
Int	A 32-bit integer type
Long	A 64-bit integer type
Short	A 16-bit integer type

Table 2.1: A list of Java's primitive types

Each primitive type also has its own reference type, which is sometimes called a **wrapper class**. These wrapper classes provide additional functionality that can be useful when converting data between types. There are additional reference types as well, like the **String** type we are about to use.

Let us make an addition to our **HelloWorld** class. We will add a new **String** variable to our class called **firstName**, which contains our own first name, like this:

```
public class HelloWorld {

private static String firstName = "Aaron";
```

```
public static void main(String[] args) {
```

Note: We need to define our variable to be static because our class is a static class. Again, this means that methods on our class can be run without the class being instantiated as an object.

We will also add a new **printf** statement:

```
System.out.print("Hello world!");
```

```
System.out.printf("Welcome to the world of Java, %s!", firstName);
```

Running this code should produce the following output:

Hello world!Welcome to the world of Java, Aaron!

So, what is the difference between **print** and **printf**? The **print** statement simply prints the text string entered in its parameter list. But the **printf** statement lets us add formatting rules to customize our output with data from variables. The format rule we used was the **%s** rule, which lets us print the data in **String** variables.

Another question is, 'Why were our text strings output on the same line?' Well, the answer is that we did not instruct our program to put those two strings on separate lines. We can do that with one simple change: using the **println** statement instead of **print**:

```
System.out.println("Hello world!");
```

```
System.out.printf("Welcome to the world of Java, %s!", firstName);
```

Now if we run our program, we should see our text output on two different lines, as follows:

Hello world!

Welcome to the world of Java, Aaron!

Let us add another variable to our **HelloWorld** class to track our age. We will define our age as a **static** integer variable right under our **firstName** variable:

```
private static String firstName = "Aaron";
```

```
private static int age = 47;
```

We also want to add our age to our output. Let us do that with another **printf** statement. This time, we will use the **%d** format specifier to show numeric, integer data:

```
System.out.println("Hello world!");
```

```
System.out.printf("Welcome to the world of Java, %s!", firstName);
```

```
System.out.printf("age = %d.  It's never too late to learn Java!", age);
```

Let us save and run our program again, which should show the following output:

Hello world!

Welcome to the world of Java, Aaron!age = 47. It's never too late to learn Java!

The output from our last two **printf** statements ended up on the same line, again. We cannot use **println**, as it does not accept format specifiers or variables.

However, we can solve this by adding a special **new line** character to our strings. The new line character is two characters, a backslash **** and the letter **n**. It looks like **\n** and is what we need to get our text on separate lines.

Let us add it to the end of the text strings for both our **printf** statements:

```
System.out.printf("Welcome to the world of Java, %s!\n", firstName);
```

```
System.out.printf("age = %d.  It's never too late to learn Java!\n", age);
```

Remember our earlier discussion on the different line endings between operating systems? Bearing that in mind, users on the Windows OS may have to use **\r\n**, instead of just **\n**.

Running our code produces the following output:

Hello world!

Welcome to the world of Java, Aaron!

age = 47. It's never too late to learn Java!

Now you might ask, 'Why does that work?'

The keyboard used with modern computers evolved from typewriters used in the 20th century. When you finished typing a line on a typewriter, you had to do two things:

- Move the carriage back to its original position at the start of the line.
- Move the paper feed to the next line.

When computers started interacting with large, data-center printers, special control codes were created to handle implementing **carriage returns and line feeds** (**CRLF**). Those control codes are still present in modern computer languages and character encoding sets. Some languages simply refer to them as a CRLF.

Another way to solve this would be to add the special line separator from the **System** library:

```
System.out.printf("Welcome to the world of Java, %s!" +

    System.lineSeparator(), firstName);
```

```
System.out.printf("age = %d.  It's never too late to learn Java!" +
```

```
System.lineSeparator(), age);
```

It is important to note that Windows and MacOS/Linux handle line endings differently. This is why we pointed out that Windows users may have to use **\r\n**, while others should be fine using **\n**. However, the advantage of using **System.lineSeparator()** or **println** is that they will automatically adjust for those subtle, OS-level differences in line endings.

Reading input

Let us create a new Java class named **ReadingInput**. It should be inside the **chapter2** package and should have a **public main** method. Before we add any code to the class, let us **import** Java's **Scanner** library to use. We can accomplish this using the **import** statement with the library name. Be sure to put this, and all other, **import** statements between the **package** definition and the **class** definition:

```
package chapter2;

import java.util.Scanner;

public class ReadingInput {

    public static void main(String[] args) {
        // TODO Auto-generated method stub


    }
}
```

We will use the **Scanner** library to read a number typed by the user. Next, we will convert that numeric code to its corresponding ASCII/UTF character. Inside the **main** method, let us remove the comment, print some quick instructions, and initialize our **Scanner** object:

```
public static void main(String[] args) {

System.out.print("Enter a number between 31 and 256: ");


    Scanner inputScanner = new Scanner(System.in);
```

Essentially, we are creating an object as a new instance of the **Scanner** class. We are naming the object **inputScanner** and then using the **new** keyword to initialize it by calling **Scanner**'s constructor.

A **constructor** is a special kind of method that is called to instantiate a new object of a class.

The constructor method(s) contain code that is run during creationtime to make sure the object is properly initialized. We have called the **Scanner** constructor by passing Java's reference to the **Standard Input (STDIN) System.in** as a parameter.

Next, we will use the **inputScanner** object to poll for keyboard input:

```
String inputStr = inputScanner.nextLine();

inputScanner.close();
```

We will set a new **String** variable named **inputStr** to capture the keyboard input. As **Scanner** works on input streams, we will call the **close** method as we will not need it again:

```
int number = Integer.parseInt(inputStr);

System.out.printf("The character for ASCII code %d is %c", number, (char)
number);
```

Next, we will convert **inputStr** into an integer variable named **number** using the **parseInt** method from the **Integer** reference class. Finally, we will print our findings, including the original numeric code (**number**) and the ASCII/UTF character for that number, by casting **number** to a character (**char**) type.

Running this program and entering the number **68** from the keyboard results in this output:

```
Enter a number between 0 and 255: 68

The character for ASCII code 68 is D
```

Error handling

So far, our program to convert numbers into their corresponding ASCII/UTF characters works great. But what happens if we give it an input it is not expecting?

Run the program again, but instead of a number, enter the letter **a**:

```
Enter a number between 31 and 256: a

Exception in thread "main" java.lang.NumberFormatException: For input string:
"a"

    at java.base/java.lang.NumberFormatException.
    forInputString(NumberFormatException.java:67)

    at java.base/java.lang.Integer.parseInt(Integer.java:665)

    at java.base/java.lang.Integer.parseInt(Integer.java:781)

    at chapter2.ReadingInput.main(ReadingInput.java:14)
```

In this case, our input caused the program to throw an exception (a **NumberFormatException**, to be specific). This happened because the **parseInt** method of the **Integer** class is expecting to output a number from a numeric text. To prevent this, we should do some input validation. Let us try surrounding our **parseInt** and **printf** statements with a **try**/ **catch**.

This way, if the **parseInt** fails, it will throw the **NumberFormatException** that we saw earlier. But we will **catch** this exception and provide a graceful failure message to our user:

```
try {

    int number = Integer.parseInt(inputStr);

    System.out.printf("The character for ASCII code %d is %c", number,
    (char) number);

} catch (NumberFormatException ex) {

    System.out.println("Sorry, only numbers are permitted.");

}
```

Now, if we rerun our program and enter the letter 'a' as input, we should see this:

```
Enter a number between 31 and 256: a

Sorry, only numbers are permitted.
```

Note that **NumberFormatException** is a Java class that inherits from the base **Exception** class. This means the code is valid:

```
} catch (Exception ex) {

    System.out.println("Sorry, only numbers are permitted.");

}
```

However, it is always better to trap for specific exceptions. We may want to handle different types of failures differently, and in this case, we might misinterpret and thus, inadvertently mask the true nature of the error. If we are going to catch the base **Exception** type, we should probably show its actual error message. Fortunately, we can do that and still catch our **NumberFormatException**:

```
} catch (NumberFormatException ex) {

    System.out.println("Sorry, only numbers are permitted.");

} catch (Exception ex) {

    System.out.println(ex.getMessage());
```

```
}
```

This ability to **daisy-chain catch** clauses together allows us to implement a very dynamic level of error handling.

> **Note: When catching multiple exceptions, remember that they are evaluated in the order listed. Therefore, the base exception type should always be the last one to be 'caught.'**

If statements

What if we enter a number less than **31**?

Enter a number between 31 and 256: 30

The character for ASCII code 30 is

Depending on the character set on your computer, you may see nothing or you may see some other strange-looking symbol. Remember when we mentioned that early character sets included special codes for printers and that those control characters are still in today's character encoding sets? Well, that is what the numbers below 32 represent. Even entering the number **32** as input here will show nothing, as **32** is the encoding code for the spacebar on your keyboard.

We should limit our numeric input to ensure that it is greater than or equal to **32**. This is because anything below that number will not display a useful character. We can accomplish this with an **if**/**else** condition:

```
if (number > 31) {

    System.out.printf("The character for ASCII code %d is %c", number,
    (char) number);

} else {

    System.out.println("Sorry, only numbers 32 or higher are permitted.");

}
```

What about our max input constraint? We mentioned earlier that we only accept numbers between 31 and 256. Let us add another conditional to our **if** statement:

```
if (number > 31 && number < 256) {

    System.out.printf("The character for ASCII code %d is %c", number,
    (char) number);

} else {
```

```
    System.out.println("Sorry, only numbers 32 or higher and 255 or less are
    permitted.");

}
```

In this case, we have added an **and** operator to our **if** statement, represented by the double-ampersand **&&**. Therefore, before converting our **number** variable to an ASCII/UTF character, we are verifying that it is *both* greater than **31** *and* smaller than **256**.

This is where you should start seeing that the **if**/**else** statement is a Boolean logic structure. We are essentially checking that everything in the **if** clause evaluates to *true* before running the code below it. If not, we run the code under the **else** clause.

> **Note: Some languages refer to the 'if statement' as an 'if/then' statement. This is because these languages will use a 'then' keyword to indicate the end of the condition and the beginning of the code to run. As Java does not have a 'then' keyword, we will just call them 'if statements.'**

However, characters above 255 are useful for other written languages, so let us comment-out that if-check, and use our original:

```
//if (number > 31 && number < 256) {

if (number > 31) {

    System.out.printf("The character for ASCII code %d is %c", number,
    (char) number);

} else {

    System.out.println("Sorry, only numbers 32 or higher are permitted.");

}
```

Switch/case statements

Another way to check for equality is to use a **switch**/**case** statement. **Switch**/**case** statements are useful when there may be several kinds of inputs we want to handle, and creating an **if** condition for all of them would be cumbersome.

Let us create a new Java class named **RandomCase**. It should be inside the **chapter2** package and should have a public **main** method. First, let us import Java's **Random** library. We will then start by creating a new object named **random** as a new instance of the **Random** class:

```
package chapter2;


import java.util.Random;
```

```java
public class RandomCase {

    public static void main(String[] args) {
        Random random = new Random();



    }

}
```

> **Note:** It is an accepted practice to name all classes using 'camel case,' where the names consist of no spaces and an uppercase character is used for the first letter of each word. Classes and variables are also named using camel case, but the first letter of the name is always lowercase.

Underneath the definition of our random object, let us use the **nextInt** method to generate a random number from one through five:

```java
int rndNumber = random.nextInt(5) + 1;
```

Calling the **nextInt** method while passing the number **5** as a parameter will generate a random integer value from **0** to **4**. We are adding the **+ 1** at the end to bring the result up to a minimum of **1** and a maximum of **5**.

Next, we will check the value of **rndNumber** using a **switch**/**case** statement and act on it:

```java
switch(rndNumber) {

case 1:

    System.out.println("One");

    break;

case 2:

    System.out.println("Two");

    break;
```

As you can see, we start with the **switch** statement and direct it to act on the **rndNumber** variable. Inside the curly braces, we use the **case** statement to check **rndNumber** for a particular value. We then write a block of code to be run for each case.

Once our code is complete, we finish it with a **break** statement. The **break** statement is important because it tells Java that we are done with the **switch**/**case** statement. If the **break** statement is not present, the Java compiler then checks the remaining cases until one of them either has a **break** statement or until the **switch**/**case** statement ends.

Sometimes, this behavior is useful. But for our purpose, for example, once we match on a **case** statement for the number **2** and we print **Two** to the terminal, we do not need to check any of the other cases.

Let us add in the rest of our cases:

```
case 3:

    System.out.println("Three");

    break;

case 4:

    System.out.println("Four");

    break;

case 5:

    System.out.println("Five");

    break;

default:

    System.out.println("Something goofy happened here...");

}
```

Once we finish checking the remaining cases, there is a **default** case. Think of it as a **catch-all** for the **switch**/**case** statement. If it makes it all the way through the **switch**/**case** statement without matching on a single case, the code inside the default block is run.

> **Note: The default case does not need to contain a 'break' statement, as no additional cases are after it.**

If we run the preceding code, we should see the word for one of the numbers printed out to the terminal.

Loops

What if we want our **RandomCase** program to run several times? We can accomplish that by using a loop. Loops are a great way to do the following:

- Repeat code for a specified number of times
- Repeat code until another condition occurs
- Iterate through a large collection of data or items

For loops

Let us say that we want our **RandomCase** program to run 10 times. We can do that by encapsulating our code inside of a **for** loop:

```java
for (int counter = 0; counter < 10; counter++) {

    int rndNumber = random.nextInt(5) + 1;


    switch(rndNumber) {

    case 1:

        System.out.println("One");

        break;

    case 2:

        System.out.println("Two");

        break;

    case 3:

        System.out.println("Three");

        break;

    case 4:

        System.out.println("Four");

        break;

    case 5:

        System.out.println("Five");

        break;

    default:

        System.out.println("Something goofy happened here...");

    }

}
```

Let us take a look at our **for** statement:

```java
for (int counter = 0; counter < 10; counter++)
```

The **for** statement operates within three parameters:

- The index or counter variable
- A condition
- A mutator for the index or counter

Essentially, we are setting our **counter** to zero and running our code while incrementing **counter**. The loop will end once **counter** is greater than or equal to the number **10**, effectively running the code in the loop 10 times (**0** through **9**). Running the program should produce results similar to the following:

```
Three

Four

Three

One

Five

Three

Three

Two

Four

One
```

Go ahead and run this program a few times. It should produce different results on each execution.

While loops

Another type of loop is a **while** loop. **While** loops are designed to run until a specified condition is met. Let us say that we want our loop to run until the number four (**4**) is randomly generated. To make this change, before the loop, we will create a new **boolean** variable named **fourFound**. Then, we will use the **while** statement to run the loop until **fourFound** becomes true:

```
boolean fourFound = false;

//for (int counter = 0; counter < 10; counter++) {

while (!fourFound) {

    int rndNumber = random.nextInt(5) + 1;
```

Note: For this example, we have simply commented-out the 'for' statement and replaced it with the 'while' statement. This way, we can leave the loop code formatted as-is.

The only other change that we need to make is in the case for when the number four is found:

```
case 4:

    System.out.println("Four");

    fourFound = true;

    break;
```

As long as we set **fourFound** to true somewhere between the **case** statement and the **break** statement, it should work. Should we forget this step, our program will run in an *infinite loop*. This means our loop code will run nonstop until our program is forced to exit. Also, if we set **fourFound** to true *after* the **break** statement, then our program will never reach that line of code, and that will also trigger it to run in an infinite loop.

Do loops

Another type of loop is known as a **do** loop or sometimes as a **do/while** loop. To change our code to a **do** loop, we need to make the following adjustment:

```
Random random = new Random();

boolean fourFound = false;


//for (int counter = 0; counter < 10; counter++) {

// while (!fourFound)

do {

    int rndNumber = random.nextInt(5) + 1;


    switch(rndNumber) {

    case 1:

        System.out.println("One");

        break;

    case 2:

        System.out.println("Two");
```

```
        break;
    case 3:

        System.out.println("Three");

        break;
    case 4:

        System.out.println("Four");

        fourFound = true;

        break;
    case 5:

        System.out.println("Five");

        break;
    default:

        System.out.println("Something goofy happened here...");


    }

} while (!fourFound);
```

The idea here is that the loop code will run at least once with a **do** loop. With a **while** loop, there could be code above the loop that sets the **while** statement's condition to **true**, which means the code would never run. On the other hand, a **do** loop will run at least once. You can test this out by changing the definition of **fourFound** to **true**. Let us try it once:

```
boolean fourFound = true;
```

With the **do** loop, our loop code runs once, prints the generated value to the terminal and ends. However, running the code with **fourFound** already set to **true** using a **while** loop prints nothing.

Files

Let us create a new Java class in our project. Name it **SimpleFileWorker**, and make sure it is a part of the **chapter2** package, and that it is created with a **public static void main** method.

Writing to a file

Add imports for the **FileWriter** and **IOException** classes from the **java.io** library. Make sure they are listed between the **package** and **class** definitions:

```
package chapter2;


import java.io.FileWriter;

import java.io.IOException;


public class SimpleFileWorker {
```

Let us instantiate a new **FileWriter** object named **writer**, passing the string **gamesCatalog. txt** as an argument. This will open the **gamesCatalog.txt** file for writing. If it does not exist, it will be created. We will also surround the definition of our **writer** object with a **try**/**catch**, trapping for an **IOException**:

```
try {

    FileWriter writer = new FileWriter("gamesCatalog.txt");


} catch (IOException writerEx) {

    System.out.println("Error occurred while writing:");

    writerEx.printStackTrace();

}
```

Now, let us write two lines of text to the file. We can use the FileWriter**'s write** method for this. Add these lines after the instantiation of the **writer** object:

```
// header

writer.write("name, company, year");


// data

writer.write("Pitfall!, Activision, 1982");
```

When working with files, it is important to close any open file handles. Let us make sure we do that:

```
writer.close();
```

This program does not have any terminal output, so we will also add a short message (after the **try**/**catch**) to let our users know when the program is finished:

```
System.out.println("Writing completed!");
```

Run this program. Once you see the **Writing completed** message, open up a terminal session and go to the directory for this project. Start by listing files in the directory.

Windows:

dir

Linux/MacOS:

ls -al

Look for the name of the file, **gamesCatalog.txt**. Now, let us display the contents of the file:

Windows:

type gamesCatalog.txt

Linux/MacOS:

cat gamesCatalog.txt

The output should look similar to this:

name, company, yearPitfall!, Activision, 1982

We forgot to add a proper line ending character (from our earlier discussion about CRLF) to our lines in the file. We can fix this by adjusting the **write** statements:

```
//header

writer.write("name, company, year\r\n");


//data

writer.write("Pitfall!, Activision, 1982\r\n");
```

> **Note: Linux and Macintosh users should only need to add the \n character.**

The **main** method of our **SimpleFileWorker** class should now look like this:

```
public static void main(String[] args) {

    try {

        FileWriter writer = new FileWriter("gamesCatalog.txt");


        // header
```

```
        writer.write("name, company, year\n");


        // data

        writer.write("Pitfall!, Activision, 1982\n");


        // close file writer

        writer.close();


    } catch (IOException writerExc) {

System.out.println("Error occurred while writing:");

        e.printStackTrace();

    }
```

Now, rerun the program and display the contents of the file. The output should look like this:

```
    System.out.println("Writing completed!");

}
```

```
name, company, year

Pitfall!, Activision, 1982
```

So, what have we accomplished here? Essentially, we have done the following:

- Opened a new file handle to the **gamesCatalog.txt** file, creating the file
- Written two lines to the file
- Closed the file

For small amounts of data, this should work just fine.

However, if we were working with large amounts of data and a high rate of write throughput, we would need to make some adjustments. The **FileWriter** class, for example, does not do any caching or buffering to help offset higher rates of write throughput. It relies on the operating system to manage the disk cache and other resources.

Therefore, for advanced applications, it makes sense to use the **BufferedWriter** class. The **BufferedWriter** class does additional cache management and backpressure mitigation within the Java heap. Fortunately, instantiating this class is easy, as it takes a **FileWriter** object as its parameter. But first, let us add it to the **import** section of our **SimpleFileWorker** class:

```
import java.io.BufferedWriter;
```

Now, let us change the name of our **writer** object to **fileWriter**. Instantiate a new **BufferedWriter** object while passing our **FileWriter** object as a parameter:

```
FileWriter fileWriter = new FileWriter("gamesCatalog.txt");
```

```
BufferedWriter writer = new BufferedWriter(fileWriter);
```

Alternatively, if we wanted to shorten this, we could do this all in one line, as follows:

```
BufferedWriter writer = new BufferedWriter(new FileWriter("gamesCatalog.txt"));
```

Let us add a few more lines to the file after the **data** comment and the entry for **Pitfall**:

```
//data
```

```
writer.write("Pitfall, Activision, 1982\r\n");
```

```
writer.write("Crackpots, Activision, 1983\r\n");
```

```
writer.write("Yars' Revenge, Atari, 1981\r\n");
```

```
writer.write("Warlords, Atari, 1981\r\n");
```

```
writer.write("Defender, Atari, 1981\r\n");
```

```
writer.write("Adventure, Atari, 1980\r\n");
```

It important to note that there is a **flush** method on both the **FileWriter** and **BufferedWriter** classes. This is useful if the file is open for both reading and writing, and you want to make sure the entire contents of the operating system's file cache are *flushed* to the disk (before attempting to read them).

For our purposes, we do not need to call this directly. A **flush** operation is also invoked from inside the **close** method. Therefore, as long as we remember to call the **close** method on our **writer** object, our data should be persisted to the disk.

After running the program, displaying the contents of the **gamesCatalog.txt** file should produce output like this:

```
name, company, year
```

```
Pitfall!, Activision, 1982
```

```
Crackpots, Activision, 1983
```

```
Yars' Revenge, Atari, 1981
```

```
Warlords, Atari, 1981
```

```
Defender, Atari, 1981

Adventure, Atari, 1980
```

Reading from a file

Now, let us try to read from the file. First, we will add two new entries to our **import** section. For the examples shown below, we will need *both* the **FileReader** and **BufferedReader** classes:

```
import java.io.BufferedReader;

import java.io.FileReader;
```

Now we could have taken the same approach that we did when looking at how to write to files. But rest assured, while the **FileReader** class is fine for reading small files, it is better to use **BufferedReader** instead. The reasons for using the **BufferedWriter** (instead of the **FileWriter**) class holds true for using the **BufferedReader** class for reading files as well.

Let us instantiate a new **BufferedReader** object named **reader** after we output our **Writing completed!** message. We will also add in a blank **println** to provide some extra line spacing in our output. Also, make sure that our new **reader** object is instantiated inside its own **try**/**catch**:

```
System.out.println("Writing completed!");

System.out.println();


try {

BufferedReader reader = new BufferedReader(new FileReader("gamesCatalog.txt"));


} catch (IOException readerEx) {

    System.out.println("Error occurred while writing:");

    readerEx.printStackTrace();

}
```

Next, inside the **try**/**catch**, we will initialize a string variable named **gameLine** to the result of the **readLine** method. Then, we will build our **while** loop with a condition to run the code inside as long as **gameLine** is not null. In our code, we will print the line from the file and then call the **readLine** method again:

```
// read the first line

String gameLine = reader.readLine();
```

```
while (gameLine != null) {

    System.out.println(gameLine);

    // read the next line

    gameLine = reader.readLine();

}
```

As the **while** loop progresses, our code continues to call the **readLine** method. Once there are no more lines remaining in the file to be read, the **readLine** method returns null. With **gameLine** set to null, the **while** condition evaluates to false, and the loop ends.

Simply put, we have written a quick program to write a header and lines into a file, and also to read those lines back out.

Reading row properties from a file

We can also direct our program to read only specific lines of the file. For example, let us read back the names of the games that were released in 1981. To make this happen, there are some basic steps we should take:

- Read all lines from the file.
- Parse each line into the following columns:
    o   name
    o   company
    o   year
- If the year is equal to 1981, we print the line from the file.

Outside the loop, the code should remain pretty much the same. But inside the loop, we will start by separating each column value from **gameLine**. We can do that with the **split** method, which can be called on any string. The **split** method returns a string array, so we will create one named **gameColumns** and initialize it with the value returned after splitting **gameLine** by a comma:

```
String[] gameColumns = gameLine.split(",");
```

We will discuss things like arrays and string methods in the later chapters of the book. For now, it is enough to say that we have separated **gameLine** into three columns. Remember that our file is delimited by commas: there are two commas on each line in the file, separating each line into three values.

As Java works on a zero-based numbering system, the three values in the array are indexed by the numbers **0**, **1**, and **2**. This puts the **year** column on index number **2**. We can set that to its own variable:

```
String strYear = gameColumns[2];
```

Values are usually easier to work with in their native data types, so let us convert year to an integer. For that, we can use the **Integer** wrapper class **parseInt** method:

```
int year = Integer.parseInt(strYear);
```

To be more efficient with our code, we can combine both of the previous lines into one:

```
int year = Integer.parseInt(gameColumns[2]);
```

With that completed, let us now create an **if** check to only print the lines from the files that have the **year** as 1981:

```
if (year == 1981) {

    System.out.println(gameLine);

}
```

Let us try running what we have so far. Unfortunately, we are going to get an exception:

```
Writing completed!


Exception in thread "main" java.lang.NumberFormatException: For input string:
" year"

    at java.base/java.lang.NumberFormatException.
    forInputString(NumberFormatException.java:67)

    at java.base/java.lang.Integer.parseInt(Integer.java:647)

    at java.base/java.lang.Integer.parseInt(Integer.java:777)

    at chapter2.SimpleFileWorker.main(SimpleFileWorker.java:49)
```

Although there is a single exception here, our code has two problems. If we look at the bottom of the exception message, we can see that the problem occurred in our **main** method on line 49. Line 49 should be this line of code:

```
int year = Integer.parseInt(gameColumns[2]);
```

The two lines above it clearly reference the **parseInt()** method.

If we look at the first line in the exception message, we can see the text that caused **parseInt()** to fail:

```
NumberFormatException: For input string: " year"
```

Ultimately, this error has been caused by our header line. The header line is the first line in our file, and it looks like this:

```
name, company, year
```

As the string for the column name **year** cannot be converted to an integer, the **NumberFormatException** is thrown. To get past this, we need to properly handle our header row. Outside our **while** loop, let us create a new **boolean** variable named **headerRead** and initialize it to **false**. This way, at the beginning of the loop, we know that the header has not yet been read:

```
boolean headerRead = false;
```

Next, let us encapsulate our code for the **split()**, **parseInt()**, and **if** logic inside another **if**. The **if** statement needs to check whether **headerRead** is equal to **true**. If **headerRead** is **false**, all we need to do is set it to **true**. This will be sufficient for our code to skip the file header:

```
if (headerRead) {

    String[] gameColumns = gameLine.split(",");

    int year = Integer.parseInt(gameColumns[2]);


    if (year == 1981) {

        System.out.println(gameLine);

    }
} else {

    headerRead = true;

}
```

But if we run our code now, we will find our *second* problem:

```
NumberFormatException: For input string: " 1982"
```

Look at the space before the numbers. The **parseInt()** method cannot convert the string **1982** to an integer as long as the string has a leading space. Fortunately, there is a simple method that can handle the **trim()** method.

The **trim()** method removes any trailing or leading spaces from a string, and we can call it on our **year** string to do that. Extra spaces have a way of causing problems, so running a **trim()** on file and user input is usually a good idea. Our parse line should now look like this:

```
int year = Integer.parseInt(gameColumns[2].trim());
```

> **Note: Similar to split(), the trim() method can be invoked on all string data in Java.**

Our complete code for the file reading portion of our program should now look like this:

```java
try {

    BufferedReader reader = new BufferedReader(new FileReader("gamesCatalog.
    txt"));

    // read the first line
    String gameLine = reader.readLine();
    boolean headerRead = false;

    while (gameLine !=  null) {

        if (headerRead) {

            String[] gameColumns = gameLine.split(",");
            int year = Integer.parseInt(gameColumns[2].trim());

            if (year == 1981) {

                System.out.println(gameLine);

            }
        } else {

            headerRead = true;

        }
        // read the next line
        gameLine = reader.readLine();

    }

} catch (IOException readerEx) {

    System.out.println("Error occurred while writing:");

    readerEx.printStackTrace();

}
```

Running this program should now produce the following output:

```
Writing completed!

Yars' Revenge, Atari, 1981

Warlords, Atari, 1981

Defender, Atari, 1981
```

Methods and constructors

Let us take a look at methods and constructors. Methods, sometimes known as **functions** or **subroutines**, are simply smaller blocks of code that are written with a specific purpose. If we find that the code in our **main** method starts to get long, it is usually a good idea to split some of it into another method or two. This is especially true if the smaller block of code is being called multiple times.

Constructors are special kinds of methods that are called when an object is instantiated. Object classes will have one or more constructors, depending on the number of different ways the object can be instantiated in.

To illustrate these concepts, let us create a few new classes inside the **chapter2** package:

- **MetricUnitConverter:** With a static void **main** method
- **MeasurementValue:** Use this class to store our measurement data
- **InvalidUOMException:** Extending the **RuntimeException** class

MetricUnitConverter sample program

We are going to build a program to take measurements in either metric or Imperial units and convert data between the two. We will support the following **units of measure (UOM):**

- **Imperial units**
  - o Inches (**in**)
  - o Feet (**ft**)
  - o Miles (**mi**)
- **Metric units**
  - o Centimeters (**cm**)
  - o Meters (**m**)
  - o Kilometers (**km**)

InvalidUOMException class

We will start with the **InvalidUOMException** class, which is a custom exception class to handle a specific type of problem. If a user passes a UOM that is not on that list (above), we want to throw our custom exception. To support this functionality, we can build our simple **InvalidUOMException** class like this:

```
package chapter2;

public class InvalidUOMException extends RuntimeException {


    public InvalidUOMException() {

        super("The UOM of this entry could not be determined.");

    }

}
```

Our **InvalidUOMException** class inherits **RuntimeException** (which itself inherits the base **Exception** class). This will allow us to work with it using Java's standard exception handling tools. It has a simple, no-argument constructor that uses the **super** statement to call the inherited class' constructor and initialize an object with our custom error message.

> Note: You may get a warning about our custom exception class not declaring a static, final serial version Universally Unique Identifier (UUID). To get around this, you can tell your IDE to generate one. Otherwise, this warning can be ignored and the JVM will generate one at runtime.

MeasurementValue POJO

Now, let us move on to our **MeasurementValue** class. We will use this class to instantiate a **Plain Old Java Object (POJO)** to keep track of our inputs, UOMs and converted values. First, we will define our class along with our object properties:

```
package chapter2;


public class MeasurementValue {

    private double inputValue;

    private String inputUOM;


    // metric

    private double centimeters;
```

```
private double meters;

private double kilometers;


// imperial

private double inches;

private double feet;

private double miles;
```

We will use the double type for our numerics to make sure we will be able to handle some of the larger numbers that could be generated. Now, let us create some constants to aid conversions between the different UOMs:

```
//conversion constants

private final int CENTIMETERS_PER_METER = 100;

private final int METERS_PER_KILOMETER = 1000;

private final int INCHES_PER_FOOT = 12;

private final int FEET_PER_MILE = 5280;

private final double METERS_PER_FOOT = 0.3048d;
```

Our constants (denoted with the **final** keyword) are whole numbers that can be defined as integers. Java will implicitly convert values from arithmetic operations between doubles and integers to doubles.

The last constant that we define will help us convert between meters and feet. As **METERS_PER_FOOT** is a decimal value, we will need to put a **d** character at the end for it to be instantiated as a double. This sets a value of **0.3048d** to our **METERS_PER_FOOT** constant.

> **Note: It is considered to be a best practice for Java style to define constant variable names using 'snake case,' where words are delimited by underscores ("_"). Additionally, constant variable names should be in all capital letters.**

For the last two variables, we need to define the **MeasurementValue** class, which will allow us to format the output of our different values properly. The **dFormat** object will be an instantiation of the **DecimalFormat** class, and we will call its constructor to indicate that we want it to limit our doubles to two points of decimal precision.

We will also instantiate a **mKmFormat** object of the **DecimalFormat** class. The difference between the level of miles and kilometers is much greater than our other, smaller UOMs. Therefore, we want to allow more precision on those UOMs to reflect that:

```
private static final DecimalFormat dFormat = new DecimalFormat("0.00");

private static final DecimalFormat mKmFormat = new DecimalFormat("0.0000");
```

With our object properties, formatters, and constants defined, let us move on to the constructors of the **MeasurementValue** class. We will build two constructors. One constructor will accept a string input of a numeric value and a UOM value, separated by a space. The other will accept parameters for the numeric value (as a double) and the UOM separately:

```
public MeasurementValue(String valueStr) throws Exception {

    parseInput(valueStr);

    runConversions();

}


public MeasurementValue(double value, String uom) throws Exception {

    inputValue = value;

    inputUOM = uom;

    runConversions();

}
```

Recall from *Chapter 1, Getting to Know Java*, that overloading constructors is a form of static polymorphism. In the business world, we would do this as a convenience to the developers using our class. They could already have the value and the UOM parsed and separated. Alternatively, they may have the raw user input. Either way, our constructors help give them options on how to build out the application. But for our purpose in this book, we will be using the constructor that accepts the user input stored in the **valueStr** string.

Both our constructor definitions include the **throws** keyword to pass any exceptions encountered *upward* to the calling method or class. We will do this because we want to focus on exception handling in our **main** method, which we will get to shortly.

In our constructors, we specified two private methods that do not yet exist: **parseInput()** and **runConversions()**. We will build them now. As our constructor relies on the **parseInput()** method, we will build that first:

```
private void parseInput(String input) {

    String[] params = input.trim().split(" ");

    inputValue = Double.parseDouble(params[0]);

    inputUOM = params[1];
```

```
}
```

Our **parseInput()** method might be small, but it does quite a bit. It is privately-scoped, as we do not want it to be called from outside the **MeasurementValue** class. Its return type is **void**, as we can set the object properties directly (so no need to return anything), and it accepts a string parameter simply named **input**.

First, it runs a **trim** on our input string and then splits it into a string array named **params**, assuming that the values are delimited by a single space. It then takes the first item in the params array (**params[0]**), converts it into a numeric type of double, and stores the result in the object property **inputValue**. It then stores the second item in the **params** array (**params[1]**) in the object property **inputUOM**.

Next, we will build the **runConversions()** method. The idea behind this method is that it will check for the UOM and then handle running the necessary conversions so that we know what our value is in **centimeters**, **inches**, **meters**, **feet**, **kilometers** and **miles**. As we have multiple UOM values to run logic on, a **switch**/**case** statement is the best approach.

Our method definition will look like this:

```
private void runConversions() throws Exception {
```

Similar to **parseInput()**, the **runConversions()** method will be privately-scoped, as we do not want it called from outside the **MeasurementValue** class. Likewise, it will not have a return type, as it will modify the object properties directly. The definition also has a **throws** statement, as we want to pass all exceptions *upward*.

We will then define our **switch**/**case** statement and code, switching on the **inputUOM** object property:

```
switch (inputUOM) {

case "in":

    inches = inputValue;

    feet = inches / INCHES_PER_FOOT;

    miles = feet / FEET_PER_MILE;

    convertImperialToMetric();

    break;
```

We will build a **case** for each of the six UOM types that we accept. In the preceding code, we are showing the code for the inches UOM, denoted by the abbreviation **in**. Essentially, if we get a value in inches, we want to set the corresponding object property (**inches** in this case) to the number stored in the **inputValue** property.

Now that we have established that the value is in inches, we can use our defined constants to compute the value in feet and miles. Likewise, we can store that data in the **feet** and **miles** object properties. We then call the **convertImperialToMetric()** method (which we will build shortly) to compute the measurement's value in **centimeters**, **meters**, and **kilometers**. Finally, we conclude the case code for inches with a **break** statement, as we will not need to check for any other UOMs.

After building out similar cases for feet (**"ft"**) and miles (**"mi"**), we would build out our metric cases, starting with a case for centimeters:

```
case "cm":

    centimeters = inputValue;

    meters = centimeters / CENTIMETERS_PER_METER;

    kilometers = meters / METERS_PER_KILOMETER;

    convertMetricToImperial();

    break;
```

Similar to our preceding case for **inches**, our **centimeters** case runs code if **inputUOM** has a string value of **cm**. Given a value in **centimeters**, we can quickly use our constants to compute **meters** and **kilometers**. We then call the **convertMetricToImperial()** method (which we will build shortly) to convert the measurement's value in **inches**, **feet**, and **miles**. Likewise, we also finish with a **break** statement to avoid spending extra processing time on conditions that we know will not be met.

We would also build out similar cases for meters (**m**) and kilometers (**km**). Finally, we would build out a **default** case:

```
default:

    throw new InvalidUOMException();

}
```

Our **default** case is triggered if the value of the **inputUOM** string does not match any of our six pre-defined UOMs. The only thing this case does is throw our **InvalidUOMException** custom exception. Obviously, if the flow of our program ends here, something is not right, so we instantiate a new object of our custom exception and then **throw** it.

The complete code for our **runConversions()** method looks like this:

```
private void runConversions() throws Exception {

    switch (inputUOM) {

    case "in":
```

```
    inches = inputValue;

    feet = inches / INCHES_PER_FOOT;

    miles = feet / FEET_PER_MILE;

    convertImperialToMetric();

    break;
case "ft":

    feet = inputValue;

    inches = feet * INCHES_PER_FOOT;

    miles = feet / FEET_PER_MILE;

    convertImperialToMetric();

    break;
case "mi":

    miles = inputValue;

    feet = miles * FEET_PER_MILE;

    inches = feet * INCHES_PER_FOOT;

    convertImperialToMetric();

    break;
case "cm":

    centimeters = inputValue;

    meters = centimeters / CENTIMETERS_PER_METER;

    kilometers = meters / METERS_PER_KILOMETER;

    convertMetricToImperial();

    break;
case "m":

    meters = inputValue;

    centimeters = meters * CENTIMETERS_PER_METER;

    kilometers = meters / METERS_PER_KILOMETER;

    convertMetricToImperial();
```

```
            break;

        case "km":

            kilometers = inputValue;

            meters = kilometers * METERS_PER_KILOMETER;

            centimeters = meters * CENTIMETERS_PER_METER;

            convertMetricToImperial();

            break;

        default:

            throw new InvalidUOMException();

    }

}
```

Moving on, let us look at the **convertImperialToMetric()** method. The idea behind this method is that we already have a value for the **feet** property. The properties of **feet** and **meters** were chosen as the basis for our **Metric**/**Imperial** conversions as they are in between the other measurements. If we chose **centimeters** and **inches**, our accuracy for **kilometers** and **miles** would be skewed. Likewise, using **kilometers** and **miles** would skew our accuracy for **centimeters** and **inches**.

So the idea with the **convertImperialToMetric()** method is that we first convert **feet** to **meters**. Then, we use **meters** to compute **centimeters** and **kilometers**:

```
private void convertImperialToMetric() {

    // use feet/meters as our conversion

    meters = feet * METERS_PER_FOOT;

    centimeters = meters * CENTIMETERS_PER_METER;

    kilometers = meters / METERS_PER_KILOMETER;

}
```

We used the same approach for the **convertMetricToImperial()** method. The **feet** property is computed first, from the value stored in the **meters** property. Once we have a value for **feet**, we use our constants to compute **inches** and **miles**:

```
private void convertMetricToImperial() {

    // use feet/meters as our conversion

    feet = meters / METERS_PER_FOOT;
```

```
    inches = feet * INCHES_PER_FOOT;

    miles = feet / FEET_PER_MILE;

}
```

Next, we will build our public methods for the **MeasurementValue** class. But we only need the **toString()** method. Now, all objects inherit a **toString()** method from the base **Object** class. But we want to make sure our property output is properly formatted, so we will *overload* that method by writing our own:

```
public String toString() {

    dFormat.setRoundingMode(RoundingMode.UP);

    mKmFormat.setRoundingMode(RoundingMode.UP);


    StringBuilder values = new StringBuilder();

    values.append("\ninches = ");

    values.append(dFormat.format(inches));

    values.append("\nfeet = ");

    values.append(dFormat.format(feet));

    values.append("\nmiles = ");

    values.append(mKmFormat.format(miles));

    values.append("\ncentimeters = ");

    values.append(dFormat.format(centimeters));

    values.append("\nmeters = ");

    values.append(dFormat.format(meters));

    values.append("\nkilometers = ");

    values.append(mKmFormat.format(kilometers));


    return values.toString();

}
```

As demonstrated, we start by setting the rounding mode on our **DecimalFormat** objects to **UP**. Next, we initialize a **StringBuilder** object with the name **values**. We build out our **StringBuilder** with text to preface our properties and the formatted properties.

> **Note: We lead each string with a newline '\n' character to ensure that our property values are easy to read.**

Note on encapsulation

Normally, POJO classes also have public methods that expose the object properties known as getters and setters. Creating getters and setters is a good way to control or allow access to data inside POJO classes. However, inputs to our class only happen through the constructors, and outputs only happen through the **toString()** method. Therefore, in the spirit of proper encapsulation for our program, we should not allow any of our individual object properties to be read or written to.

MetricUnitConverter (main) class

With our supporting classes written, let us build our **MetricUnitConverter** class and combine it. Our class definition will look like this:

```
package chapter2;


import java.util.Scanner;


public class MetricUnitConverter {
```

We will want to make sure that it has a **main** method as well. We will start by printing out some quick instructions to help our users provide input in the correct format:

```
public static void main(String[] args) {

    // instructions

    System.out.println("This program converts units of measure (UOM) between metric and imperial units.");

    System.out.println("Valid UOMS: (in, ft, mi, cm, m, km");

    System.out.println("Examples: (14 ft, 5 km)");

System.out.print("Enter a number with its UOM: ");
```

Next, we will want to build an **InputScanner**, grab the input from the **STDIN** and close the scanner:

```
// get input

Scanner inputScanner = new Scanner(System.in);

String inputStr = inputScanner.nextLine();

inputScanner.close();
```

Once we have input from the user, we will want to validate that it contains a space. This is because our accepted input is a numeric value and a UOM, delimited by a space. If that space is not there, we do not want to proceed:

```
// check for space

int spacePos = inputStr.indexOf(" ");
```

Once we know that we have an input string that contains a space, we can proceed. The first thing we will want to do is surround our logic with a **try**/**catch**. Recall that the **MeasurementValue** class contained a few **throws** statements. Our **try**/**catch** statement will need to check for those exceptions.

Inside the **try**/**catch** statement, we will instantiate a new **MeasurementValue** object named **measurement** and call its first constructor with our **inputStr**. Next, we can print out the results of all the measurement UOMs using the object's **toString()** method (which we overloaded):

```
if (spacePos > 0) {

    try {

        MeasurementValue measurement = new MeasurementValue(inputStr);

        System.out.print(measurement.toString());

    } catch (Exception ex) {

        System.out.println(ex.getMessage());

    }
```

Next, we want to build an **else** block to trap for the possibility that **inputStr** did not contain a space:

```
} else {

    System.out.println("Check your input; there should "

            + "be a space between the value and the UOM.");

}
```

The code for the complete **MetricUnitConverter** class should look like this:

```
package chapter2;


import java.util.Scanner;
```

```java
public class MetricUnitConverter {

    public static void main(String[] args) {

        // instructions
        System.out.println("This program converts units of measure (UOM)
        between metric and imperial units.");

        System.out.println("Valid UOMS: (in, ft, mi, cm, m, km");

        System.out.println("Examples: (14 ft, 5 km)");

        System.out.print("Enter a number with its UOM: ");

        // get input
        Scanner inputScanner = new Scanner(System.in);

        String inputStr = inputScanner.nextLine();

        inputScanner.close();

        // check for space
        int spacePos = inputStr.indexOf(" ");

        if (spacePos > 0) {

            try {

                MeasurementValue measurement = new MeasurementValue(inputStr);

                System.out.print(measurement.toString());

            } catch (Exception ex) {

                System.out.println(ex.getMessage());

            }
        } else {

            System.out.println("Check your input; there should "
                    + "be a space between the value and the UOM.");
```

```
        }
    }
}
```

Running this code and providing an input of **8 m** should produce this output:

```
This program converts units of measure (UOM) between metric and imperial
units.

Valid UOMS: (in, ft, mi, cm, m, km

Examples: (14 ft, 5 km)

Enter a number with its UOM: 8 m


inches = 314.97

feet = 26.25

miles = 0.0050

centimeters = 800.00

meters = 8.00

kilometers = 0.0080
```

You can try other inputs and inputs that can cause exceptions (for example, enter **8m** without the space).

Conclusion

In this chapter, we covered the fundamental statements and structures for Java. We discussed printing output to the terminal and reading input from the keyboard, along with leveraging loops to accomplish simple tasks. We also worked with files and introduced more advanced topics like string parsing and exception handling.

The topics covered in this chapter will be heavily referenced and used in the upcoming chapters. These fundamental topics are relevant for building all kinds of applications, from simple interactions to the most complex integrations.

In the next chapter, we will take a closer look at the character and string data types. We will also examine some of the methods which are a part of the String class, and even use some simple regular expressions.

Points to remember

- Classes are named using camel case, starting with a capital letter.
- Variables are named using camel case, starting with a lower case letter.
- Constants are named using snake case, with all capital letters.
- When working with **File** or **Scanner** (or any other **stream** object), do not forget to close it when finished.
- Exceptions can be handled immediately or **thrown** upward, but they should be handled before reaching the user.
- **For** loops are good for handling a pre-determined number of iterations.
- **While** loops are good for handling an unknown number of iterations.
- The code inside a **Do**/**While** loop will run at least once, but the code in a **While** loop may not.

Join our book's Discord space

Join the book's Discord Workspace for Latest updates, Offers, Tech happenings around the world, New Release and Sessions with the Authors:

https://discord.bpbonline.com

CHAPTER 3
Strings, Characters, and Regular Expressions

Introduction

This chapter will focus on working with text-based data. We will introduce strings and characters and understand how to leverage them with techniques for parsing and equality. We will also focus on regular expressions and see how powerful they can be for string equality and pattern matching.

Structure

In this chapter, we will discuss the following topics:

- Characters
- Strings
- String equality
- Regular expressions

Objectives

As we are still building up on our fundamental knowledge of Java, the objective of this chapter is to help you understand how to work with character and string data. We will explore some of the **String** class methods and put them to use. We will also learn about regular expressions and when to use them.

Characters

A character is a data type designed to hold a single alphanumeric character. However, behind the scenes, a character is stored as an integer value. When the character is displayed or read in Java, that integer is converted to a character using the JVM's character encoding set (also known as a **charset**). The default **charset** for Java (as of Java 18) is UTF-8.

So far, we have worked mostly with strings. Strings are essentially arrays of characters. Some implementations of string libraries in other languages build and treat strings as arrays of characters.

Let us create a new Java class. We will name this class **FunWithCharacterCodes** and ensure that it is in the **chapter3** package. Do not forget to create a **main()** method in this class as well. Inside the **main()** method, let us define three strings and three characters for the uppercase letters **A**, **B**, and **C**. Then we will simply print them, along with the default **charset**:

```java
import java.nio.charset.Charset;


public class FunWithCharacterCodes {

    public static void main(String[] args) {

        String strA = "A";

        String strB = "B";

        String strC = "C";


        char upperA = 'A';

        char upperB = 'B';

        char upperC = 'C';


        System.out.println(strA);
```

```
        System.out.println(strB);

        System.out.println(strC);


        System.out.println(upperA);

        System.out.println(upperB);

        System.out.println(upperC);


        System.out.println(Charset.defaultCharset());

    }

}
```

Running the preceding code should produce these results:

A

B

C

A

B

C

UTF-8

Now, we will adjust two lines of code. Let us print our value for the letter **A** twice. First, we will adjust the line that prints the **strA** string:

```
System.out.println(strA + strA);
```

Next, we will also adjust the line that prints the **upperA** string:

```
System.out.println(upperA + upperA);
```

It appears to be the same. However, running that code produces this output:

AA

B

C

130

B

C

UTF-8

The preceding output may not be what we expected, but we will take a detailed look at the code to understand what happened and why this output was shown.

We have used the plus (**+**) operator on strings before, so the concatenated output of **AA** should be expected. Using the plus operator on two **A** characters produced a numeric value of **130**.

This happened because Java parsed the plus operator, which means that in the absence of any overloading (as the **String** class does), it expects to work with numeric operands. Java did not know what to do with the two primitive characters, so it went through a **binary numeric promotion**.

Binary numeric promotion is the process of changing a small numeric type into a larger type. This is usually done when performing an operation on two numeric types that do not match. Java deals with characters in this process by converting them to integers. The ASCII/UTF character code for the capital letter **A** is **65**. Thus, *adding* the characters (**A + A**) is the same as adding *65* and *65*, or *130*.

We can leverage this when reading and verifying character input. Let us use the **Scanner** class to read a single character from the keyboard and verify its range in the alphabet:

```
// read a character from keyboard

Scanner inputScanner = new Scanner(System.in);

System.out.println("\nEnter a single character.");

String inputStr = inputScanner.nextLine();
```

Next, we will create a new character variable named **inputChar** and set its value using the string **charAt()** method to grab the first character from **inputStr**:

```
char inputChar = inputStr.charAt(0);
```

Now, let us close our scanner and verify whether **inputChar** is between the letters **A** and **K**, **L** and **Q**, or **R** and **Z**:

```
inputScanner.close();

if (inputChar >= 'A' && inputChar < 'L') {

    System.out.println("Character is between A and K.");

} else if (inputChar >= 'L' && inputChar < 'R') {

    System.out.println("Character is between L and Q.");
```

```
} else {

    System.out.println("Character must be between R and Z.");

}
```

```
System.out.println(inputChar + " = " + (int)inputChar);
```

We will finish by printing the character entered and its UTF code. Running this program should produce similar output:

AA

B

C

130

B

C

UTF-8

Enter a single character.

F

Character is between A and K.

F = 70

This works well, until we try entering a lowercase character:

Enter a single character.

a

Character must be between R and Z.

a = 97

A lower case **a** is not between **R** and **Z**. This is a failing in our **if** check. Yes, lowercase characters have a UTF index that is higher than uppercase characters. Let us expand our **if** statement to account for this:

```
if (inputChar >= 'A' && inputChar < 'L') {

    System.out.println("Character is between A and K.");

} else if (inputChar >= 'L' && inputChar < 'R') {
```

```java
    System.out.println("Character is between L and Q.");
} else if (inputChar >= 'R' && inputChar < 'Z') {
    System.out.println("Character must be between R and Z.");
} else if (inputChar >= 'a' && inputChar < 'l') {
    System.out.println("Character is between a and k.");
} else if (inputChar >= 'l' && inputChar < 'r') {
    System.out.println("Character is between l and q.");
} else {
    System.out.println("Character must be between r and z.");
}
```

Now, entering a lower case character should produce the correct results:

Enter a single character.

a

Character is between a and k.

a = 97

ASCII art

Some ASCII/UTF character codes point to lines and shapes, which can be used to create simple images. This is called **ASCII art**, and it has been used for decades to add an *extra flair* to programs.

To use it, we will create a new Java class named **CharacterArt** inside the **chapter3** package; make sure it has a **main()** method. Specify these three imports between the package and class definitions:

```java
import java.io.BufferedReader;

import java.io.FileReader;

import java.io.IOException;
```

Our program is going to read UTF codes from a file named **commandKeyCodes.txt**.

Our code will expect this file to be in the **data**/directory of our project. The file is a comma-separated text file, and it can be easily viewed from a terminal session in our project directory:

Windows:

```
type data\commandKeyCodes.txt
```

Linux/MacOS:

```
cat data/commandKeyCodes.txt
```

The contents of the file look like this:

```
9484,9472,9472,9488,9484,9472,9472,9488

9474,9484,9488,9474,9474,9484,9488,9474

9474,9492,9524,9524,9508,9500,9496,9474

9492,9472,9516,9516,9508,9500,9472,9496

9484,9472,9508,9500,9524,9524,9472,9488

9474,9484,9508,9500,9516,9516,9488,9474

9474,9492,9496,9474,9474,9492,9496,9474

9492,9472,9472,9496,9492,9472,9472,9496
```

To process it, let us build out a **BufferedReader** (for the file) inside a **try**/**catch** and read the first line:

```java
public static void main(String[] args) {

    try {

        BufferedReader reader = new BufferedReader(new FileReader("data/
        commandKeyCodes.txt"));


        // read the first line

        String dataLine = reader.readLine();
```

Like before, we will write a **while** loop to process the lines in the file, *splitting* them by a comma. The numeric codes in this file do not contain any spaces, so we do not need to run a **trim()** this time. We will split the **dataLine** string into an array named **data**:

```java
while (dataLine != null) {

    String[] data = dataLine.split(",");
```

Inside the **while** loop, we will use a **for** loop to iterate through the items in the **data** array. Then, we will use our **Integer** wrapper class to parse the code into an integer named **number**. Finally, we will print **number** to the screen while casting it as a character:

```java
    for (String strNumber : data) {

        int number = Integer.parseInt(strNumber);


        System.out.print((char)number);

    }
```

As we are now done with the current line, we need to run a **println()** to jump to the next line. We will also read the next file from the file into **dataLine**, which will start the **while** loop's logic all over again:

```java
    System.out.println();


    dataLine = reader.readLine();

}
```

With that complete, we have to close our **reader** and handle our exception:

```java
        reader.close();

    } catch (IOException ex) {
        ex.printStackTrace();

    }

}
```

Running this program should produce the following output:

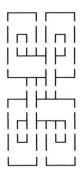

We have drawn a symbol that resembles the Macintosh *command* key. Given what we have accomplished with a few lines of code and an eight-by-eight file of comma-delimited numbers, it is easy to see how the possibilities of what to print are only limited by our imagination.

Note: A UTF conversion chart can be found in the appendices.

Strings

We have worked with strings in the previous chapters. But now, we will take a closer look at the powerful functions that we can use on strings.

Create a new Java class named **WorkingWithStrings** inside the **chapter3** package. This class will also require a **main()** method. Inside our **main()** method, define a string named **email**.

```
String email = "victoria.ploetz@largecorp.com";
```

As we can see, the employee email addresses for *Large Corp* are built in the following pattern:

- First name
- A dot or period
- Last name
- An *at-sign* ("**@**")
- **largecorp** in all lower case
- A dot or period, and then the suffix of **com**

We will start by splitting the email into smaller parts. To do that, we first need to figure out the positions of two characters:

- The **@**
- The first dot

indexOf

Once we know the positions of characters in the **email** string, we can use the string manipulation methods to parse them. We can do this with the **indexOf()** method:

```
// get string positions

int dotPos = email.indexOf('.');

int atPos = email.indexOf('@');
```

This way, the **indexOf()** method returns an integer value to indicate the position of the requested character. The possible range of return values is zero through the end of the string. If the character or string requested is not found, a value of **-1** is returned. Remember, Java uses zero-based indexes and numbering, which means the character positions of the **email** string resemble what is shown in *Table 3.1*:

v	i	c	t	o	r	i	a	.	p	l	o	e	t	z	@	l	a	r	g	e	c	o	r	p	.	c	o	m
0	1	2	3	4	5	6	7	8	9	10	11	12	13	14	15	16	17	18	19	20	21	22	23	24	25	26	27	28

Table 3.1: *The character index positions of the email string*

In the mapping shown in *Table 3.1*, the value stored in **atPos** should be 15, and the value stored in **dotPos** should be 8.

> **Note: By default, indexOf() will return the index of the first occurrence of the character or string passed in.**

substring

Now, we will use the **substring()** method to parse out the employee's first name and save it in a variable named **firstName**:

```
String firstName = email.substring(0, dotPos);
```

We are providing the substring with a start index and a stopping point after the last character that we want. We can build variables for **lastName** and **company** in the same way:

```
String lastName = email.substring(dotPos + 1, atPos);
```

```
String company = email.substring(atPos + 1, dot2Pos);
```

Let us add statements to output the string values:

```
System.out.println("First name: " + firstName);
```

```
System.out.println("Last name: " + lastName);
```

```
System.out.println("Company: " + company);
```

Running our code should produce results similar to this:

```
First name: victoria
```

```
Last name: ploetz
```

```
Company: largecompany
```

toUpperCase

Our user's name is not in the proper case, that is, with a capital letter at the beginning of each name. We can fix that by writing a new method called **properCase**:

```
private static String properCase(String name) {

    char firstLetter = Character.toUpperCase(name.charAt(0));


    return firstLetter + name.substring(1);

}
```

Our **properCase()** method accepts a string variable named **name** and starts by defining a character named **firstLetter** set to the value of the first letter in the **name** string. We also run the **toUpperCase()** method on that letter, forcing it to be in upper case. We then return the value of **firstLetter** concatenated with the substring of **name** from position 1 through to the end of the **name** string.

When the **substring()** method is called with a single numeric parameter, it is essentially running with a starting position to bisect the string, but no end. Therefore, it will return the entire remaining string value from that index on.

> **Note: The toUpperCase() method is a part of both the String and Character classes. Also, running toUpperCase() on a string in all or partial upper case will have no effect on the upper case characters, while any lower case characters will be converted to upper case.**

We can now call our **properCase()** method before our **System.out.println** statements:

```
firstName = properCase(firstName);
```

```
lastName = properCase(lastName);
```

Rerunning our code should produce results similar to this:

First name: Victoria

Last name: Ploetz

Company: largecompany

toLowerCase

Since there is a **toUpperCase()** method, we also have a **toLowerCase()** method on the Java **String** class. This method can be useful when processing user input fields like email addresses. Email addresses are case-insensitive and should be stored and processed in lowercase.

However, sometimes we may encounter a user who enters them as all uppercase or even in mixed-case:

```
String messedUpEmail = "bObJoNeS@BIGGERCOMPANY.com";
```

```
System.out.println("messedUpEmail.toLower() = " +

        messedUpEmail.toLowerCase());
```

This way, we can easily apply the **toLowerCase()** method to show the string in the desired case.

If we were to add this code to the end of our **main()** method and run it, our output would look like this:

```
First name: Victoria

Last name: Ploetz

Company: largecompany


messedUpEmail.toLower() = bobjones@biggercompany.com
```

As shown, string methods like **charAt()**, **toUpperCase()**, **toLowerCase()**, **indexOf()**, and **substring()** can be very useful when parsing streams of incoming data.

String equality

Equality of characters and other primitive types is straightforward. However, string equality can be a little tricky.

After our **println** statements, let us add an if-check to see if our user's first name is **Victoria**:

```
if (firstName == "Victoria") {

    System.out.println("Your name is Victoria!");

} else {

    System.out.println("Sorry, your name is NOT Victoria.");

}
```

Running this code yields the following output:

```
First name: Victoria

Last name: Ploetz

Company: largecompany


messedUpEmail.toLower() = bobjones@biggercompany.com


Sorry, your name is NOT Victoria.
```

The **firstName** variable is definitely equal to a string value of **Victoria**, so what could be the issue? The problem is that since strings are not primitive types, string variables only store a pointer to a location in memory. Here, we are comparing the reference identifier that points to each string value. In this case, that is not going to do what we want.

Fortunately, strings have their own operator for equality, known as the **equals()** method:

```
if (firstName.equals("Victoria")) {

    System.out.println("Your name is Victoria!");

} else {

    System.out.println("Sorry, your name is NOT Victoria.");

}
```

Now when we run our code, we get the expected results:

First name: Victoria

Last name: Ploetz

Company: largecompany

messedUpEmail.toLower() = bobjones@biggercompany.com

Your name is Victoria!

As we can see, the string **equals** operator is what we want to use when checking whether strings are of equal *value*, which is most of the time.

Equality of string suffixes

We may need to check whether the end of a string is equal to a certain value. Fortunately, Java's delivered **String** class has a method to accommodate this requirement as well.

We will start by creating a new method named **isBusinessEmail**. This method will return a **boolean** value and accept a string email address as a parameter. The idea behind this method is to check the ending of the email address string to see if it matches some known endings that indicate whether:

- The user is a student
- The user has submitted a personal email address

This is a common filter used on web forms when businesses want to focus their efforts on individuals who could possibly be good leads for sales:

```
private static boolean isBusinessEmail(String email) {

    boolean validEmail = true;


    if (email.endsWith("@gmail.com")) {
```

```
        validEmail = false;

    } else if (email.endsWith(".edu")) {

        validEmail = false;

    }


    return validEmail;

}
```

The logic behind this method is that we first initialize the **validEmail** boolean to a value of **true**. Next, we check whether the email address provided is a Gmail address (ending in @gmail.com), and then set **validEmail** to **false**. This indicates that a user has provided a *personal* email address, when our page wants their *business* email address instead. After that, we have another if-check to see whether the email address ends with the **.edu** string, indicating that the user is likely a student at a university. In this case, **validEmail** will also be set to **false**. Finally, we return the value of **validEmail** to the calling method.

To test this out (at the end of our **main()** method), we can define a new email named **email2** to have one of these invalid endings:

```
String email2 = "khadiya8821@mnsu.edu";
```

Then, we can create two if-checks for our email addresses:

```
if (isBusinessEmail(email)) {

    System.out.println(email + " is valid!");

} else {

    System.out.println(email + " is not valid!");

}


if (isBusinessEmail(email2)) {

    System.out.println(email2 + " is valid!");

} else {

    System.out.println(email2 + " is not valid!");

}
```

If we ran our complete code (so far), it would look something like this:

First name: Victoria

```
Last name: Ploetz

Company: largecompany


messedUpEmail.toLower() = bobjones@biggercompany.com


Your name is Victoria!


victoria.ploetz@largecompany.com is valid!

khadiya8821@mnsu.edu is not valid!
```

As shown, Khadiya's email is not valid (ends in **.edu**), while Victoria's email meets our requirements for a valid business email address.

Equality of string prefixes

We can also verify the beginning of a string value. Let us say we wanted to do some special processing on users whose last names start with **Pl**. For that, we can use the Java **String** class **startsWith()** method.

This can be accomplished with a simple if-check at the end of the code in our **main()** method:

```
if (lastName.toUpperCase().startsWith("PL")) {

    System.out.println(firstName + "'s last name of "

            + lastName + " does indeed start with Pl.");

}
```

As shown, we are simply checking whether the **lastName** string has a prefix of **PL** and are writing an output to the screen if it does.

> **Note: Remember that Java strings are indeed case-sensitive. Therefore, when checking equality for a string retrieved from a user's input, it is a good idea to force the casing to either upper or lower. This way, we do not have to account for multiple types of casing (upper or lower) for each character in a string.**

Now when we run our code, the last line of our output reads the following:

```
Victoria's last name of Ploetz does indeed start with Pl.
```

contains

Another useful method in the Java **String** class is the **contains()** method. This method can be used to verify whether or not a smaller string exists within a larger string. A phone number might be a good way to use this. Let us assume that we want to apply some special processing to phone numbers with a central office code of **188**. To test this, we could define a couple of phone numbers (as strings) on the end of our **main()** method and check:

```java
String phoneNumber = "444-867-5309";

String phoneNumber2 = "444-188-2300";


if (phoneNumber.contains("-188-")) {

    System.out.println(phoneNumber + " is a valid 188 number!");

}


if (phoneNumber2.contains("-188-")) {

    System.out.println(phoneNumber2 + " is a valid 188 number!");

}
```

If we execute our code, the end of our output would look like this:

444-188-2300 is a valid 188 number!

This output occurs because only **phoneNumber2** contains a string that matches **"-188-"**, which means that the if-check for the other variable (**phoneNumber**) does not process anything. In this case, it is important to include the dashes (**-**) around the **188** so that our **contains()** do not match on other occurrences of **188**.

Regular expressions

So far, we have shown easy ways to check the prefix or suffix of a string for a particular value. But what if our needs are more complicated? Regular expressions are a powerful tool that enables fast and efficient verification of strings.

> **Note: The term** *regular expression* **is often abbreviated as or shortened to regex or regexes (plural).**

To utilize regular expressions (*Baeldung 2022b*), we will import two Java standard library classes: **Pattern** and **Matcher**. Let us go ahead and add these imports to our **WorkingWithStrings** class:

```
package chapter3;
```

```
import java.util.regex.Pattern;
```

```
import java.util.regex.Matcher;
```

```
public class WorkingWithStrings {
```

To apply a regular expression to a string, we first define a pattern, and then we try to match a string to that pattern. Keeping with our **contains** example on a phone number, we could build our pattern (on the end of our **main()** method) like this:

```
Pattern phone188Pattern =
```

```
Pattern.compile("[0-9]{3}\\-188\\-[0-9]{4}");
```

Let us break it down one part at a time:

- **[0-9]{3}:** The **[0-9]** in brackets indicate that we are looking for a single numeric digit from zero to nine. The **{3}** immediately afterward indicates that we are looking to perform the previous match three times. Essentially, this means we are looking for our string to start with any three numbers.
- **\\-:** This indicates that we want to look for a literal dash - after the first three digits. As the dash character has special meaning inside regular expression syntax, we must escape it with two backslash **** characters.
- **188:** Here, we have a literal string of **188** as we want to match on phone numbers with a **188** central office code.
- **\\-:** Once again, we need a dash character.
- **[0-9]{4}:** Similar to the first numeric pattern in this regex, this part is looking to match on four consecutive numeric digits.

With our pattern defined, let us instantiate two objects of the **Matcher** class:

```
Matcher phone188Matcher = phone188Pattern.matcher(phoneNumber);
```

```
Matcher phone188Matcher2 = phone188Pattern.matcher(phoneNumber2);
```

Essentially, we need a **Matcher** object for each string we are trying to match. Now, we can build our if-checks using the **find()** method on each **Matcher** object:

```
if (phone188Matcher.find()) {

    System.out.println(phoneNumber + " is a valid 188 number! (regex)");

}
```

```
if (phone188Matcher2.find()) {
```

```
    System.out.println(phoneNumber2 + " is a valid 188 number! (regex)");
}
```

Running our code should show this at the end of the output:

444-188-2300 is a valid 188 number! (regex)

Essentially, we performed the same operation performed earlier with the **contains()** method, but with more finely-tuned control. The advantage of using a regular expression is that we can be more abstract about what we want to match on. For instance, the **contains()**, **endsWith()**, and **startsWith()** methods all require explicit strings to match on. But regular expressions allow us to say things like *I want to make sure that we match on three numbers,* so it definitely offers a great deal of flexibility. We could use a regular expression to verify that the phone numbers were entered correctly:

```
Pattern validPhonePattern = Pattern.compile("[0-9]{3}\\-[0-9]{3}\\-[0-9]{4}");

Matcher phoneMatcher = validPhonePattern.matcher(phoneNumber);

Matcher phoneMatcher2 = validPhonePattern.matcher(phoneNumber2);


if (phoneMatcher.find()) {

    System.out.println(phoneNumber + " is a valid phone number! (regex)");

}


if (phoneMatcher2.find()) {

    System.out.println(phoneNumber2 + " is a valid phone number! (regex)");

}
```

Running this code should produce the following at the end of our output:

444-867-5309 is a valid phone number! (regex)

444-188-2300 is a valid phone number! (regex)

Regular expressions also give us a wide range of flexibility with strings. Let us say that some of our users decide to log in or use an email with their **nickname** instead of their given first name. Can regular expressions help us with that?

Let us start by defining some **nickname** strings at the end of our **main()** method. We will use two for **Victoria**, and a new user named **Robert** (some people named **Robert** like to go by **Rob** or **Bob**):

```
String nickname = "Toria";
```

```
String nickname2 = "Vicky";

String robert = "Robert";

String nickname3 = "Rob";

String nickname4 = "Bob";
```

We will start by verifying **Robert**. This pattern is not difficult:

```
System.out.println("\nBob pattern:");

Pattern bobPattern = Pattern.compile("[B|R]ob");
```

This pattern is simple. We want to match on strings of either **Bob** or **Rob**. The single pipe character '**|**' is the regular expression **or** operator. Therefore, an opening pattern of **[B|R]** looks to see if the first character in the string is a capital **B** or a capital **R**. The next two characters of **ob** are literals, looking to match on the second and third characters matching on a lower case **o**, followed by a lower case **b**.

As we are going to perform a regex operation multiple times here, let us build a method to do the *heavy lifting* for this task. We will name this method **matchName**, and it will accept an object of the **Pattern** class and a name as a string:

```
private static void matchName(Pattern pattern, String name) {

    Matcher matcher = pattern.matcher(name);

    if (matcher.find()) {

        System.out.println("Match found!  Welcome " + name + "!");

    } else {

        System.out.println("Sorry " + name + ", no match found.");

    }

}
```

We will start off our method by taking the **pattern** object that was passed in and instantiating an object of the **Matcher** class, using **name** as a parameter. With matcher defined, we will invoke the **find()** method in our if-check and output the appropriate message.

Now, we can call this method for all the six names we have defined:

```
matchName(bobPattern, nickname);

matchName(bobPattern, nickname2);

matchName(bobPattern, nickname3);
```

```
matchName(bobPattern, nickname4);
```

```
matchName(bobPattern, robert);
```

```
matchName(bobPattern, firstName);
```

If we run our code, we see the following at the end of our output:

Bob pattern:

Sorry Toria, no match found.

Sorry Vicky, no match found.

Match found! Welcome Rob!

Match found! Welcome Bob!

Match found! Welcome Robert!

Sorry Victoria, no match found.

As the output shows, **Rob**, **Bob**, and **Robert** all matched! **Victoria** and her nicknames were not matched, which is correct.

So how do we match Victoria's nicknames? We will start by creating an instance of the pattern object to define how they should be matched:

```
System.out.println("\nVictoria pattern:");
```

```
Pattern victoriaPattern = Pattern.compile("[Vic|][[T|t]oria]");
```

This pattern has two distinct parts:

- **[Vic|]:** This part is looking to match either on a string starting with **Vic** or nothing. Note that the pipe (**or** operator) is after the **Vic** string, and it has nothing afterward. Essentially, if our string starts with **Vic**, then we have a match. If it does not, then the next part is assumed to be the *start* of the string.
- **[[T|t]oria]:** This part is looking to match on the strings **Toria** or **toria**. In the latter case, it is assumed that it is the suffix (end) of the string.

Now, we will call the **matchName()** method while passing our **victoriaPattern** for the same six names:

```
matchName(victoriaPattern, nickname);
```

```
matchName(victoriaPattern, nickname2);
```

```
matchName(victoriaPattern, nickname3);
```

```
matchName(victoriaPattern, nickname4);
```

```
matchName(victoriaPattern, robert);
```

```
matchName(victoriaPattern, firstName);
```

Running our code should produce the following at the end of the output:

Victoria pattern:

Match found! Welcome Toria!

Match found! Welcome Vicky!

Sorry Rob, no match found.

Sorry Bob, no match found.

Sorry Robert, no match found.

Match found! Welcome Victoria!

All the **Bob** failed to match, **Toria** matched because of the second part of the pattern, **Vicky** matched because of the **[Vic|]** pattern definition, and **Victoria** matched because it matched *both* parts of our pattern definition.

As shown, regular expressions can quickly get complicated, but they are a great way to validate input rules with powerful yet abstract tools.

Conclusion

In this chapter, we discussed different ways to handle character and string data. First, we discussed character data types and saw how they work with concatenation and ASCII/UTF codes. We looked at different methods from the Java **String** class, providing many tools to manage and parse text-based data. Finally, we worked on string equality, highlighting how it differs from checking for equality on primitive types. Part of our work with string equality led us to look at regular expressions and ways to wield them as powerful tools.

In the next chapter, we will continue to work with string data as we explore structures like arrays and collections. We will have a look at Java records as well.

Points to remember

- The default character set for Java (as of Java 18) is UTF-8.
- The **Character wrapper** class has many useful methods to help us parse and work with character data.
- There are several ASCII/UTF characters that can be used to add *extra flair* to your programs.
- The first occurrence of a character in a string can be found using the **indexOf()** method.

- Character positions in Java strings are zero-based (first index at zero, not one).
- A smaller part of a string can be retrieved using the **substring()** method.
- Complicated, regular expressions give us extremely high levels of flexibility and customizability for performing string equality operations.

Join our book's Discord space

Join the book's Discord Workspace for Latest updates, Offers, Tech happenings around the world, New Release and Sessions with the Authors:

https://discord.bpbonline.com

CHAPTER 4
Arrays, Collections, and Records

Introduction

This chapter will focus on different ways of storing and grouping data together. We have already discussed some of the focal points of this chapter. Now, we will take a deep dive and further explore concepts like arrays, collection types, and records.

We will also discuss sequenced collections, a new feature in Java 21. This feature will allow us to track the order in which items are added to a collection and greatly enhance the ways we work with lists, sets, and maps.

Structure

In this chapter, we will discuss the following topics:

- Arrays
- Sets
- Lists
- Maps
- Records

Objectives

In this chapter, we are going to take a close look at the ways in which Java allows us to group data together and work with it in memory. We will focus on the following:

- Building arrays of data types that we are already familiar with
- Understanding the different behaviors and capabilities of sets, lists, and maps
- Learning how to store data in and retrieve it from the different collection types
- Exploring and understanding the Java record type

Arrays

Arrays are a simple way of storing multiple indexed values of the same data type. We have already used arrays a few times in the previous chapters. While working with files and reading lines of input, we have defined arrays as follows:

```java
String[] gameColumns = gameLine.split(",");
```

As we have seen, using arrays created by the **split()** method has helped us divide file lines into columns. Additionally, every time we start a new program, we define an array:

```java
public static void main(String[] args) {
```

That's right, The **args** parameter that we define in every **main()** method is a string array. So far, we have not done anything with this array. However, it is an easy way to accept and organize inputs into our programs.

Create a new Java class named **JavaArguments** in the **chapter4** package, and make sure it has a **static void main** method:

```java
package chapter4;


public class JavaArguments {

    public static void main(String[] args) {

        System.out.println("You have supplied " + args.length
                + " arguments:");

        for (int index = 0; index < args.length; index++) {
            System.out.printf("Argument #%d:",index);
```

```
        System.out.println(args[index]);
    }

  }

}
```

The idea here is simple. We are outputting the number of arguments (**args.length**) and iterating it through the **args** array. Then we print each argument, along with its numeric **index**. If we run this program without providing any arguments, it yields the following output:

You have supplied 0 arguments:

So, how do we pass arguments to a Java program? There are two ways to do this. The first is from the command line. If we open up a terminal session, pass arguments to a Java program from within the project directory. We will need to be in the **target/classes** subdirectory. Once inside that directory, we can use the main Java executable to run our compiled class with as many arguments as we decide to add:

cd target/classes

pwd

/Users/aaronploetz/Documents/workspace/CodeWithJava21/target/classes

java chapter4.JavaArguments The cake is a lie!You have supplied 5 arguments:

Argument #0:The

Argument #1:cake

Argument #2:is

Argument #3:a

Argument #4:lie!

> **Note: Depending on how our IDE builds the class files in the target directory, we may have to compile our JavaArguments.java file with the javac command.**

The second method to pass in arguments is from within your IDE. Eclipse, for example, allows us to use Run Configurations. This feature allows us to save and reuse runtime arguments and environment variables. In Eclipse, this can be found within the project properties, as shown in *Figure 4.1*:

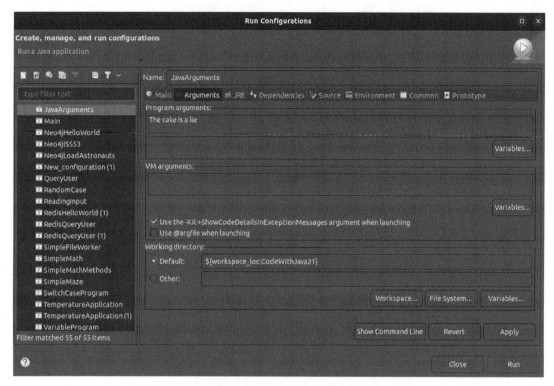

Figure 4.1: *The Arguments tab of the Run Configurations window in the Eclipse IDE*

For our program arguments, we will enter a simple sentence: **The cake is a lie**. If we run our program with this string as arguments, we get the following output:

```
You have supplied 5 arguments:
```

```
Argument #0:The
```

```
Argument #1:cake
```

```
Argument #2:is
```

```
Argument #3:a
```

```
Argument #4:lie
```

An argument array can be a useful tool to pass in a limited number of parameters to our Java programs.

We can also iterate through our **args** array backward if we want. A simple adjustment of the **for** loop is all it would take:

```
for (int index = args.length - 1; index > -1; index--) {
```

Running our code should now produce the following output:

You have supplied 5 arguments:

Argument #4:lie

Argument #3:a

Argument #2:is

Argument #1:cake

Argument #0:The

Multi-dimensional arrays

Arrays can also have multiple dimensions to their indexes. To demonstrate this, let us create a new Java class. We will call it **CoordinateArrays** and make sure it is in the **chapter4** package and that it contains a **main()** method.

Let us start by defining a private, two-dimensional array in our class to store the location of heroes on a game grid:

```
public class CoordinateArrays {

    private static String [][] gameGrid = new String[5][5];

    public static void main(String[] args) {
```

This statement defines a new **gameGrid** array to hold a maximum of *5x5 (25)* values. With the array defined, we can add the position of our heroes:

```
gameGrid[3][2] = "Byorki - Ranger";

gameGrid[3][3] = "K'lar - Fighter";

gameGrid[4][3] = "Tyrenni - Wizard";

gameGrid[1][3] = "Athena - Rogue";

gameGrid[0][1] = "Jarrod - Cleric";
```

Now our `gameGrid` holds location data for our heroes, as shown in *Figure 4.2*:

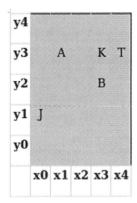

Figure 4.2: *A grid showing the X,Y coordinates for our heroes, denoted by the first letter in their name*

We can display the position of a specific hero by referencing their grid coordinates:

```
System.out.println(gameGrid[4][3]);
```

If we run this code, we should see the following output:

Tyrenni - Wizard

> **Note: Java allocates memory based on the maximum possible size of the defined variable. With multi-dimensional arrays, we need to be careful not to define them to be too big, or they will consume most (or all) of the available memory on the Java heap.**

Let us write a new, private, and static method to print out the grid:

```
private static void printGrid() {

    System.out.println();
```

We will start by printing an empty line to keep our outputs appropriately spaced. Next, we will use a pair of nested **for** loops to iterate through both dimensions of our **gameGrid** array. The problem is that our grid (as shown in *Figure 4.2*) works from zero to four, increasing from left-to-right, and down-to-up. But our standard output works from left-to-right and up-to-down. Therefore, we will have to iterate through the Y-axis *backward*:

```
for (int indexY = 4; indexY > -1; indexY--) {

        // print column axis key

        System.out.print(indexY);

        for (int indexX = 0; indexX < 5; indexX++) {
```

Next, we should check whether the current **gameGrid** entry is null or empty. If it is, then it is an unoccupied space, and we will print a square outline. We will run this check because programs tend to run a little faster if we are checking for the conditions that are most likely to be true:

```java
        if ((gameGrid[indexX][indexY] == null)
|| (gameGrid[indexX][indexY].equals(""))) {

            // print a square character

            System.out.print((char)9634);
```

Next, we will build our else clause to print the value for our current gameGrid entry:

```java
} else {

            // prints first character in hero's name

            System.out.print(
gameGrid[indexX][indexY].charAt(0));

        }

    }

    System.out.println();

}
    // print row axis key
    System.out.println(" 01234");

}
```

We finish the inner loop with a **println()** to jump to the next line. Finally, we finish the outer loop by printing the numbers for the X-axis as a **key** at the bottom of the grid. Now go back to our **main()** method and add a call to the new **printGrid()** method at the end.

Running this code should then produce the following output:

```
Tyrenni - Wizard


4◻◻◻TO◻

3◻◻BK◻

2◻◻◻◻◻◻
```

1☐☐☐A☐

0☐J☐☐☐

```
01234
```

We can also move one of our heroes quite easily. Create a new private, static method named **movePlayer** and have it accept the following three parameters:

- **char direction**
- **int currentX**
- **int currentY**

In the **movePlayer** method, we will begin by initializing two new variables to the values of the **currentX** and **currentY** coordinates:

```
private static void movePlayer(char direction,

int currentX, int currentY) {


    int newX = currentX;

    int newY = currentY;
```

Next, we will have a **switch**/**case** statement on the direction variable and adjust our new coordinates appropriately:

```
        switch (Character.toUpperCase(direction)) {

        case 'N':

            // north

            newY++;

            break;

        case 'S':

            // south

            newY--;

            break;

        case 'W':

            // west

            newX--;

            break;
```

```
    default:

        // east

        newX++;

}
```

Basically, our hero can move north and south by incrementing and decrementing (respectively) the **newY** axis value. We move east (by default) and west by incrementing and decrementing (respectively) the **newX** axis value. For the actual movement, we will save off the value stored at the **currentX** and **currentY** coordinates:

```
String hero = gameGrid[currentX][currentY];


// move player

gameGrid[newX][newY] = hero;


// erase old location

gameGrid[currentX][currentY] = "";
```

We then set the **hero** value to our new location on the grid and finish by setting our current location to an empty string. Finally, we will print a line describing the movement activity:

```
System.out.println("Moved " + hero + " from ("

        + currentX + "," + currentY

        + ") to " + "(" + newX + "," + newY + ")");
```

Back in our **main()** method, let us add a call to **movePlayer()**, giving it a direction of **N** (North) and **Athena**'s current location:

```
// move player Athena from 1,3 to 1,4

movePlayer('N', 1, 3);

printGrid();
```

Running our code should now print the following output:

Tyrenni - Wizard

4⬜⬜⬜⬜⬜

3⬜A⬜KT

2⬜⬜⬜B⬜

```
1J☐☐☐☐

0☐☐☐☐☐

 01234
```

Moved Athena - Rogue from (1,3) to (1,4)

```
4☐A☐☐☐

3☐☐☐KT

2☐☐☐B☐

1J☐☐☐☐

0☐☐☐☐☐

 01234
```

If we examine the grid at the bottom, we can see that **Athena** (represented by the **A**) has moved north (up) from a Y-axis of **3** to a Y-axis of **4**.

Collections and maps

Java provides a few other data structures capable of storing multiple data points of the same type but with much more functionality and versatility. These structures are known as **collections**.

There are three main types of Java collection structures that we will discuss:

- Sets
- Lists
- Maps

As with all things in Java, everything is an object. That means everything inherits the **Object** base class. In addition to that, sets and lists both inherit the **Collection** base class. While maps may not inherit **Collection**, they are still a part of the Java **Collection** framework and have similar methods and ways of working with the data inside.

For our examples with collections, we will create a new Java class named **WorkingWithCollections**. It should be inside the **chapter4** package, have a **main()** method, and contain the specified imports:

```
package chapter4;


import java.util.Collections;
```

```
public class WorkingWithCollections {

    public static void main(String[] args) {

    }

}
```

Before we get too far, let us create a new static method to output the contents of whichever collection we happen to be working with. Add a new method named **printCollection** to the end of our new class. It should be of type **void** (no return type) and should accept an object of type **Collection** as its only parameter:

```
private static void printCollection(Collection collection) {

    for (Object element : collection) {

        System.out.printf("%s, ", element.toString());

    }

    System.out.println();

}
```

> **Note: Technically, we could omit the call to the toString() method on element. The print(), printf(), and println() methods will all implicitly convert their output parameter to a string.**

This method should be able to display the contents of any set or list, as they all inherit from the **Collection** base class.

Sets

The simplest **collection** type is a set. A set is a unique collection of multiple items of data. There are different types of sets with some subtle differences, which we will examine.

Let us start by creating a new string array and initializing it with the names of our heroes:

```
String[] heroes = {"Byorki", "K'lar", "Tyrenni", "Athena", "Jarrod"};
```

For the following examples, we should use the following imports:

```
import java.util.HashSet;
```

```
import java.util.LinkedHashSet;
```

```
import java.util.Set;

import java.util.TreeSet;
```

HashSet

Next, we will create a new **HashSet** and load it with data from the **heroes** array (using the **Collections addAll()** method):

```
Set<String> heroSet = new HashSet<>();

Collections.addAll(heroSet, heroes);

printCollection(heroSet);
```

First, we declared **heroSet** to be of type **Set<String>**. This code informed Java that **heroSet** will be a *set of string values*. However, **Set** is an abstract class. We still need to initialize it with a concrete class, like **HashSet**.

With **HashSet**, we gave it an empty set of angle brackets (**<>**). This way, it inherits the same element class (**String**) that we defined for the abstract **Set** class. It is worth noting that older versions of Java required the inner element class to be specified in the implementation as well. Consider this example:

```
Set<String> heroSet = new HashSet<String>();
```

Fortunately, this is no longer the case, as you will see with all the collection implementations in this chapter and throughout the book.

With **heroSet** initialized as an empty **HashSet**, we then used the **addAll()** method from the **Collections** class to fill **heroSet** with the values in the **heroes** array. As **heroes** is defined as an array of type string (which matches our element class), it loads **heroSet** with the values from **heroes**. Running our code should produce the following output:

Byorki, K'lar, Tyrenni, Athena, Jarrod,

Let us add an element to **heroSet**:

```
heroSet.add("Byorki");
```

Byorki is already there, but we will add her again. Now let us run our code and check the output:

Byorki, K'lar, Tyrenni, Athena, Jarrod,

That's right! The output is the same. The values inside sets must be unique, so our call to the **add()** method silently fails. Let us add a different name:

```
heroSet.add("Rik");
```

Running our code produces these results:

Byorki, K'lar, Rik, Tyrenni, Athena, Jarrod,

Remember that a **HashSet** does not maintain any order.

LinkedHashSet

Let us modify the definition of **heroSet**. We will comment it out and redefine its implementation to use **LinkedHashSet** instead:

```
// Set<String> heroSet = new HashSet<>();
```

```
Set<String> heroSet = new LinkedHashSet<>();
```

We will also need to import LinkedHashSet:

```
import java.util.LinkedHashSet;
```

If we make no other changes, running our code produces the following output:

Byorki, K'lar, Tyrenni, Athena, Jarrod, Rik,

Note how **Rik** has moved to the end of the set. This is because a **LinkedHashSet** maintains the order in which the elements were added. As **Rik** was added last, he is at the end of the set.

TreeSet

We will again modify the definition of **heroSet**, this time altering its implementation to be a **TreeSet**:

```
// Set<String> heroSet = new HashSet<>();
```

```
// Set<String> heroSet = new LinkedHashSet<>();
```

```
Set<String> heroSet = new TreeSet<>();
```

Remember to **import TreeSet** as well:

```
import java.util.TreeSet;
```

Again, without any other changes, running our code produces these results:

Athena, Byorki, Jarrod, K'lar, Rik, Tyrenni,

The values of **heroSet** are now in alpha-numeric order. A **TreeSet** implements a binary sort on its elements. The order in which they were added is not maintained, but sometimes we do have a need for a **collection** to be in its sorted, alpha-numeric order.

Removing an item from a set is a simple task:

```
heroSet.remove("Rik");
```

Adding **remove()** for **Rik** and running our code produces this output:

Athena, Byorki, Jarrod, K'lar, Tyrenni,

Lists

Let us move on to work with lists. Lists are a simple collection of items, ordered by index. They function much like arrays do, and likewise, they allow duplicate entries. Similar to sets, there are a few different implementations of lists that will be examined here.

The following imports will help with the upcoming examples:

```
import java.util.ArrayList;

import java.util.List;

import java.util.LinkedList;
```

The different types of sets have some subtle differences that we will examine. Let us start by creating a new string array and initializing it with the names of our heroes:

```
String[] heroes = {"Byorki", "K'lar", "Tyrenni", "Athena", "Jarrod"};
```

ArrayList

Let us define a new list of string named **monsterList**, with an implementation type of **ArrayList**:

```
List<String> monsterList = new ArrayList<>();
```

With that defined, we will add a few elements to it:

```
monsterList.add("Kobald");

monsterList.add("Skeleton");

monsterList.add("Zombie");

monsterList.add("Rats");

monsterList.add("Skeleton");
```

We will follow that by calling **printCollection()** to output our list to the console:

```
printCollection(monsterList);
```

Running our code adds this line to our output:

Kobald, Skeleton, Zombie, Rats, Skeleton,

Note how our **monsterList** is in the order that we entered the elements, and that **Skeleton** is in there twice. Now, we will use the **sort()** method from the **Collection** class to put **monsterList** in order:

```
Collections.sort(monsterList);
```

Running our code now shows the contents of **monsterList** to be this:

Kobald, Rats, Skeleton, Skeleton, Zombie,

As you can see, the elements in **monsterList** are now sorted alpha-numerically. This works, because the **List** is defined to hold string values, and Java's **String** class implements the comparable interface for use with strings.

Removing an element from a list is identical to how an element is removed from a **Set**. Here, we will issue a **remove()** for **Skeleton**:

```
monsterList.remove("Skeleton");
```

Running our code leads the contents of **monsterList** to look like this:

Kobald, Rats, Skeleton, Zombie,

As you can see, the first occurrence of **Skeleton** was removed from the list. However, the second occurrence of **Skeleton** remains. This is an important aspect to consider when running a **remove()** on a list. While the first occurrence is removed, any duplicates of the named element are not.

The **remove()** method also works by numeric index. If we wanted to remove the **Skeleton** element by index, we could do so like this:

```
monsterList.remove(2);
```

We can also access the individual elements in an **ArrayList** by using an element's numeric index. At the end of our code, we will output the second item in the list (index of 1) using the **get()** method:

```
System.out.println(monsterList.get(1));
```

Running our code shows the following output for **monsterList** and the element at **monsterList** position 1:

Kobald, Rats, Skeleton, Zombie,

Rats

> **Note: Remember that Java works from zero-based numeric indexes. The first element in a list is index 0, the second element is at index 1, the third at index 2, and so on.**

Vector

We can also define **monsterList** using the **Vector** concrete class. We will not be showing any examples for it, as its behavior is similar to that of **ArrayList**. This is how the instantiation would look:

```
List<String> monsterList = new Vector<>();
```

There is no difference in the functional behavior between **ArrayList** and **Vector**. The advantage of creating a list of type **Vector** would be that **Vector** is known to be **thread-safe**. As a result, while using **Vector**, we may incur a small performance hit. Therefore, if the application is not using threads, **ArrayList** is the better option.

Thread safety

Essentially, the state of an object can become corrupted or inconsistent if it is being used by many processes threads simultaneously. Objects and types that are thread-safe employ techniques like synchronization to ensure that they are only accessed by one thread at a time.

LinkedList

Java's **LinkedList** is an implementation of the traditional linked list data structure. Essentially, elements in a linked list are sorted by their insertion position relative to the other elements. Elements are always added at the end of a linked list.

What makes a linked list unique is that the elements maintain limited knowledge about the other elements of the list. In our case, Java's **LinkedList** class is known as a **doubly linked list**. It is considered to be doubly linked because each element has a pointer to both the next and previous elements of the list.

We will create a **LinkedList** to hold data on the cities that our heroes encounter in their travels. To gain the full functionality of the available methods, we will need to specify **LinkedList** as both the base and concrete classes:

```
LinkedList<String> cityList = new LinkedList<>();

cityList.add("Elddim");

cityList.add("Crystwind");

cityList.add("Fallraen");

cityList.add("Meren");

cityList.add("Lang");


printCollection(cityList);
```

Running our code shows these values for `cityList`:

```
Elddim, Crystwind, Fallraen, Meren, Lang,
```

As we can see, they are indeed listed in the order that they were added. This can be seen in *Figure 4.3*:

LinkedList<String> cityList

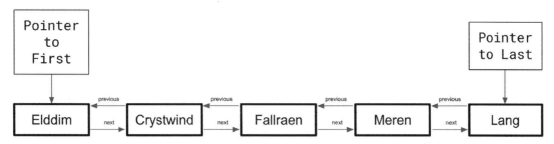

Figure 4.3: *A visual representation of the cityList linked list*

Similar to **ArrayList**, elements in a **LinkedList** can be referenced by numeric index:

```
System.out.println(cityList.get(3));
```

Running this code adds the following line to our output:

Meren

As we have seen with an **ArrayList**, we can also remove by index or by element:

```
cityList.remove("Meren");

printCollection(cityList);
```

The difference here is that the following steps had to happen behind the scenes:

- The element **Meren** was located.
- The element **Meren** was removed.
- The element **Lang** set its **previous element** pointer to **Fallraen**.
- The element **Fallraen** set its **next element** pointer to **Lang**.

Running our code now returns this output:

```
Elddim, Crystwind, Fallraen, Meren, Lang,
```

Meren

```
Elddim, Crystwind, Fallraen, Lang,
```

The **LinkedList** also provides other unique and useful methods. If we wanted to **peek** at the top of the list and output that element, we could use this:

```
System.out.println(cityList.peek());
```

```
printCollection(cityList);
```

The code adds these lines to our output:

Elddim

Elddim, Crystwind, Fallraen, Lang,

We can do the same with the last element:

```
System.out.println(cityList.peekLast());
```

```
printCollection(cityList);
```

This yields the following output:

Lang

Elddim, Crystwind, Fallraen, Lang,

Additionally, we can **poll** the list:

```
System.out.println(cityList.poll());
```

```
printCollection(cityList);
```

The last two lines of our output are as follows:

Edam

Crystwind, Fallraen, Lang,

There is also a **pollLast()** method, which exhibits similar behavior on the last element in the list. The difference between the **peek()** and **poll()** methods is as follows:

- **poll()** returns the value of the first element in the list.
- **peek()** returns the value of the first element in the list and removes that element from the list.

We will discuss **pollLast()** and its counterpart **pollFirst()** in the section on **Sequenced Collections**.

> **Note: In addition to each element having pointers to the previous and next elements, a LinkedList maintains pointers to the first and last elements in the list.**

It is important to understand when to use an **ArrayList** versus a **LinkedList**. It all comes down to the number of items and type of operation. In tech, there is a concept known as **Big O notation**. Essentially, it is a way of thinking about the operational complexity behind an operation or algorithm. Adding an item to an **ArrayList** is an **O(n)** operation. The time it takes for the operation **(O)** to complete is proportional to the number **(n)** of elements in the list. This is because an addition into an **ArrayList** has to run through a seek on the indexes before knowing where to insert the new element.

On the other hand, adding an item to a **LinkedList** is (using Big O notation) an O(1) operation. This means that the time it takes for the operation (O) to complete is consistent, regardless of the number of items on the list. This is because (by default) all new elements in a **LinkedList** go to the end. Java does not have to spend extra time figuring out where to put them.

The result is that if we plan on using large lists and adding more to the list than reading from the list, it makes more sense to use a **LinkedList**. On the other hand, if we are going to spend most of our time reading list items (and not adding too many more), then an **ArrayList** or **Vector** should do just fine.

We will discuss linked lists in further detail in a later chapter.

Maps

One of the more unique collection types is maps. Maps are useful for storing small amounts of key/value-based data. Some databases like **Apache Cassandra** use maps to provide smaller levels of denormalization (storing additional properties with a data row) to prevent the need for an additional query.

Before we start working with maps, we will create a small, static method to output our map contents to the console. We cannot use the **printCollection()** method, as the **Map** class does not inherit from the **Collection** base class.

Add a new method named **printMap** to the end of our class. It should be of type **void** (no return type) and accept an object of type **Map** as its only parameter:

```java
private static void printMap(Map map) {

    System.out.println();

  Set<Object> keys = map.keySet();

    for (Object key : keys) {

      System.out.printf("%s: %s\n", key, map.get(key));

    }

}
```

As shown, the **printMap()** method works unlike the **printCollection()** method. We start by initializing a **Set** named **keys** with the value returned from map's **keySet()** method. The **keys** set has an inner element type of **Object**, as we will not know what type the map's key is. Therefore, we use the base **Object** class so that it can handle just about anything. Then, we iterate through each **key** of **keys** with a **for** loop, using **map**'s **get()** method in our **printf()** to output the value associated with that key.

We will also create a method called **printKeys**, which will only output a map's keys. As we will have a few examples where the output of keys and values could be verbose, this will give us the advantage of brevity.

Our **printKeys()** method bears some similarity to the **printMap()** method, shown as follows. Add the following method to the end of our **WorkingWithCollections** class:

```java
private static void printKeys(Map map) {

    System.out.println();

    Set<Object> keys = map.keySet();

    for (Object key : keys) {
        System.out.printf("%s, ", key);
    }

    System.out.println();

}
```

In Java, there are multiple types of **Map** implementations. The most commonly used is the **HashMap**, which we will start now.

The following imports will allow us to complete the examples to follow:

```java
import java.util.HashMap;

import java.util.LinkedHashMap;

import java.util.Map;

Import java.util.TreeMap
```

HashMap

At the end of our **main()** method, let us create a new map named **spellbook**. It should have a key type of **String** and a value type of **String**. We will then use map's **put()** method to add key/value pairs into **spellbook**, and finish with a call to our **printMap()** method:

```java
Map<String,String> spellbook = new HashMap<>();
```

```
spellbook.put("Fireball",
    "A ball of fire that inflicts 8 damage per level of magic.");
spellbook.put("Healing Touch",
    "Touching an injured player recovers 5 hit points per
     character level.");
spellbook.put("Lightning Bolt",
    "A stream of lightning that inflicts 10 damage per level
     of magic.");
spellbook.put("Create Water",
    "Creates 10 liters of water per level of magic.");
spellbook.put("Transmutation",
    "Converts common items into gold.");

printMap(spellbook);
```

Running our code should produce this new output at the end:

Fireball: A ball of fire that inflicts 8 damage per level of magic.

Transmutation: Converts common items into gold.

Create Water: Creates 10 liters of water per level of magic.

Healing Touch: Touching an injured player recovers 5 hit points per character level.

Lightning Bolt: A stream of lightning that inflicts 10 damage per level of magic.

Fireball, Transmutation, Create Water, Healing Touch, Lightning Bolt,

If we examine the output, we can see that the key/value pairs in **spellbook** are not shown in the order that they were added (put).

A **HashMap** also offers additional constructors/parameters, which can be advantageous for certain requirements:

```
HashMap<>(initialSize, customLoadFactor)
```

The additional constructor parameters are described here:

- **initialsize:** This is an integer representing the number of elements that the **LinkedHashMap** will contain at first.

- **CustomLoadFactor:** This is a float indicating a specific percent capacity of the initial size should trigger an expansion of the **LinkedHashMap**'s memory usage. The default is *75%*, specified as **.75f**.

These additional parameters can be used to fine-tune the memory usage and ultimately, the performance of a **HashMap**. Resize operations can be expensive, so if the maximum size of the map is known ahead of time, specifying it can yield performance benefits.

> **Note: While a HashMap can be instantiated with only the initial size parameter, it cannot be instantiated with the custom load factor alone. The initial size must always be present when specifying a custom load factor.**

Hashtable

Similar to a vector's relationship with **ArrayList**, the **Hashtable** implementation is a thread-safe alternative to a **HashMap**. If we require the functionality of **HashMap** to support interaction with multiple threads, a **Hashtable** is the way to go:

```
Map<String,String> spellbook = new Hashtable<>();
```

LinkedHashMap

Next, we will change **spellbook** to a **LinkedHashMap**. **LinkedHashMaps** are similar to **LinkedLists** in that each entry has pointers to the next and previous elements:

```
Map<String,String> spellbook = new LinkedHashMap<>();
```

Running our code will show that the map keys are in the following order:

Fireball, Healing Touch, Lightning Bolt, Create Water, Transmutation,

As shown, they are now in the order that they were added.

Similar to **HashMap**, a **LinkedHashMap** also offers additional constructors/parameters, which can be advantageous for certain requirements. A **LinkedHashMap** also has one more parameter to allow a reorder to be triggered on access.

```
LinkedHashMap<>(initialSize, customLoadFactor, accessOrderEnabled)
```

These additional constructor parameters are described as follows:

- **Initial size:** This is an integer representing the number of elements that the **LinkedHashMap** will contain at first.
- **Custom load factor:** This is a float indicating a specific percent capacity of the initial size should trigger an expansion of the **LinkedHashMap**'s memory usage. The default is *75%*, specified as **.75f**.

- **Access order enabled:** This is a **boolean** indicating whether accessing (get) an element should trigger a reorder operation. This puts the most recently accessed key/value pair at the bottom of the list.

We can demonstrate this differently by redefining our **LinkedHashMap** instantiation:

```
Map<String,String> spellbook = new LinkedHashMap<>(5,.8f,true);
```

Now, comment-out our call to **printMap()** and output the value from the **Lightning Bolt** key:

```
//printMap(spellbook);
```

```
System.out.print(spellbook.get("Lightning Bolt"));
```

```
printKeys(spellbook);
```

Running this code shows the new key order:

Fireball, Healing Touch, Create Water, Transmutation, Lightning Bolt,

As shown, the key for **Lightning Bolt** now appears at the end, as it was accessed most recently.

ConcurrentModificationException

For the preceding example, we commented-out our call to the **printMap()** method. If we fail to comment-out that line, our code fails with a **ConcurrentModificationException**.

Remember that our for-each in **printMap()** first fetches the keys and then executes a **get()** on each key. By passing a value of **true** to enable access order, a **get()** call effectively modifies the map, continually placing the most-recently accessed key/value pair at the end of the map. Java recognizes this and throws the **ConcurrentModificationException** to prevent us from falling into an infinite loop.

TreeMap

Now we will alter our **spellbook** implementation to use a **TreeMap**:

```
Map<String,String> spellbook = new TreeMap<>();
```

Running our code now shows this list of keys at the end:

Create Water, Fireball, Healing Touch, Lightning Bolt, Transmutation,

As shown, the map has been sorted by the keys in alpha-numeric order. This happens because a **TreeMap** implements a (*JavaTPoint 2021*) binary search, red-black tree behind the scenes to speed up operation time.

> **Note: Unlike the previous map implementations, a TreeMap will not permit a key/ value pair to be added with a null key.**

Sequenced collections

A new feature with Java 21 is (*Parlog 2023*) sequenced collections. Essentially, this feature exposes what is known as **encounter order**. Lists now also inherit a new class known as **SequencedCollection**, which provides many new methods to make working with the first and last entries of a list much easier. This allows new behaviors, similar to what is possible with a linked list:

- **getFirst()**: Returns the first element in the collection
- **getLast()**: Returns the last element in the collection
- **addFirst(element)**: Adds a new element to the beginning of the collection
- **addLast(element)**: Adds a new element to the end of the collection
- **reversed()**: Returns a view of the list in reverse order

> **Note: The addFirst() and addLast() method will throw exceptions if the collection is unmodifiable or if the add would violate the current order of a sorted collection.**

While sets did not see the same level of improvement, they did gain access to the **reversed()** method. Calling the **reversed()** method on a set will return a **SequencedSet** object containing a view of the set in reverse order.

> **Note: This view for sets and lists does reflect the state of the underlying collection, and any changes to it will also be reflected there.**

Maps also benefited by inheriting a new class in Java 21, and this one is named **SequencedMap**. This class extends the following methods to all map implementations:

- **putFirst()**: Adds a new key/value pair to the beginning of a map
- **putLast()**: Adds a new key/value pair to the end of a map
- **firstEntry()**: Returns the first key/value pair on the map
- **lastEntry()**: Returns the last key/value pair on the map
- **pollFirstEntry()**: Removes and returns a key/value pair from the beginning of a map
- **pollLastEntry()**: Removes and returns a key/value pair from the end of a map
- **sequencedKeySet()**: Returns a **sequencedSet** view of the map's keys
- **sequencedValues()**: Returns a **sequencedSet** view of the map's values
- **sequencedEntrySet()**: Returns a **sequencedSet** view of the key/value pairs in the map

These methods are great to have in our *developer toolbox*, as they lower the learning curve to working with collections in Java.

Records

The concept of records was introduced in Java 14. Records are essentially immutable **Plain Old Java Objects (POJOs)**. One of the criticisms with POJOs is that there is a lot of *boilerplate code* with their creation, as all POJOs need things like constructors, private properties, and pairs of getters/setters.

> **Note: In this sense, the term *boilerplate code* refers to standard code that is entered into every object, the creation of which is considered to be tedious.**

We will create a record to keep track of room objects for our heroes to explore. Our **Room** record certainly qualifies as immutable, as typically, rooms in an adventure game are defined ahead of time and do not change.

We will start by defining our **Room record**:

```
record Room(String name, String description, List<String> exits) {

}
```

Inside the braces, we can define any additional code that we need to round out the **Room record**. One common requirement for adventure games is knowledge of the possible exits from the room. Therefore, we will build a public **getExits()** method. We will also implement an **if-else** check to format our output based on how many exits are present inside the list:

```
public String getExits() {

    StringBuilder exitDesc = new StringBuilder();


    if (exits.isEmpty()) {

        exitDesc.append("There are no obvious exits.");

    } else if (exits.size() == 1) {

        exitDesc.append("There is an exit to the ");

        exitDesc.append(exits.get(0));

    } else if (exits.size() == 2) {

        exitDesc.append(exits.get(0));

        exitDesc.append(" and ");
```

```
        exitDesc.append(exits.get(1));

    } else {

        exitDesc.append("There are exits to the ");

        boolean first = true;

        for (String exit : exits) {
            if (!first) {
                exitDesc.append(", ");
            } else {
                first = false;
            }
            exitDesc.append(exit);
        }

    }

    exitDesc.append(".");

    return exitDesc.toString();
}
```

The idea here is that we first check whether or not the **exits ArrayList** has records by calling the **isEmpty()** method and providing an appropriate response. Likewise, there are appropriate ways of specifying a response if there are only one or two exits, so we will cover that as well. Finally, we will iterate through the exits and prepend them with commas (except for the first exit).

With the **Room** **record** defined, we will now build our **cabinExits ArrayList** and instantiate a **Room** named **lakeCabin**:

```
List<String> cabinExits = new ArrayList();

cabinExits.add("South");

cabinExits.add("West");


Room lakeCabin = new Room("Lake cabin",
```

```
"You are standing outside of a cabin"

+ " on a lake, with water visible to the South and East. There is"

+ " a red dock to the South.", cabinExits);
```

Finally, we will output **lakeCabin**'s description and call our **getExits()** method:

```
System.out.println(lakeCabin.Description());

System.out.println(lakeCabin.getExits());
```

Running our code should produce an output that looks similar to this:

You are standing outside of a cabin on a lake, with water visible to the South and East. There is a red dock to the South.

There are exits to the South and West.

As shown, records are a quick way to define small, immutable POJOs without the need for lots of standard boilerplate methods.

Building a simple example

Let us say that we want to build a short **role-playing game** (**RPG**) simulation. To work with this example, we will need to create three classes:

- **RPGSimulation**: Our main class
- **Player:** Our base player class, which holds most of the common info for player objects
- **Hero**: Our hero class, which will inherit the **Player** class

RPGSimulation class

Let us start by creating a new static class in the **chapter4** package, with a **main()** method, and name it **RPGSimulation**:

```
package chapter4;

import java.util.ArrayList;

import java.util.List;

import java.util.Map;

import java.util.Random;

import java.util.TreeMap;
```

```java
public class RPGSimulation {

record Monster (String name, int attack, int maxDamage,

int defense) {

    static Random random = new Random();

        static int hitPoints = 2;

    static boolean alive = true;

public int rollAttack() {

        return random.nextInt(attack) + 1;

    }


public int rollDamage() {

        return random.nextInt(maxDamage) + 1;

    }


    public boolean isAlive() {

        return alive;

    }

}


    public static void main(String[] args) {


        Random randomNumber = new Random();

        int monsterCount = randomNumber.nextInt(4) + 1;
```

After defining our class, we will build our **Monster** record *outside* the **main()** method. This will allow the **Monster** record to be called from our other private methods.

The **Monster** record will define properties for **name**, **attack**, **maxDamage**, and **defense**. It will also default to a **hitPoints** value of **2**, and the **alive boolean** will be given a default value of **true**. After that, we will build two public methods named **rollAttack** and **rollDamage**, which will produce a random value based on the values contained in attack or **maxDamage**. We will finish the method with one list method named **isAlive** to expose the **alive boolean** property.

Inside the **main()** method, we will implement a random number generator named **randomNumber** and start by randomly generating the number of monsters that will be present in our RPG simulation. This generated value will be a random number between 1 and 4, and it will be stored in the **monsterCount** integer variable.

Next, we will build a new **ArrayList** named **monsters**, which will hold values for several **Monster** records:

```
List<Monster> monsters = new ArrayList<>();


for (int monsterIdx = 0; monsterIdx < monsterCount; monsterIdx++) {


    int typeIdx = randomNumber.nextInt(4);


    switch (typeIdx) {
    case 0:
        monsters.add(new Monster("Kobald", 2, 8, 1));
break;
    case 1:
        monsters.add(new Monster("Skeleton", 2, 8, 2));

        break;
    case 2:
        monsters.add(new Monster("Zombie", 1, 6, 2));

        break;
    default:
        monsters.add(new Monster("Rats", 1, 4, 1));
}

}
```

The preceding code will iterate through the number of monsters with a **for-each** loop. Inside the loop, it randomly picks a number from 0 through 3 for the type of monster to generate. It will then use a **switch-case** to call the **Monster** constructor with the appropriate values and add the monster's name to the **monsterNames** list.

Next, we will reuse code from our **WorkingWithCollections** class for the **spellbook**, because we have one hero who will use it:

```
Map<String,String> spellbook = new TreeMap<>();

spellbook.put("Fireball",

    "A ball of fire that inflicts 8 damage per level of magic.");

spellbook.put("Healing Touch",

    "Touching an injured player recovers 5 hit points per

      character level.");

spellbook.put("Lightning Bolt",

    "A stream of lightning that inflicts 10 damage per level

      of magic.");

spellbook.put("Create Water",

    "Creates 10 liters of water per level of magic.");

spellbook.put("Transmutation",

    "Converts common items into gold.");
```

Player class

Next, we will create two new classes in the **chapter4** package (without a **main** method), named **Player** and **Hero**.

We will start with the **Player** class:

```
package chapter4;


import java.util.Random;


public class Player {

    private Random random = new Random();

    private String name;

    private int attack;

    private int maxDamage;

    private int defense;
```

```
    private int hitPoints;

    private boolean alive;


}
```

As shown, we will start by defining our private properties. Next, we will build our constructor:

```
public Player(String name, int attack, int maxDamage, int defense) {

        this.name = name;

        this.attack = attack;

        this.maxDamage = maxDamage;

        this.defense = defense;

        this.alive = true;

}
```

For the **Player** constructor, we will store property values passed for **name**, **attack**, **maxDamage**, and **defense**. We will also initialize **alive** to a value of **true**.

Moving on, we will need public methods to generate values based on the **attack** and **maxDamage** values:

```
public int rollAttack() {

    return random.nextInt(attack) + 1;

}


public int rollDamage() {

    return random.nextInt(maxDamage) + 1;

}
```

Next, we will build our getters and setters. Remember we discussed Java records and mentioned the tedious amounts of boilerplate code earlier in the chapter? This is what was meant by that:

```
public String getName() {

    return name;

}
```

```java
public void setName(String name) {

    this.name = name;

}


public int getAttack() {

    return attack;

}


public void setAttack(int attack) {

    this.attack = attack;

}


public int getMaxDamage() {

    return maxDamage;

}


public void setMaxDamage(int maxDamage) {

    this.maxDamage = maxDamage;

}


public int getDefense() {

    return defense;

}


public void setDefense(int defense) {

    this.defense = defense;

}


public int getHitPoints() {

    return this.hitPoints;

}
```

```
protected void setHitPoints(int hitPoints) {

    this.hitPoints = hitPoints;

}


public boolean isAlive() {

    return this.alive;

}
```

Fortunately, most IDEs have a quick way to generate getters and setters.

> **Note: The Eclipse IDE can automatically generate getters and setters for you. Simply right-click in the middle of a class file, select Source and then Generate Getters and Setters.**

Finally, we will need a public method that decrements **hitPoints** by a certain damage amount:

```
public void decrementHitPoints(int damage) {

    this.hitPoints = this.hitPoints - damage;

}
```

Hero class

Next, we will build our **Hero** class. The **Hero** class definition will extend the **Player** class to inherit it as a base class:

```
package chapter4;


import java.util.Map;


public class Hero extends Player {

    private Map<String,String> spellbook;
```

We will also define **spellbook** as a private property. With the **Hero** class, we will define two constructors:

```
    public Hero(String name, int attack, int maxDamage, int defense) {

        super(name, attack, maxDamage, defense);
```

```
        super.setHitPoints(5);

    }
```

The first constructor accepts parameters for **name**, **attack**, **maxDamage**, and **defense**. It then uses the **super** keyword to pass those parameters to the base class, **Player** in this case. It also initializes the **hitPoints** property to a value of **5** for all heroes, using the appropriate setter method.

The second constructor is similar, except that it accepts a parameter for the **spellbook**:

```
    public Hero(String name, int attack, int maxDamage, int defense,
            Map<String,String> spellbook) {
        this(name, attack, maxDamage, defense);
        this.spellbook = spellbook;
    }
```

As shown earlier, the second constructor uses **this** keyword to call the first constructor with the first four parameters that were passed in. It then initializes the **spellbook** property with the **spellbook** map passed in as the last parameter.

Since our properties are all inherited from the **Player** class, we only need to generate getters and setters for the **spellbook** property:

```
    public Map<String, String> getSpellbook() {
        return spellbook;
    }

    public void setSpellbook(Map<String, String> spellbook) {
        this.spellbook = spellbook;
    }
}
```

RPGSimulation class continued

With our **Player** and **Hero** classes built, we can return to our **RPGSimulation** class. At the end of our **main()** method (after the **spellbook** code), we will define our heroes:

```
Hero byorki = new Hero("Byorki", 8, 5, 5);

Hero klar = new Hero("K'lar", 10, 12, 3);

Hero tyrenni = new Hero("Tyrenni", 6, 2, 6, spellbook);
```

With our three heroes instantiated as objects, we will now add them to a new **ArrayList** named **heroes**:

```
List<Hero> heroes = new ArrayList<>();

heroes.add(byorki);

heroes.add(klar);

heroes.add(tyrenni);
```

Now, we will add a new method to the end of the **RPGSimulation** class. It will be a static method named **generatePlayerOrder** that returns an **ArrayList** of **String** and accepts a list of **Hero** and a list of **Monster** as parameters. The point of this method is to take the names of our heroes and the monsters, and randomly combine them into a single list.

To do this, we will define **playerCount** as the total number of elements in both lists. The **returnValue** list should be of the same size as **playerCount** once all players have been assigned to the main list. Essentially, we will randomly decide to pick from the **heroList** or **monsterList**, and then randomly pick a valid index from that list:

```
private static List<Object> generatePlayerOrder(List<Hero> heroList,

List<Monster> monsterList) {

    List<Hero> tempHeroList =
new ArrayList<Hero>(List.copyOf(heroList));
    List<Monster> tempMonsterList =
new ArrayList<Monster>(List.copyOf(monsterList));

    List<Object> returnValue = new ArrayList<>();
    Random random = new Random();
    int playerCount = heroList.size() + monsterList.size();

    while (returnValue.size() < playerCount) {
        if (random.nextBoolean()) {
            if (!tempHeroList.isEmpty()) {
                int heroIndex =
random.nextInt(tempHeroList.size());
```

```
            returnValue.add(tempHeroList.get(heroIndex));

            tempHeroList.remove(heroIndex);

        }

    } else {

        if (!tempMonsterList.isEmpty()) {

            int monsterIndex =
random.nextInt(tempMonsterList.size());


            returnValue
.add(tempMonsterList.get(monsterIndex));

            tempMonsterList.remove(monsterIndex);

        }

    }

}


    return returnValue;

}
```

The first thing we do is create two new **ArrayLists**, named **tempHeroList** and **tempMonsterList**. This allows us to remove objects as a way to keep track of who has been selected, without affecting the main **heroList** and **monsterList**. Then, we define a few variables to help us along the way, including an **ArrayList** named **returnValue** which is a **List** of **Object**, so we can add objects of any class to it.

We then build a **while** loop that keeps running as long as the size of our **returnValue** list is smaller than the total number of elements present in **heroList** and **monsterList** combined (**playerCount**). Inside our **while** loop, we flip between pulling random elements (using two randomly generated values) from **tempHeroList** and **tempMonsterList**. This way, we have a list of all players in the game (heroes and monsters) that is in as random of an order as possible.

> **Note: Random's nextBoolean() method does exactly as it suggests, in that it randomly returns either a true or false value.**

With our **returnValue** list generated, we return it to the calling method. Back in our **main()** method, we create a new **List** of **Object**, and set it to the value returned by the **generatePlayerOrder()** method:

```
List<Object> playerOrder = generatePlayerOrder(heroes, monsters);
```

We then iterate through **playerOrder** to simulate a round of action in an RPG adventure game. The first thing that we need to do is check whether the current **player** object is a **Hero** or a **Monster**. We can do this using the **instanceof** keyword. We also want to make sure our **hero** is alive before allowing them to act, and we can do that by calling the **isAlive()** method inherited from the **Player** class:

```
for (Object player : playerOrder) {

    System.out.println();

    if (player instanceof Hero hero) {
        if (hero.isAlive()) {
            String name = ((Hero) player).getName();

            int monsterIndex =
randomNumber.nextInt(monsters.size());
            Monster targetMonster = monsters.get(monsterIndex);

            System.out.println(name
                    + " attacks " + targetMonster.name());

            int attack = hero.rollAttack();
            if (attack >= targetMonster.defense) {
                int damage = hero.rollDamage();
                System.out.println(name
                        + " rolls a " + attack + " and hits "
                        + targetMonster.name() + " for "
                        + damage + " points.");
                targetMonster.decrementHitPoints(damage);

                if (!targetMonster.isAlive()) {
                    System.out.println(targetMonster.name()
```

```
                            + " is down!");

}

            } else {

                System.out.println(name + " rolls a "

                    + attack + " and misses "

                    + targetMonster.name());

            }

        }
```

Within our nested **if** checks, we will prepare for the main action logic by defining variables for the hero's name, the random index of the target **monster**, and an object for the target **monster** itself. The action commences by storing the result of the hero's **attack** roll. As long as the **attack** value is greater than or equal to the **targetMonster**'s **defense**, a *hit* is scored and appropriate messages are output to the console. There is also an appropriate message if the **targetMonster**'s **isAlive()** method should return a **false** value after the action.

Following the logic for the hero's action is an **else** check (from the root **if (player instanceof Hero)** statement in the preceding code), if the current **player** is of type **Monster**. The logic is similar to what we have done with the **Hero** objects, except that it makes calls to the **Monster** record properties and methods, and selects a random index of a target **hero**:

```
} else if (player instanceof Monster monster) {

    if (monster.isAlive()) {

        String name = monster.name();

        int heroIndex = randomNumber.nextInt(heroes.size());

        Hero targetHero = heroes.get(heroIndex);

        String heroName = targetHero.getName();

        System.out.println(monster.name()

                + " attacks " + heroName);

        int attack = monster.rollAttack();

        if (attack >= targetHero.getDefense()) {
```

```
    int damage = monster.rollDamage();

    System.out.println(name

        + " rolls a " + attack + " and hits " + heroName

        + " for " + damage + " points.");

    targetHero.decrementHitPoints(damage);


    if (!targetHero.isAlive()) {

        System.out.println(heroName + " is down!");

    }

} else {

    System.out.println(name

            + " rolls a " + attack

            + " and misses " + heroName);

    }

  }

}
```

Running this code should build our list of heroes, put together a random list of monsters, and step through one round of their actions in an RPG. Given the random components, the output will vary, but it should look something like this:

```
Rats attacks Tyrenni

Rats rolls a 5 and misses Tyrenni


Byorki attacks Skeleton

Byorki rolls a 7 and hits Skeleton for 4 points.

Skeleton is down!


Tyrenni attacks Kobald

Tyrenni rolls a 3 and hits Kobald for 2 points.

Kobald is down!
```

```
K'lar attacks Kobald
```

```
K'lar rolls a 6 and hits Kobald for 10 points.
```

```
Kobald is down!
```

In this section, we used much of what was covered earlier in this chapter. We also learned a few new tricks and keywords:

- Calling a constructor from another in the same class using **this()**
- Building lists of base classes that can hold different types of objects
- Checking the type of an object using **instanceof**
- Generating a random **boolean** with Random's **nextBoolean()** method
- Comparing the definition and implementation of records versus POJOs

Conclusion

In this chapter, we discussed arrays, collections, and records in detail. We also went into the details of different types of collection implementations and their uses, advantages, and disadvantages. Additionally, we discussed sequenced collections and some of the new methods and capabilities shipped with Java 21. Finally, we utilized much of our learnings by writing a quick RPG simulation to practice leveraging collections and other concepts differently.

In the next chapter, we will discuss how Java processes arithmetic operations. We will examine integer operations (which we used in this chapter) and operations on floating point types.

Points to remember

- Arrays are simple structures that allow us to store multiple values in a single variable.
- Arrays are indexed by integers and must have their max size defined during initialization.
- Array values can be indexed by multiple dimensions. We demonstrated two-dimensional arrays in our examples, but more are certainly possible.
- Sets contain only unique elements, while lists allow duplicates.
- **HashSets** maintain the order of the elements added in, while **TreeSets** put the elements into alpha-numeric order.
- The **sort()** method from the **Collections** class is a good way to sort elements in a collection, as long as the element type comparator is supported or defined.

- When working with elements in a **List** with threads, use **Vector** as the implementation. **ArrayList** does not support thread safety.

- **LinkedList** should be used with many elements and frequent adds.

- A map stores small amounts of data in key/value pairs and does not inherit the **Collection** base class.

- **HashMap**s are not ordered, **LinkedHashMap**s are ordered by entry, and **TreeMap**s are ordered by keys.

- Sequenced collections allow developers easy access to the *encounter order* of the underlying collection, including new access methods for the first and last elements.

- Records are a great way to define small, immutable objects without having to create a separate POJO with a lot of verbose, boilerplate code.

Join our book's Discord space

Join the book's Discord Workspace for Latest updates, Offers, Tech happenings around the world, New Release and Sessions with the Authors:

https://discord.bpbonline.com

CHAPTER 5

Arithmetic Operations

Mathematics is the language with which God has written the universe.

— *Galileo Galilei*

Introduction

In this chapter, we will understand how to perform arithmetic in Java. This will lead us to discuss some nuances of how computers process math. We will also take a quick look at how to build simple unit tests, as the deterministic nature of arithmetic makes a good backdrop for teaching the basics of unit testing.

While some may find math daunting, as software developers, we must embrace it. Understanding how computers execute arithmetic operations is central to learning about software development and, as *Galileo* inferred, the universe as well.

Structure

In this chapter, we will cover the following topics:

- Integer arithmetic
- Floating point arithmetic

Objectives

The primary aim of this chapter is to build a foundational understanding of how to leverage arithmetic operations in Java code. We will also take the opportunity to introduce unit testing. This leads to the following objectives for this chapter:

- Learn how to perform integer arithmetic in Java.
- Learn how to perform floating point arithmetic in Java.
- Understand how computers process arithmetic *under the hood*.
- Learn a little about unit testing and how to use it to ensure consistent method behavior.

Integer arithmetic

We will start by showing some simple arithmetic with integers (whole numbers). First, create a new Java class named **MathExamples** in a new package named **chapter5**. Make sure this class has a **main()** method:

```
package chapter5;


public class mathExamples {


    public static void main() {


    }

}
```

Inside our **main()** method, let us define two integer variables:

```
int intNumA = 5;
int intNumB = 3;
```

Addition

Now, let us add them together and print the result:

```
System.out.println(intNumA + " + " + intNumB + " = "
    + intNumA + intNumB);
```

If we run our code, the output should be as follows:

5 + 3 = 53

However, this output is not what we expected. After all, **5** plus **3** is equal to **8**, not **53**.

Remember that numeric variables in a **println** statement are implicitly converted into strings. Ultimately, we do want that. But first, we want the numbers to be added together. To that end, we will encapsulate **intNumA** and **intNumB** inside an additional set of parentheses:

```
System.out.println(intNumA + " + " + intNumB + " = "
     + (intNumA + intNumB));
```

Now, when we run our code, the order of operations takes place, and the parenthesis is evaluated before being converted to a string:

5 + 3 = 8

Now, let us look at what is happening behind the scenes.

Both **intNumA** and **intNumB** are integers. As integers are a primitive type, the values are stored in the base-2 (also known as **binary**) system, as shown here:

```
intNumA = 5 = 1 0 1
     place = 4 2 1

intNumB = 3 = 0 1 1
     place = 4 2 1
```

The base-10 (decimal) number of **5** becomes **101**, because there is a **1** in the four's place and another **1** in the one's place. Likewise, the decimal number **3** becomes **011**, because there is a **1** in the two's place and a **1** in the one's place. Essentially, this means that we are adding **101** and **011**:

```
      101
     +011
     ----
     1000


answer = 1 0 0 0 = 8
 place = 8 4 2 1
```

Our binary addition is done with the following steps:

1. In the one's place, we add **1** and **1**, which in binary is **10**. So, we record the **0**.
2. In the two's place, we carry the **1** and add **1**, which is **10**. Again, we record the **0**.
3. In the four's place, we carry the **1** and add **1**, which is **10**. Once again, we record the **0**.
4. In the eight's place, we carry the **1** and add **0**. Now we record the **1**, and we have the complete answer.

With a **1** in the eight's place and 0s in the four's, two's, and one's places, it gives us a decimal value of **8** for the answer.

Now, as we are planning on building a few of these operations, we will build a public **add** method instead:

```
public static int add(int intNum1, int intNum2) {

    return intNum1 + intNum2;

}
```

Now, let us modify our **println** statement from above:

```
System.out.println(intNumA + " + " + intNumB + " = "

    + add(intNumA,intNumB));
```

Running our code should produce the same output as above. Note that as **intNumA** and **intNumB** are computed in the **add()** method, we do not need extra parenthesis inside the **println()** method.

Testing add() with JUnit

Building methods for arithmetic operations offers us the opportunity for a natural detour into unit testing. Unit testing is a systematic form of testing that involves creating small tests for the individual parts of an application. This usually means that software developers create a test for each method of a class.

Unit tests work well with **deterministic operations**. In software development, a deterministic operation is one that (given a set of inputs) will return the same, predictable result on every execution. As arithmetic operations are deterministic in nature, they should make for great examples of simple unit tests.

In our case, we will use the JUnit testing library to create a unit test for our **add()** method.

Create a new **JUnit Test Case**. If that is not an available option under the **File | New menu**, then select **Other**. In the next dialog, scroll down to **JUnit** and select **JUnit Test Case**, as shown in *Figure 5.1*:

Figure 5.1: *Creating a new JUnit Test Case in the Eclipse IDE*

We need to specify the package, name, and class under test in the next dialog. Refer to *Figure 5.2,* and add the entries shown here:

- **Package: chapter5**
- **Name: MathExamplesTests**
- **Class under test: MathExamples**

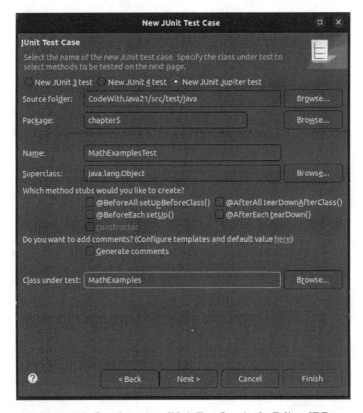

Figure 5.2: Creating a new JUnit Test Case in the Eclipse IDE

There is another dialog, but we can click **Finish** at this point. This will create the **MathExamplesTests** class file.

> **Note: We may have to acknowledge a dialog to allow JUnit5 to be added to the build path.**

Recall from *Chapter 2, Fundamental Programming Structures,* where we created our **Maven pom.xml** file. We need to modify that file to include one new property and one new dependency.

Open the **pom.xml** file and add the current version for **junit.jupiter.version** in the **properties** section:

```
<properties>

    <java.version>21</java.version>

    <maven.compiler.source>21</maven.compiler.source>

    <maven.compiler.target>21</maven.compiler.target>
```

```
<junit.jupiter.version>5.9.3</junit.jupiter.version>
```

```
</properties>
```

Next, scroll down to the bottom of the **pom.xml** file and add a new dependency. As this is the first dependency we are adding, we will need to add a new section for **dependencies**. We will need to add the **JU**nit dependency by specifying the following additional properties:

- **Group ID: org.junit.jupiter**
- **Artifact ID: junit-jupiter-api**
- **Version: ${junit.jupiter.version}**
- **Scope: test**

The dependency section code in the **pom.xml** should look like this:

```
<dependencies>

    <dependency>

        <groupId>org.junit.jupiter</groupId>

        <artifactId>junit-jupiter-api</artifactId>

        <version>${junit.jupiter.version}</version>

        <scope>test</scope>

    </dependency>

</dependencies>
```

With these settings in place, we can shift our attention back to the **MathExamplesTests** class:

```
package chapter5;


import static org.junit.jupiter.api.Assertions.assertEquals;


import org.junit.jupiter.api.Test;


class MathExamplesTests {


}
```

The important points of the preceding code (aside from the class definition) are the imports. We have an **import** for the **org.junit.jupiter.api.Test** class and a **static import** for `org.junit.jupiter.api.Assertions.assertEquals`. The **static** keyword allows us to include the **assertEquals()** method from the **Assertions** static class.

Let us create a new method named **testAdd** inside the class:

```
@Test

void testAdd() {

    assertEquals(8,MathExamples.add(5,3));

}
```

Simply put, the **@Test** annotation identifies this method as a **JUnit** test. Inside the **testAdd()** method, we are simply calling the **assertEquals()** method to indicate that the value of **8** should be equal to the result of calling our **add()** method with parameters of **5** and **3**.

To test the **testAdd()** method, we can right-click on the **MathExamplesTests** class in our project explorer and select **Run As followed by JUnit Test**. If everything mentioned is done correctly, our JUnit tests should report 1/1 successful runs, without any errors or failures.

JUnit tests are executed during the **Maven** process before the code is actually run. If the test fails, our code will not run. This becomes useful in large production environments. If changes are made to a method, a unit test can assure that the method will still produce the same results.

> **Note: Sometimes, unit tests are written before the logic in the class under test. This is called Test Driven Development (TDD), and it helps ensure that the methods are written to meet certain, specific requirements.**

Subtraction

Getting back to our **MathExamples** class, we will write a method for subtraction:

```
public static int subtract(int intNum1, int intNum2) {

    return intNum1 - intNum2;

}
```

In our **MathExamplesTests** class, we can write a short unit test for the **subtract()** method, named **testSubtract**:

```
@Test

void testSubtract() {

    assertEquals(2,MathExamples.subtract(5,3));
```

```
}
```

Back in our **main()** method, add a new **println** statement:

```
System.out.println(intNumA + " - " + intNumB + " = "
    + subtract(intNumA,intNumB));
```

Now, running our code should produce this output:

```
5 + 3 = 8
5 - 3 = 2
```

Multiplication

While the two previous examples were fairly straightforward, Java does use some different symbols for multiplication and division (as do most programming languages). We will start with a new method for multiplication. As shown here, instead of an **x**, Java uses the asterisk (*****) for a multiplication operation:

```
public static int multiply(int intNum1, int intNum2) {
    return intNum1 * intNum2;
}
```

In our **MathExamplesTests** class, we can write a short unit test for the **multiply()** method named **testMultiply**:

```
@Test
void testMultiply() {
    assertEquals(15,MathExamples.multiply(5,3));
}
```

Back in our **main()** method, we will add a **println** statement for this:

```
System.out.println(intNumA + " x " + intNumB + " = "
    + multiply(intNumA,intNumB));
```

Running our code should produce the following output:

```
5 + 3 = 8
5 - 3 = 2
5 x 3 = 15
```

Division

Division is also different, as instead of a (÷), Java uses the forward-slash **/** for division operations. This makes more sense, as the (÷) symbol is not present on most keyboards. We will build a simple method for this as well:

```java
public static int divide(int intDividend, int intDivisor) {

    return intDividend / intDivisor;

}
```

In our **MathExamplesTests** class, we can write a short unit test for the **divide()** method. For our **testDivide()** method, we will assert that **8** divided by **2** equals **4**:

```java
@Test

void testDivide() {

    assertEquals(4,MathExamples.divide(8,2));

}
```

Back in our **main()** method, we will add a **println** statement for this as well:

```java
System.out.println(intNumA + " " + (char)247 + " " + intNumB + " = "

    + divide(intNumA,intNumB));
```

Running our code should now produce this output:

5 + 3 = 8

5 - 3 = 2

5 x 3 = 15

5 ÷ 3 = 1

Wait a minute, what happened here? Why does $5 \div 3$ result in a value of 1?

Many readers were probably expecting 1.6667 or 1⅔. Remember that integer arithmetic only works with whole numbers. As a divisor of **3** goes into a dividend of **5** only **1** time, a quotient of **1** is the correct answer here. Refer to *Figure 5.3*:

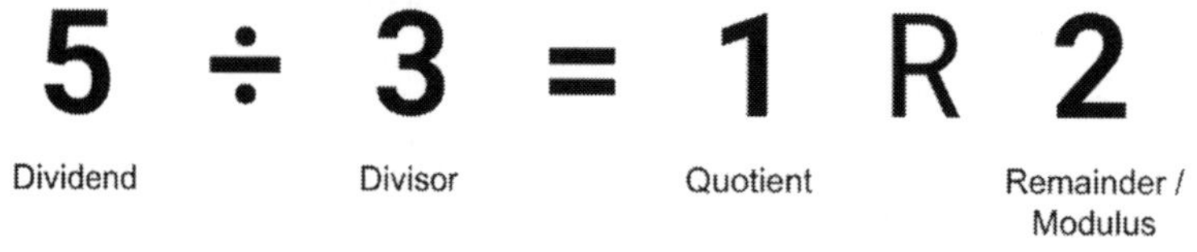

$$5 \div 3 = 1 \text{ R } 2$$

Dividend   Divisor   Quotient   Remainder / Modulus

Figure 5.3: A quick refresher on the parts of a division operation

Modulo

A common question about integer division is, *'What happened to the remainder?'*. Java absolutely computed the entire answer; both the quotient and the remainder. But with integer division, the (**/**) operator only returns the quotient (the whole number portion of the answer). The remainder (or modulus), that is the portion of the answer that is left over, is still there; but we cannot see it. To perform integer division and only have the remainder returned, we need to execute a modulo operation. To return a modulus in Java, we need to use the **%** operator.

In our **MathExamples** class, let us create a method to return the modulus of a dividend and a divisor:

```java
public static int modulo(int intDividend, int intDivisor) {

    return intDividend % intDivisor;

}
```

In our **MathExamplesTests** class, we can create a unit test for the **modulo()** method as well:

```java
@Test

void testModulo() {

    assertEquals(2,MathExamples.modulo(5,3));

}
```

Likewise, we will add a **println** statement in our **main()** method:

```java
System.out.println(intNumA + " mod " + intNumB + " = "

    + modulo(intNumA,intNumB));
```

Running our code should produce this output:

5 + 3 = 8

5 - 3 = 2

5 x 3 = 15

5 ÷ 3 = 1

5 mod 3 = 2

Exponent

Another common arithmetic operation that software developers need to know about is how to evaluate a number against an exponent. This is sometimes referred to as **raising a number to a power**. Unfortunately, Java does not have a native operator for exponent functions, so we will need to use the **pow()** method from the **Math** library. We will start by writing an **exponent()** method on our **MathExamples** class to take a **base** number and raise it to the **power** exponent:

```java
public static int exponent(int base, int power) {

    return (int) Math.pow(base, power);

}
```

> Note: The Math.pow() method expects type double parameters and returns a value of type double. While the method will implicitly convert its parameters from integers to doubles, we need to cast the return value as an integer.

We can perform a unit test for our **exponent()** method using the same numbers mentioned above. This could test for the same operation where **5** to the power of **3** equals a value of **125**:

```java
@Test

void testExponent() {

    assertEquals(125,MathExamples.exponent(5, 3));

}
```

Now we can add a **println** statement to the end of our **main()** method in the **MathExamples** class:

```java
System.out.println(intNumA + " to the power of " + intNumB + " = "

    + exponent(intNumA,intNumB));
```

Running our code will produce the following output:

```
5 + 3 = 8

5 - 3 = 2

5 x 3 = 15

5 ÷ 3 = 1

5 mod 3 = 2

5 to the power of 3 = 125
```

Floating point arithmetic

Now that we have a good understanding of integer arithmetic, let us move on to floating point arithmetic. Floating point numbers (like floats and doubles) are different because they have to account for the **main** number and its decimal precision points. Additionally, there is a fixed amount of precision points for them to work with, which is why they are also known as **fixed precision types**.

Before we go further, let us define two terms: accuracy and precision. **Accuracy** is a measure of error, whereas **precision** is a degree of distinction. When working with arithmetic operations, we want accuracy and precision. However, the restrictions of the binary numeric system (and, ultimately, the underlying computer hardware) will force us to trade one for the other in some circumstances.

We will find that this leads to some nuances when rounding numbers that do not fit well into fractions of base-2 (binary) numbers. This leads to estimation at some of the precision points, which is why many developers describe floating point arithmetic as (*Darcy 2021*) an approximation of real arithmetic.

Let us start by defining two new **double** variables in our **MathExamples** class:

```
double dblNumC = 5.2d;

double dblNumD = 3.1d;
```

Addition

Now, we will overload our **add()** method to accept and return doubles:

```
public static double add(double dblNum1, double dblNum2) {

    return dblNum1 + dblNum2;

}
```

> **Note: It is considered good coding practice to put overloaded methods next to each other inside of a class. This makes it easier for other developers in a shared codebase to understand what is happening, so they can clearly see that a method has been overloaded.**

Let us add a **println** statement to the end of our **main()** method:

```
System.out.println(dblNumC + " + " + dblNumD + " = "

    + add(dblNumC,dblNumD));
```

Running our code should yield these results at the end of our previous output:

```
5.2 + 3.1 = 8.3
```

Nuances with floating point arithmetic

Now, let us try something slightly different. Define two more double variables with the values of **0.1** and **0.2**, and add a **println** statement to show the result of the **add()** method:

```
double dblNumE = 0.1d;

double dblNumF = 0.2d;


System.out.println(dblNumE + " + " + dblNumF + " = "

    + add(dblNumE,dblNumF));
```

Now, let us run our code:

3.1 + 5.2 = 8.3

0.1 + 0.2 = 0.30000000000000004

This output was probably not expected.

Recall us mentioning that floating point arithmetic is an approximation. The problem is that a decimal value of **0.1** (also represented as a fraction of $1/10$) is a repeating fraction when expressed in binary. Similar to how a decimal fraction of ⅓ is a non-terminating expansion (0.3333), $1/10$ can be tersely and accurately expressed as **0.1**. On the other hand, a binary representation of **0.1** is a non-terminating expansion and looks like this:

Decimal: 0.1 = Binary: 0.0001100110011001100110011001100110011

This phenomenon occurs because of each numeric system's *prime factors*. Prime numbers are numbers that can only be divided by one and themselves. Therefore, the prime factors of a number are the prime numbers by which it can be evenly divided.

With the decimal system (*Wiffin 2017*), the prime factors of 10 are 2 and 5. Therefore, fractions such as ½, ¼, ⅕, ⅛, and $1/10$ can be accurately represented. This means that the remaining fractions of ⅓, ⅙, $1/7$, and $1/9$ are non-terminating expansions, as their denominators (3, 6, 7, 9) use 3 or 7 as their greatest prime factor.

However, in binary, the only primary factor of 2 is 2. Therefore, fractions of ½, ¼, and ⅛ can be accurately represented. But other common fractions, such as 0.1 ($1/10$) or 0.2 (⅕), are non-terminating.

Unfortunately, this means that the conversion between the decimal and binary numeric systems introduces varying degrees of approximation. As software developers, we need to be sure we account for that.

The float representation of **0.1** decimal in Java comes out to this:

0.1f = 0.100000001490116119384765625

However, as we are using a double, our example's representation of 0.1 decimal in Java looks like this instead:

```
0.1d = 0.1000000000000000055511151231257827021181583404541015625
```

This indicates yet another nuance between primitive types, in that **0.1f** and **0.1d** are not technically equal. In fact, we can test this by adding this line of code to the end of our **main()** method:

```
System.out.println((0.1f == 0.1d));
```

Running our code should now produce the following output:

```
3.1 + 5.2 = 8.3
```

```
0.1 + 0.2 = 0.30000000000000004
```

```
false
```

As shown, using a **println** statement to display whether or not **0.1f** and **01.d** are equal gives a Boolean response of **false**. We can also see this difference if we go back to our definition of **dblNumE** and **dblNumF**, and adjust them as shown here:

```
double dblNumE = 0.1f;
```

```
double dblNumF = 0.2f;
```

Now, running our code displays this output:

```
3.1 + 5.2 = 8.3
```

```
0.10000000149011612 + 0.20000000298023224 = 0.30000000447034836
```

```
false
```

The difference is that a 64-bit double has the ability to provide a lot more precision and accuracy than a 32-bit float does. In fact, a double allows 54 bits for precision, while a float only provides 24 bits for precision. Using a type with more precision helps us provide a more accurate result.

> Note: More information on this problem can be found at https://0.30000000000000004.com/.

Unit Testing

In the previous section, where we overloaded our **add()** method to work with floating point types, we did not create a corresponding unit test in our **MathExamplesTests** class. This was not an oversight. Caution should be used with unit tests built around floating point results, as we have shown that they should not be considered deterministic.

BigDecimal

One way around this problem is to use the **BigDecimal** class. This class is useful when performing operations on currency, as it is deterministic and will give an accurate result. **BigDecimal** stores base-10 values natively, so we are not at risk of the floating point approximations that happen during decimal-to-binary conversions.

First, we will import the **BigDecimal** and **RoundingMode** classes:

```
import java.math.BigDecimal;
```

```
import java.math.RoundingMode;
```

Next, we will overload our **add()** method one more time:

```
public static BigDecimal add(BigDecimal bdNum1, BigDecimal bdNum2) {

    return bdNum1.add(bdNum2);

}
```

Back in our **main()** method, we will redefine **0.1** and **0.2** as **BigDecimals**, instantiate a **RoundingMode** object, and display our output:

```
RoundingMode rmHalfUp = RoundingMode.HALF_UP;

BigDecimal bdNumE = new BigDecimal(0.1).setScale(1, rmHalfUp);

BigDecimal bdNumF = new BigDecimal(0.2).setScale(1, rmHalfUp);


System.out.println(bdNumE + " + " + bdNumF + " = "

    + add(bdNumE,bdNumF));
```

Running our code now produces this output:

```
5.2 + 3.1 = 8.3
```

```
0.10000000149011612 + 0.20000000298023224 = 0.30000000447034836
```

```
false
```

```
0.1 + 0.2 = 0.3
```

Excellent! That is what we expect to see when trying to add **0.1** and **0.2**.

The **RoundingMode** class offers several options to control rounding behaviors on **BigDecimal** numbers. These options (*IBM 2022*) are detailed in *Table 5.1*:

Mode	Description
CEILING	Rounds in the direction of positive infinity
DOWN	Rounds toward zero
FLOOR	Rounds toward negative infinity
HALF_DOWN	Rounds to the closest neighbor; if both neighbors are at the same distance away, rounds down
HALF_EVEN	Rounds to the closest neighbor; if both neighbors are at the same distance away, rounds toward the even neighbor
HALF_UP	Rounds to the closest neighbor; if both neighbors are the same distance away, rounds up; this is BigDecimal's default behavior
UNNECESSARY	No rounding
UP	Rounds away from zero

Table 5.1: A short description of the options available in the Java RoundingMode class

Subtraction

Let us return to our floating point arithmetic methods. At the end of the **MathExamples** class, we will add a new method to subtract two doubles and return the answer as a double. As with the **add()** method, this method should overload our existing **subtract()** method:

```
public static double subtract(double dblNum1, double dblNum2) {

    return dblNum1 - dblNum2;

}
```

Likewise, we will add a **println** statement in our **main()** method to call it:

```
System.out.println(dblNumC + " - " + dblNumD + " = "

    + subtract(dblNumC,dblNumD));
```

Running our code should produce these results:

```
5.2 + 3.1 = 8.3

0.1 + 0.2 = 0.30000000000000004

false

5.2 - 3.1 = 2.1
```

Multiplication

Similar to what we did with the subtraction operation, we will now overload our **multiply()** method:

```
public static double multiply(double dblNum1, double dblNum2) {

    return dblNum1 * dblNum2;

}
```

Additionally, we will add a **println** statement to the end of our **main()** method to call and display the result:

```
System.out.println(dblNumC + " x " + dblNumD + " = "

    + multiply(dblNumC,dblNumD));
```

Running our code should produce the following result:

5.2 + 3.1 = 8.3

0.1 + 0.2 = 0.30000000000000004

false

5.2 - 3.1 = 2.1

5.2 x 3.1 = 16.12

Division

Moving on, we will also overload our **divide()** method to handle floating point numbers:

```
public static double divide(double dblNum1, double dblNum2) {

    return dblNum1 / dblNum2;

}
```

We will also add a **println** statement to the end of our **main()** method:

```
System.out.println(dblNumC + " " + (char)247 + " " + dblNumD + " = "

    + divide(dblNumC,dblNumD));
```

Running this code should produce the following output:

5.2 + 3.1 = 8.3

0.1 + 0.2 = 0.30000000000000004

false

```
5.2 - 3.1 = 2.1

5.2 x 3.1 = 16.12

5.2 ÷ 3.1 = 1.6774193548387097
```

Formatting floating point values

In this case, we will see the remainder of our division operation. Here, it is expressed in a decimal representation. However, we will often be required to show a cleaner representation of a floating point number. We can do this by restricting the precision points to be displayed.

printf

Let us say that we only want to show the first three decimal precision points of the remainder. There are a couple of ways to achieve this. The first is to use a **printf** statement instead of a **println** statement:

```
System.out.printf("%1.3f " + (char)247 + " %1.3f = %1.3f \n",

    dblNumC, dblNumD, divide(dblNumC,dblNumD));
```

With the **printf** statement, we essentially provide markers (known as **formatting rules**) where our numeric values are supposed to go. As they are floating point types, we denote them with **%f**, with the desired precision to the left and right of the decimal point interspersed between the **%** symbol and the **f**.

Running our code should now produce slightly different output:

```
5.200 ÷ 3.100 = 1.677
```

We can further fine-tune this by adjusting the number of precision points on our inputs, as we know that they only need one decimal place:

```
System.out.printf("%1.1f " + (char)247 + " %1.1f = %1.3f \n",

    dblNumC, dblNumD, divide(dblNumC,dblNumD));
```

Now our output looks cleaner:

```
5.2 ÷ 3.1 = 1.677
```

> **Note: Remember that the printf statement does not include an end-of-line character, so we need to make sure to include that ourselves.**

The **printf** statement supports the following formatting rules listed in *Table 5.2*:

Rule	Description
%b	Output placeholder for a Boolean variable
%B	Output placeholder for a Boolean variable, forced to uppercase
%c	Output placeholder for a character variable
%C	Output placeholder for a character variable, forced to uppercase
%d	Output placeholder for a decimal integer variable
%1.1f	Output placeholder for a decimal floating point variable; the number of digits on both the right and left of the decimal point can also be specified
%n	Injects a new line
%1s	Output placeholder for a string variable, which also allows an optional, minimum width to be specified
%t	Output placeholder for a date/time variable

Table 5.2: Available formatting rules to be used with the 'printf' statement

DecimalFormat

Sometimes, using a **printf** statement is not a viable option. We can also use the **DecimalFormat** class. First, we will import the **DecimalFormat** class:

```
import java.text.DecimalFormat;
```

Then, we can instantiate a new **DecimalFormat** object with a desired format string and use it to limit what is shown with our floating point variables:

```
DecimalFormat dFormat = new DecimalFormat("#,###.###");


System.out.println(dblNumC + " " + (char)247 + " " + dblNumD + " = "
    + dFormat.format(divide(dblNumC,dblNumD)));
```

Now, when we execute our code, **dblNumC** and **dblNumD** should be formatted the same as they were with the **printf** statement:

```
5.2 + 3.1 = 8.3

0.10000000149011612 + 0.20000000298023224 = 0.30000000447034836

false

0.1 + 0.2 = 0.3

5.2 - 3.1 = 2.1

5.2 x 3.1 = 16.12
```

```
5.2 ÷ 3.1 = 1.677

5.2 ÷ 3.1 = 1.677
```

Exponent

Next, we will overload our **exponent()** method to provide a way to determine exponents of floating point values. This will be easier than it was with integers, as the **Math.pow()** method naturally returns a type of double:

```
public static double exponent(double base, double power) {

    return Math.pow(base, power);

}
```

We will also add a **println** statement to the end of our **main()** method, making sure it also uses our **dFormat** object:

```
System.out.println(dblNumC + " to the power of " + dblNumD + " = "

    + dFormat.format(exponent(dblNumC,dblNumD)));
```

Running our code should produce the following output:

```
5.2 + 3.1 = 8.3

0.10000000149011612 + 0.20000000298023224 = 0.30000000447034836

false

0.1 + 0.2 = 0.3

5.2 - 3.1 = 2.1

5.2 x 3.1 = 16.12

5.2 ÷ 3.1 = 1.677

5.2 ÷ 3.1 = 1.677

5.2 to the power of 3.1 = 165.81
```

Square root

We did not cover square roots under integer operations, as executing a square root usually requires the use of floating point types. Let us create a new method in our **MathExamples** class to determine square roots. There is not a native operator for determining square roots in Java, so we will need to use the **Math.sqrt()** method:

```
public static double squareRoot(double number) {
```

```
    return Math.sqrt(number);
}
```

We can also add **println** to our **main()** method to show the result:

```
System.out.println("The square root of " + dblNumC + " = "
    + dFormat.format(squareRoot(dblNumC)));
```

Running our code should produce the following output:

```
5.2 + 3.1 = 8.3
0.10000000149011612 + 0.20000000298023224 = 0.30000000447034836
false
0.1 + 0.2 = 0.3
5.2 - 3.1 = 2.1
5.2 x 3.1 = 16.12
5.2 ÷ 3.1 = 1.677
5.2 ÷ 3.1 = 1.677
5.2 to the power of 3.1 = 165.81
The square root of 5.2 = 2.28
```

Cube root

We will not show an example here (as the code is similar to how we performed a square root), but Java's **Math** library also contains a third/cube root method. We can use that library to easily write a method of our own:

```
public static double cubeRoot(double number) {
    return Math.cbrt(number);
}
```

Absolute value

Sometimes it is helpful to show a value without the influence of its sign bit. In those cases, we do not care if a variable is positive or negative, so we run an absolute value operation to eliminate the sign (essentially forcing it to be positive). For this, the **Math.abs()** method will come in handy:

```
public static double absoluteVal(double number) {
```

```
        return Math.abs(number);

}
```

To demonstrate this functionality, we will call our **absoluteVal()** method twice, once each for a positive and a negative number:

```
System.out.println("The absolute value of " + dblNumC + " = "

        + dFormat.format(absoluteVal(dblNumC)));


double dblNumG = -9f;


System.out.println("The absolute value of " + dblNumG + " = "

        + dFormat.format(absoluteVal(dblNumG)));
```

Now when we execute our code, we will see the following two statements at the end:

```
The absolute value of 5.2 = 5.2

The absolute value of -9.0 = 9
```

Conclusion

In this chapter, we discussed both integer and floating point arithmetic. We demonstrated how Java's **Math** library can be leveraged for some of the more advanced arithmetic operations. We also looked at different ways to format floating point values for appropriate types of output.

We looked at unit testing and learned how to leverage it to show that our arithmetic methods produced the expected results. It is important to point out that unit testing is its own discipline. Entire books have been written on unit testing and test-driven development, and we have only spent a portion of a chapter on it. It is highly recommended to explore unit testing more on your own, as there is so much more to it than the small part that we discussed here.

Some of the nuances with both integer and floating point arithmetic were discussed. It is extremely important for us, as developers, to understand how arithmetic operations behave in certain circumstances. Many developers have gone to work on complex, distributed systems and been confused by how integer division is used to compute things like replica quorums. Understanding the material in this chapter is not only foundational to Java programming but also to the larger world of computers.

In the next chapter, we will discuss data structures like stacks, queues, and linked lists. We will also look at binary trees and show an example of how they can be used.

Points to remember

- When performing an operation in a string or **print** statement, remember to wrap the operation inside an extra set of parentheses to avoid premature **String** casting.

- Primitive types are operated on and stored in the binary (base-2) numeric system.

- The **junit** library can write unit tests to ensure consistent behavior from individual methods.

- Multiplication and division operations use ***** and **/** instead of **x** and ÷, respectively.

- The remainder of an integer division operation can be obtained with the modulo operator **%**.

- Java does not have a native operator for some of the more advanced arithmetic operations. For those operations, we can check the Java **Math** library for additional methods like **pow()**, **sqrt()**, **abs()**, and many others.

- Floating point arithmetic is largely an approximation and should be used with caution.

- If precise figures are required (as with currency calculations), the **BigDecimal** type should be used instead of a **float** or a **double**.

- Floating point output formats can be influenced by using either the **printf** statement or the **DecimalFormat** class.

Join our book's Discord space

Join the book's Discord Workspace for Latest updates, Offers, Tech happenings around the world, New Release and Sessions with the Authors:

https://discord.bpbonline.com

CHAPTER 6
Common Data Structures

Introduction

In this chapter, we will look at how to build and use some common, fundamental structures to handle and work with data in Java. First, we will talk about stacks and queues and walk through building each one of them. Then, we will discuss the different types of linked lists. Finally, we will examine binary trees and demonstrate their use with a simple example.

Structure

In this chapter, we will discuss data structures that are commonly used in software development and low-level computing. This includes the following:

- Stacks
- Queues
- Linked lists
- Binary trees

Objectives

The primary goal of this chapter is to build an understanding of common underlying data structures. We will take the approach of discussing each data structure, building it, and then processing an example. Our objectives are to:

- Understand the behaviors of stacks and queues,
- Learn how stacks and queues are used, and
- Understand linked lists and binary trees and how to traverse them.

Stacks

We will start by building a stack, a fundamental structure used in many different levels of computing. It is characterized by its **last-in-first-out (LIFO)** behavior. Items can only be added to the top of the stack in an operation known as a **push**. If another item is added or *pushed* to the stack, then the most recent item is moved-downward, and the new item is now at the *top* of the stack. Refer to *Figure 6.1*:

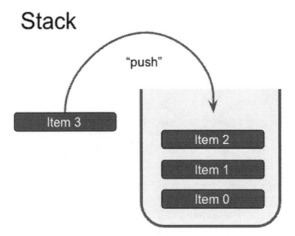

Figure 6.1: *Demonstrating the push operation of adding an item onto the stack*

Regardless of where items may be in the stack, only the topmost item can be accessed. If a **pop** operation is executed, the topmost item is removed from the top of the stack and returned. Refer to *Figure 6.2*:

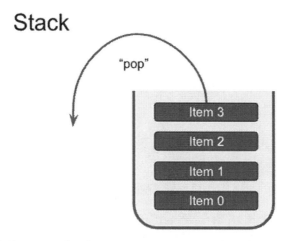

Figure 6.2: Demonstrating the 'pop' operation of removing an item from the stack

In our IDE, we will create a new class named **Item** and ensure it is in a new package named **chapter6**. This class should not have a **main** method:

```
package chapter6;


public class Item {
```

Our **Item** class should have a privately-scoped **String** property named **name** and a no-argument constructor:

```
    private String name;


    public Item() {

    }
```

Note: We could also define Item as a Record. However, in this case, defining it as a POJO gives us the additional flexibility required to use it with stacks, queues, and linked lists.

We will also create a single-argument constructor that takes a **String name** variable as a parameter and sets it to the **name** property. The **Item** class will also need a getter/setter pair for the **name** property:

```
    public Item(String name) {

        this.name = name;

    }
```

```
public String getName() {

    return this.name;

}


public void setName(String name) {

    this.name = name;

}

}
```

Next, we will build a new class in the **chapter6** package named **Stack**. Like the **Item** class, it should not have a **main** method. Make sure to define properties for an array of **Item** named **items,** as well as integers named **maxCount** and **stackCount**:

```
package chapter6;


public class Stack {


    private Item[] items;

    private int maxCount;

    private int stackCount = 0;
```

We want our **Stack** class to have two constructors. One that accepts an integer for the expected number of items. The other does not accept any parameters but simply calls the other constructor with an integer value of **10**:

```
public Stack() {

    this(10);

}


public Stack(int numItems) {

    maxCount = numItems;

    items = new Item[maxCount];

}
```

Next, we will need a **private void** method named **resizeArray**. If we increase our stack beyond the max size of the underlying **items** array, we will need a way to **resize** it. By default, we will increase it by **5** each time.

Resizing an array is not possible in Java. We will simply create a new array and copy the current **items** array to it:

```
private void resizeItemsArray() {

    maxCount = maxCount + 5;


    Item[] newArray = new Item[maxCount];


    for (int counter = 0; counter < stackCount; counter++) {

        newArray[counter] = items[counter];

    }


    items = newArray;

}
```

In the preceding code, we are doing the following:

- Creating **newArray** with space for five more items than the current **maxCount**
- Copying one item from the **items** array to **newArray**
- Overwriting **items** with **newArray**

> **Note: This would be a great time to use the Collections.copy() method, but arrays do not inherit the Collection base class.**

Next, we will write a **public** method to handle the **push** operation for adding new items to the stack. First, we need to check whether or not the new size of the array exceeds the current **maxCount**, and then we need to call our **resizeItemsArray()** method if it does. Once that is done, we will increment **stackCount** by one and then set the new **item** to **stackCount** minus one (because of zero-based indexing):

```
public void push(Item item) {

    if (stackCount + 1 >= maxCount) {

        resizeItemsArray();

    }


    stackCount++;

    items[stackCount - 1] = item;

}
```

Stacks also have a **peek** operation, providing a window to the top item on the stack. This allows the top item to be viewed without being removed:

```java
public Item peek() {

    Item returnVal = items[stackCount - 1];


    return returnVal;

}
```

We will then write a **public** method to handle the **pop** operation. The **pop()** method is fairly straightforward. We define a new **Item** object as our return value and instantiate with the result of our **peek()** method, which should be the top item. Next, we decrement **stackCount** and return the **popped** item:

```java
public Item pop() {

    Item returnVal = peek();

    stackCount--;

    return returnVal;

}
```

> **Note: We do not remove the item from the list. We simply decrement stackCount (number of items in the stack) so that it is out of range for our stack-based operations. Now, we could remove the item by setting that location to a null or empty string. We could even shrink or reduce the size of itemsArray if we wanted to be efficient with our memory footprint.**

However, executing those operations comes with a cost that can be measured in both performance and increased code complexity. It is simpler to decrease the workable range of items and ignore anything outside of that range.

To complete the **Stack** class, we simply need to add two more methods:

- A *getter* for **stackCount**
- An overload of the **toString()** method, so we have control over default formatting

The **getStackCount()** method is used to return the privately scoped **stackCount** integer variable. It is important to note that we do not want to build out a *setter* for **stackCount**, as it is used internally by the **Stack** class, and the calling method should not have the ability to set that value directly:

```java
public int getStackCount() {

    return stackCount;
```

}

For the overloaded **toString()** method, we iterate through the **items** array and show both the item and its index on the same line. As a stack has the first item (**index == 0**) at the *bottom*, we will iterate through **items** in reverse order:

```
public String toString() {

    StringBuilder returnVal = new StringBuilder("\n");

    for (int counter = stackCount - 1; counter >= 0; counter--) {

        returnVal.append(counter);

        returnVal.append(" - ");

        returnVal.append(items[counter].getName());

        returnVal.append("\n");

    }

    return returnVal.toString();

    }

}
```

With our two supporting classes built, we create a new class named **DataStructuresExamples** inside the **chapter6** package. Make sure that this class has a **main()** method. The first thing we will do in our **main()** method is to instantiate a **new Stack** object named **stack**:

```
package chapter6;


public class DataStructuresExamples {

    public static void main(String[] args) {

        Stack stack = new Stack();
```

To show how our stack works, we can instantiate several new objects of the **Item** class using an example of building a stack to manage a playlist of movies:

```
Item martian = new Item("The Martian");

Item patriotGames = new Item("Patriot Games");

Item bladerunner = new Item("Blade Runner");
```

```
Item bladerunner2049 = new Item("Blade Runner 2049");

Item apollo13 = new Item("Apollo 13");

Item firstMan = new Item("First Man");

Item empireStrikesBack = new Item("The Empire Strikes Back");

Item rogueOne = new Item("Rogue One");

Item alexander = new Item("Alexander");

Item starwars = new Item("Star Wars");

Item runningMan = new Item("Running Man");
```

With our movie items created, we will display output indicating that we are working with a stack and then **push** six of the movies (individually) onto the **stack**:

```
System.out.println("Stack example:");


stack.push(firstMan);

stack.push(apollo13);

stack.push(rogueOne);

stack.push(empireStrikesBack);

stack.push(bladeRunner2049);

stack.push(bladeRunner);


System.out.println(stack);
```

Running our code produces the following output:

5 - Blade Runner

4 - Blade Runner 2049

3 - The Empire Strikes Back

2 - Rogue One

1 - Apollo 13

0 - First Man

If our output matches what was just shown, then everything looks good so far. Now (between our push operations and our **println**), we will **pop** a movie from the stack, **push** a few more, and maybe **pop**/**push** another:

```
System.out.println(stack.pop().getName() + " was popped from the stack.");
```

```
stack.push(patriotGames);
```

```
stack.push(martian);
```

```
stack.push(alexander);
```

```
stack.push(runningMan);
```

```
System.out.println(stack.pop().getName() + " was popped from the stack.");
```

```
stack.push(starwars);
```

Now, executing our code should produce these results:

Blade Runner was popped from the stack.

Running Man was popped from the stack.

8 - Star Wars

7 - Alexander

6 - The Martian

5 - Patriot Games

4 - Blade Runner 2049

3 - The Empire Strikes Back

2 - Rogue One

1 - Apollo 13

0 - First Man

As shown, we have worked with our stack object by pushing several movies to it, popping two from it, and then displaying the results.

Recall the beginning of this chapter, when we discussed that stacks were used in many different levels of computing. Well, Java has stack structures that we work with all the time, and we do not notice because they are abstracted away from us.

Consider the program we just wrote. As we execute our **DataStructureExamples** class, our **main()** method is pushed onto a stack for holding methods and their data that ensure that the methods are run to completion in a LIFO approach. For example, as our

main() method continues, its execution is often postponed until a newly called method is completed, as shown in *Figure 6.3*:

Figure 6.3: A visualization of how the JVM uses a stack to manage the order of method execution

As we have shown, stacks are useful data structures prevalent in computing.

Queues

Next, let us move on to building a queue. Unlike a stack, a queue is more universally understood. New items are added at the back of the queue, and the oldest items are operated on from the front in a FIFO order.

We can find many examples of queues being used in computing. Event streaming message brokers like *Apache Kafka* and *Apache Pulsar* store data in structures called **topics**, which are essentially distributed queues. Ever wonder which song is coming up next in a music streaming service? That is also backed by a queue. Sending a job to a printer at work? We might have to contend with our co-workers doing the same, as our job is put into the print queue.

Let us create a new class named **Queue** inside the **chapter6** package. As we did with our **Stack** class, our **Queue** class should not have a **main** method. Likewise, we will add privately-scoped properties for the **items** array, and the **maxCount** and **queueCount** integers:

```
package chapter6;


public class Queue {

    private Item[] items;

    private int maxCount;

    private int queueCount = 0;
```

We are also going to take the same approach with the constructors. Essentially, a no-argument constructor can be called to build the **items** array with room for 10 **items** by default. That constructor will call our other constructor, which accepts a number of items as its lone argument and uses it to initialize both **maxCount** and **items**:

```
public Queue() {

    this(10);

}


public Queue(int numItems) {

    maxCount = numItems;

    items = new Item[maxCount];

}
```

We will also repurpose the **resizeItemsArray()** private method from the **Stack** class, adjusting the code to use **queueCount**:

```
private void resizeItemsArray() {

    // increase the max number of items by 5

    maxCount = maxCount + 5;


    // instantiate larger items array

    Item[] newArray = new Item[maxCount];


    // copy current items array to new

    for (int counter = 0; counter < queueCount; counter++) {

        newArray[counter] = items[counter];

    }


    // override current items array with new array

    items = newArray;

}
```

Queues typically have methods that allow the front and back items in the queue to be viewed. We will create two *getters* to handle that:

```
public Item getFront() {

    if (queueCount > 0) {
```

```java
            return items[0];
        } else {
            return null;
        }
    }

    public Item getBack() {
        if (queueCount > 0) {
            return items[queueCount - 1];
        } else {
            return null;
        }
    }
```

Both methods will only return a valid item if the **items** array is not empty. If the array is empty, a value of null is returned.

> **Note: Be careful when returning null from a method. In this case, the calling method needs to be extra careful in how the return values are processed, or a null pointer exception could occur.**

Next, we will create the **enqueue()** method. This method is similar to the **push()** method from the **Stack** class, where we will first check the new size of the **items** array and increase it if necessary. Either way, we will increment **queueCount** and add the new item to the back of the queue:

```java
public void enqueue(Item item) {
    if (queueCount + 1 >= maxCount) {
        resizeItemsArray();
    }

    queueCount++;
    items[queueCount - 1] = item;
}
```

Removing an item with the **dequeue()** method is a little tricky. First, we need to make sure the queue is not empty. If it is, calling the **dequeue()** method should return null.

Once we have the **front** item set as our return value, we need to move each item down one index position. With that complete, we can decrement **queueCount** and return the front item:

```java
public Item dequeue() {

    if (queueCount == 0) {

        return null;

    } else {

        Item returnVal = getFront();

        // move all other items down

        for (int counter = 1; counter < queueCount; counter++) {

            items[counter - 1] = items[counter];

        }

        queueCount--;

        return returnVal;

    }

}
```

We can finish the **Queue** class by creating a public *getter* method for **queueCount** and overloading the **toString()** method (similar to the **Stack** class):

```java
public int getQueueCount() {

    return queueCount;

}


public String toString() {

    StringBuilder returnVal = new StringBuilder("\n");

    for (int counter = 0; counter < queueCount; counter++) {
```

```
        returnVal.append(counter);

        returnVal.append(" - ");

        returnVal.append(items[counter].getName());

        returnVal.append("\n");

    }


    return returnVal.toString();

}
```

Next, we will go back to our **DataStructuresExamples** class and add the following to the end of the **main()** method:

```
System.out.println("Queue example:");


Queue queue = new Queue();


queue.enqueue(starwars);

queue.enqueue(bladeRunner);

queue.enqueue(empireStrikesBack);

queue.enqueue(patriotGames);

queue.enqueue(bladeRunner2049);


System.out.println(queue);
```

If we run our code, we should see the previous output from the stack example, and this output:

Queue example:

0 - Star Wars

1 - Blade Runner

2 - The Empire Strikes Back

3 - Patriot Games

4 - Blade Runner 2049

Based on this output, our queue is indeed indexing the items as they are added, with the front item (**Star Wars**) at index position **0** and the back item (**Blade Runner 2049**) at index position **4**.

Let us make one more adjustment to the **main()** method for the **Queue** example, calling the **dequeue()** method twice and then printing the contents of the queue one more time:

```
System.out.println(queue.dequeue().getName() + " was dequeued.");

System.out.println(queue.dequeue().getName() + " was dequeued.");


System.out.println(queue);
```

Running our code should then produce these results for the **Queue** example:

```
Queue example:


0 - Star Wars

1 - Blade Runner

2 - The Empire Strikes Back

3 - Patriot Games

4 - Blade Runner 2049


Star Wars was dequeued.

Blade Runner was dequeued.


0 - The Empire Strikes Back

1 - Patriot Games

2 - Blade Runner 2049
```

Notice how after the first two items were dequeued, the item indexes have all been shifted downward twice (once for each dequeue).

Linked lists

Let us move on to linked lists. We discussed linked lists back in *Chapter 4, Arrays, Collections, and Records*. We are going to build our own linked list class to make sure we understand the concepts at work here.

First, we need to make some adjustments to our **Item** class. We are going to build a doubly-linked list. As mentioned in *Chapter 4*, this is a list where the items are linked to the next and previous items. To support this, our **Item** class needs those *links* as well. In the **Item** class, let us add two more class properties:

```java
private Item prevItem;

private Item nextItem;
```

We will also add both *getter* and *setter* methods to support those properties:

```java
public Item getPrevItem() {

    return this.prevItem;

}


public void setPrevItem(Item item) {

    this.prevItem = item;

}


public Item getNextItem() {

    return this.nextItem;

}


public void setNextItem(Item item) {

    this.nextItem = item;

}
```

Now, this may seem like a lot to be adding to the **Item** class; especially since our **Stack** and **Queue** implementations will not use any of this. If not used, the **prevItem** and **nextItem** properties will be null, and null pointer references in Java consume a trivial amount of memory on the JVM heap.

> **Note: The addition of these properties makes Item a self-referential class.**

Next, we will create a new class in the **chapter6** package, named **LinkedList**. This class should not have a **main** method. We will create three class properties to handle references to the first and last items, and an integer to keep a count of how many items are in the list:

```java
package chapter6;
```

```
public class LinkedList {

    private Item firstItem;

    private Item lastItem;

    private int listCount = 0;
```

Note how we have not defined an array this time. Our **LinkedList** class only requires definitions for the first and last items. The **firstItem** property will contain a reference to the second item, and that will contain a reference to the third, and so on, until we finally reach the last item.

Our **LinkedList** class will have the following two constructors:

- A no-argument constructor without any code
- A single-argument constructor that instantiates the list with a single item

Let us build the constructors now:

```
public LinkedList() {

}


public LinkedList(Item item) {

    addItem(item);

}
```

> **Note: Even though our no-argument constructor does not contain code, its definition is still necessary to allow the class to be instantiated (as an object) without parameters.**

Next, we will work on adding items to the list. For now, our items will be added only to the *front* of the list. To support our new **add()** method, we need to have a way to handle adding a single item to an empty list, as we will be performing actions that will only be necessary in that case. Therefore, we will write a special, privately-scoped method named **setWithOneItem** to handle this:

```
private void setWithOneItem(Item newItem) {

    firstItem = newItem;

    lastItem = newItem;

}
```

Our **setWithOneItem()** method does not need to do much. But it is the only time we will need to set both **firstItem** and **lastItem** to the *same* item.

Next, we will build a new method named **addItem**. It will accept an **Item** named **newItem** as its lone parameter, check for empty list conditions, and call the **setWithOneItem()** method if necessary. If **listCount** is not zero, then there are three actions that we need to take to add the new item:

- Set the current **firstItem** as the **next** item on **newItem**.
- Set the **previous** item on the original **firstItem** to be **newItem**.
- Set **newItem** as the new **first** item in the list.

And let us not forget to increment **listCount**, no matter which logic is applied:

```java
public void addItem(Item newItem) {

    if (listCount == 0) {

        setWithOneItem(newItem);

    } else {

        newItem.setNextItem(firstItem);

        firstItem.setPrevItem(newItem);

        firstItem = newItem;

    }


    listCount++;

}
```

We also want the ability to locate an item by name. In this method, we will iterate through the list, starting with **firstItem**. The iteration happens by calling each item's **getNextItem()** method. If an item that matches our **name** string is found, we short-circuit the loop and return the item. If we make it through to the last item (which has a null value for its **nextItem**), we **return null**:

```java
public Item findItemByName(String name) {

    Item currentItem = firstItem;

    while (currentItem != null) {
        if (currentItem.getName().equals(name)) {
            // found!
            return currentItem;
```

```
    }


        currentItem = currentItem.getNextItem();

    }


    return null;

}
```

Similarly, we also want the ability to *remove* an item by name. We can leverage the **findItemByName()** method that we wrote to locate the item by name. Removing the item from the list is a simple task of *orphaning* the item by re-pointing its **nextItem** and **previousItem** to each other:

```
public boolean removeItemByName(String name) {

    Item itemFound = findItemByName(name);

    if (itemFound != null) {

        Item previous = itemFound.getPrevItem();

        Item next = itemFound.getNextItem();


        previous.setNextItem(next);

        next.setPrevItem(previous);


        listCount--;

        return true;

    }


    return false;

}
```

We will also need *getter* methods for our properties. All three of them are managed internally, so we do not need to expose any *setter* methods for them publicly:

```
public Item getFirstItem() {

    return firstItem;
```

```
}


public Item getLastItem() {

    return lastItem;

}


public int getListCount() {

    return this.listCount;

}
```

Finally, our **LinkedList** class needs an overloaded **toString()** method, allowing us to apply some formatting to the item names:

```
public String toString() {


    StringBuilder returnVal = new StringBuilder("\n");


    Item item = firstItem;


    while (item != null) {
        returnVal.append(item.getName());
        returnVal.append("\n");
        item = item.getNextItem();

    }


    return returnVal.toString();

}
```

Going back to our **DataStructureExamples** class, we can now implement our **LinkedList**. To be consistent with our earlier example, in *Chapter 4, Arrays, Collections, and Records*, we will use the same data elements (fictitious city names) as our items. This will lead to a logical structure similar to what is shown in *Figure 6.4*:

chapter6.LinkedList linkedList

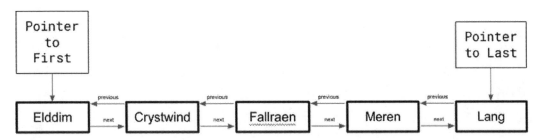

Figure 6.4: *A visual representation of our linked list that contains the same city names we used in Chapter 4*

To that end, we will create our city items, add them to our **LinkedList**, and display their contents:

```
System.out.println("Linked List example:");

LinkedList linkedList = new LinkedList();

Item elddim = new Item("Elddim");
Item crystwind = new Item("Crystwind");
Item fallraen = new Item("Fallraen");
Item meren = new Item("Meren");
Item lang = new Item("Lang");
Item hiroth = new Item("Hiroth");

linkedList.addItem(lang);
linkedList.addItem(meren);
linkedList.addItem(fallraen);
linkedList.addItem(crystwind);
linkedList.addItem(elddim);

System.out.println(linkedList);
```

If we run the preceding code, we should see the following output at the bottom:

Linked List example:

Elddim

Crystwind

Fallraen

Meren

Lang

Now, let us check to see if two cities exist inside the list. We can do that by adding this code to the end of the **DataStructuresExamples'** **main()** method:

```
if (linkedList.findItemByName(crystwind.getName()) != null) {

    System.out.println("Yes!");

} else {

    System.out.println("No, not found.");

}


System.out.println("Does the list contain " + hiroth.getName() + "?");

if (linkedList.findItemByName(hiroth.getName()) != null) {

    System.out.println("Yes!");

} else {

    System.out.println("No, not found.");

}
```

Running our code should produce the following output:

Linked List example:

Elddim

Crystwind

Fallraen

Meren

Lang

Does the list contain Crystwind?

Yes!

Does the list contain Hiroth?

No, not found.

Now, let us adjust the **DataStructuresExamples** one last time, removing the town of **Meren**:

```
System.out.println("Now remove " + meren.getName());

linkedList.removeItemByName(meren.getName());


System.out.println(linkedList);
```

Then, let us execute the code to check the output:

Linked List example:

Elddim

Crystwind

Fallraen

Meren

Lang

Does the list contain Crystwind?

Yes!

Does the list contain Hiroth?

No, not found.

Now remove Meren

Elddim

Crystwind

```
Fallraen
```

```
Lang
```

As shown, we have successfully removed one of the cities.

An important concept to understand here is that a true linked list does not need (or have) an index to pull back a particular item quickly. All our **LinkedList** class has are objects that point to the first and last item in the list. The rest of the list is maintained in the relationships between the next and previous properties of each item.

Note that we have created a doubly-linked list, which means our linked list items are aware of both the *next* and the *previous* items. This also means that we could work with our list starting from the front or from the back. For example, if we wanted to add items at the back of the list, we could do something like this:

```java
public void addItemAtBack(Item newItem) {

    if (listCount == 0) {

        setWithOneItem(newItem);

    } else {

        newItem.setPrevItem(lastItem);

        lastItem.setNextItem(newItem);

        lastItem = newItem;

    }

}
```

The advantages of a linked list become clear when we realize that it is not confined to an array or collection. This also means that items in a linked list do not have to be stored contiguously in memory (on the heap). When we add to the list, we do not have to resize it. Also, in this case, we are only adding to the front of the list, which means (coupled with not having to resize) **add** operations are very fast.

Linked lists are commonly used in computing. A good example is a web browser, which uses a linked list behind the back and forward buttons to allow users to retrace their steps between web pages quickly. Music playlists are another type of linked list. We can set a music playlist to *loop*, in which case the last item would have the first item as its *next*, creating a **circular linked list**.

Binary trees

Another common data structure is a binary tree. Binary trees are data collections known as **nodes** that are interrelated by their branch. The first node added to a binary tree is called the **root**. The root node, like all nodes, can link to two other nodes on both the left and the right.

If a node is tasked with inserting a new node, it checks the new node's value. If the new node's value is less than that of the current node, it is linked to the left. If it is greater than the current node's value, it is linked to the right. This way, a binary tree can quickly sort a set of data.

First, we will start with the **Node** class. Create a new class named **Node** inside the **chapter6** package. This class should not have a **main** method. We will create private properties for the integer value, and two more **Node** objects named **leftNode** and **rightNode**:

```
package chapter6;


public class Node {


    private int value;

    private Node leftNode;

    private Node rightNode;
```

> **Note: The definition for the Node class contains two objects of the Node class: leftNode and rightNode. This is known as a self-referential class. This is how one node will maintain references to other nodes in the tree.**

Our **Node** class will have one constructor, which will accept a single integer parameter. That integer will be used to initialize the node's **value** property:

```
public Node (int number) {

    this.value = number;

}
```

Next, a node needs to know how to insert a new node. Therefore, we will need to build an **insert()** method. This method will take an integer as its parameter, named **newNumber**. If **newNumber** is less than the value of the current node, our logic moves down the left side of the node. If **newNumber** is greater than the value of the current node, our logic moves down the right side of the node:

```
public void insert(int newNumber) {
```

```
    if (newNumber < this.value) {

        if (leftNode == null) {

            leftNode = new Node(newNumber);

        } else {

            leftNode.insert(newNumber);

        }

    } else if (newNumber > this.value) {

    if (rightNode == null) {

            rightNode = new Node(newNumber);

        } else {

            rightNode.insert(newNumber);

        }

    }

}
```

Regardless of which side we move down (right or left), if that side's node is null (does not have a value), we have reached a **leaf** node. This means that we can set that side's node to the new node (initialized with **newNumber**). However, if that node has a value, then we call the **insert()** method on that node, and the process repeats until a leaf node is found and the new node is inserted.

Note: In looking at the preceding code, note that we do not have an 'if' condition to check if newNumber is equal to the current node's value. The binary tree node in its current state does not accept duplicates. If a duplicate is added, it will simply be ignored.

We can finish the **Node** class by building three *getter* methods for our properties:

```
public Node getLeftNode() {

    return this.leftNode;

}


public Node getRightNode() {

    return this.rightNode;
```

```
}
```

```
public int getValue() {

    return this.value;

}
```

Next, we will build our **Tree** class. Make sure this class is named **Tree**, does not have a **main** method, and is inside the **chapter6** package. It should only have one property, that is, an object of type **Node** named **root**:

```
package chapter6;
```

```
public class Tree {

    private Node root;
```

Our **Tree** class will have two constructors:

- A no-argument constructor
- A single-argument constructor that takes an integer and initializes **root** as a **new Node** with the integer value

Let us build the constructors now:

```
public Tree() {

}
```

```
public Tree(int number) {

    root = new Node(number);

}
```

Our **Tree** class will also have an **insert()** method, which will set the **root** node if it is null or call the **root** node's **insert()** method if it has a value:

```
public void insert(int number) {

if (root == null) {

        root = new Node(number);

    } else {
        root.insert(number);
```

```
    }

}
```

Now, let us look at traversing the tree. We will build two methods: a **private** method named **traverse** and a **public** method named **traverseFromRoot**. The **traverseFromRoot()** method will call our **private traverse()** method while passing the **root** node as a parameter. The **traverse()** method checks if the node it passed is null. If so, it simply returns with no further action. If it has a value, **traverse()** calls itself recursively on the left and right nodes until it reaches a leaf node:

```java
public void traverseFromRoot() {

    traverse(root);

}


private void traverse(Node node) {

    if (node == null) {

        return;

    }


    traverse(node.getLeftNode());

    System.out.println(node.getValue());

    traverse(node.getRightNode());

}
```

Now, let us return to our **DataStructuresExamples** class, and add the following lines at the bottom of our **main()** method:

```java
System.out.println("Tree example:");


Tree tree = new Tree(47);


tree.insert(48);

tree.insert(20);

tree.insert(15);

tree.insert(26);
```

```
tree.insert(18);

tree.traverseFromRoot();
```

Essentially, we are creating a new **Tree** and instantiating it to contain a single node with the integer value of **47**. We are then calling the tree's **insert()** method with five new integers in no particular order. Finally, we call the tree's **traverseFromRoot()** method to display its contents.

Running this code should produce the following output:

Tree example:

15

18

20

26

47

48

By building the **traverse()** method to favor the left-sided nodes first, we have essentially written a binary sorting operation. A visual representation of our binary tree can be seen in *Figure 6.5*:

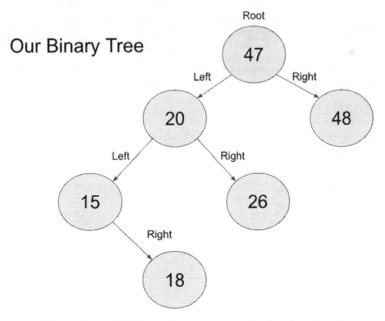

Figure 6.5: The numbers added in our binary tree example, showing 47 as the root node

If we wanted to get the values stored in the tree in *reverse* order, we could have built two new methods in our **Tree** class. The only difference is that we would have to traverse the right side first:

```java
public void reverseFromRoot() {

    reverse(root);

}


private void reverse(Node node) {

    if (node == null) {

        return;

    }

    reverse(node.getRightNode());

    System.out.println(node.getValue());

    reverse(node.getLeftNode());

}
```

We can then add two lines of code to the end of the **DataStructureExamples'** **main()** method:

```java
System.out.println();

tree.reverseFromRoot();
```

Running our code should now produce the following output:

Tree example:

15

18

20

26

47

48

48

47

26

20

18

15

With these examples, we can clearly see that trees are powerful data structures that allow us to quickly store and retrieve ordered information. Binary trees are also commonly used in computing behind implementations such as file systems and email storage.

Conclusion

In this chapter, we discussed several common data structures, such as stacks, queues, linked lists, and binary trees. With the help of examples shown in this chapter, you understood that these structures are fundamental building blocks for data processing and storage methodologies.

It bears mentioning that many companies use these structures and concepts in technical interviews and coding challenges for prospective new hires. Therefore, understanding the concepts in this chapter will not only make us better programmers but might also help us land a job.

In the next chapter, we will discuss building web applications in Java. We will include restful web services and user interfaces, as well as how to use them to build a complete application.

Points to remember

- Stacks are useful structures for keeping track of things that need to be processed in a nested, **last-in-first-out** (**LIFO**) fashion. Method calls on a program stack is a good example of this.

- Queues are meant for storing data to be processed in a **first-in-first-out** (**FIFO**) fashion.

- Linked lists have faster add times and fewer memory constraints as compared to other data structures.

- Singly-linked lists are only aware of the *next* item in the list and can only be traversed one way.

- Doubly-linked lists are aware of both the *next* and *previous* items in the list and can be traversed from the front or from the back.

Binary tree nodes can be quickly navigated based on their value, which are stored in linked nodes on either the left or the right sides.

Join our book's Discord space

Join the book's Discord Workspace for Latest updates, Offers, Tech happenings around the world, New Release and Sessions with the Authors:

https://discord.bpbonline.com

Chapter 7
Working with Databases

Introduction

In this chapter, we will discuss how to build Java applications that use databases. First, we will give a brief introduction to databases, including the history and computer science theory behind them. Then, we will talk about how to connect with databases. Finally, we will explore how to connect and work with two different types of databases by building out examples to perform some simple **Create, Read, Update, and Delete (CRUD)** operations.

Structure

The world of databases and database development is quite large. We will approach this topic from the perspective of a developer, discussing ways to accomplish our tasks of learning how to build data-intensive Java applications.

To that end, this chapter will cover the following topics:

- Introduction to databases
- CAP theorem
- PostgreSQL
- Apache Cassandra
- Choosing the right database

Objectives

This chapter is about building a base of knowledge about how to work with and think about databases as a Java developer. To that end, our learning objectives are to:

- Understand the major differences between a relational database and a NoSQL database.
- Learn how to connect to databases without hard-coding access credentials.
- Understand the benefits of using prepared statements.
- Learn how to perform basic queries and operations.
- Understand that tables for a relational database need to be modeled differently from how the same tables would look in a NoSQL database.

Introduction to databases

Databases are software applications that serve, organize, and persist data on disk. A database is designed to work with its local operating system to provide the best possible read-and-write performance. This way, an application can connect to a database to quickly look up or store data without understanding the intricacies of working with the native file system.

There are several types of databases and several database products to choose from. Understanding the goals and requirements of the application to be built is essential to selecting the right database. It also helps to know how the current selection of database products came into existence.

Short history of databases

Databases emerged in the late 1960s, as the need for data persistence became apparent. Before that, developers simply wrote data out to files, which were organized by the calling application and varied widely in formatting. Two main types of **database management systems (DBMS)** arose during this time: hierarchical and network databases.

However, these approaches to data storage were susceptible to many problems. It was difficult to maintain the integrity and consistency of commonly used data points. Data relations were also problematic, especially in the hierarchical model.

In 1970, *Dr. Edgar F. Codd* (then a consultant for IBM) wrote a paper named *A Relational Model for Large, Shared Data Banks*. This paper is widely considered to mark the invention of the **relational database management system (RDBMS)**. Shortly afterward (*Oracle 2004*), IBM released the **Structured English Query Language (SEQUEL)** to work with Codd's designed model. This language was later renamed as the **Structured Query Language (SQL)**.

In 1979, *Relational Software, Inc.* released its flagship product *Oracle V2*, the first commercially-available RDBMS. Other relational database products emerged, with databases like *Sybase*, *FoxBase*, and *Microsoft SQL Server* taking their place in the enterprise in the early 1990s.

Until the early 2000s, relational databases did well in solving the problems put before them. With the sudden rise of the internet, it soon became apparent that databases built to operate within the bounds of a single machine were having difficulty keeping up with the demands of large-scale internet applications.

It was at this time that researchers took inspiration from a then-recent paper written by *Dr. Eric Brewer* and *Dr. Armando Fox* called *Harvest, Yield, and Scalable Tolerant Systems*. In this paper, *Brewer* and *Fox* postulated that (*Brewer, Fox 1999*) all distributed systems attempted to achieve three properties: consistency, availability, and tolerance of network partitions. However, they further stated that it was only realistically possible to achieve two of those three properties and that distributed system architects would have to consider trading off one to achieve their goals. This idea became known as the *CAP theorem*. Furthermore, the ideas presented by *Brewer* and *Fox* in this paper are widely considered to indicate the beginning of the distributed or non-relational database movement.

In the late 2000s and early 2010s, several new and distributed database products arose. These databases took a different approach to solving problems than the traditional RDBMSs. When RDBMS needed more resources, the only way was to add more within the bounds of the single system by adding more disk, RAM, or a faster CPU. This process is known as **vertical scaling**. However, vertical scaling has limits, as a single system can only address or support so much RAM, disk, or even certain CPUs without replacing the motherboard.

The new databases became known as the **Not only SQL (NoSQL)** databases. NoSQL databases embraced the idea of architecting for partition tolerance (and then either high availability or strong consistency) by allowing a single database to exist across multiple physical machines. When the database was low on resources, a NoSQL database was capable of quickly using the additional resources of another newly added machine. This process is known as **horizontal scaling**. It became even faster as cloud services rose to prominence in the 2010s, allowing another machine instance to be added to a NoSQL database cluster with just a few mouse clicks.

Today, both NoSQL and RDBMS databases are commonly used. Large enterprises typically use several database products, allowing application developers to select the correct tool for the task at hand.

CAP theorem

In the previous section, we briefly mentioned the CAP theorem and its origins in *Dr. Brewer* and *Dr. Fox*'s paper *Harvest, Yield, and Scalable Tolerant Systems*. It is key to understanding how modern distributed systems are architected.

First, let us define each of the CAP properties to be clear on the operational goals of certain databases.

Consistency

NoSQL databases (and even primary / secondary failover RDBMSs) typically keep multiple copies of all data points. Consistency is a measure of a database's ability to:

- Perform updates and keep all copies of each data replica in sync.
- Prevent a user from reading an old or stale value.

Databases that can perform these two tasks are considered to be **strong-consistent**.

Availability

We all know that performance in our code matters, and database software is no different. All database queries suffer from varying degrees of latency, especially when multiple data replicas are stored on different physical or logical machines. Availability measures a database's ability to (*Brewer, Fox 1999*) always read and return data on request. Essentially, if we run a query and the data exists, we should get an answer to that query. Databases that can do this are considered to be **highly available**.

Partition tolerance

Hardware failures can and do happen. Consider a hypothetical cloud provider with data centers and compute regions located around the world. Cloud providers at that scale usually have tens of thousands of servers running to support customer operations. When an organization has a sheer amount of hardware scale, there is almost never a time when 100% of all available hardware is running reliably.

Databases operating in these environments need to account for small amounts of localized hardware failure. Databases that can successfully serve results during a hardware failure are considered to be **partition tolerant**.

CAP designations

Let us offer a visualization of this topic. Suppose we put each of the CAP properties (Consistency, Availability, and Partition Tolerance) on the corners of a triangle. In that case, each side of the triangle represents the current paradigm for the distributed system or database in question. This is because it is only possible to support two of these properties at any given time. Refer to the following *Figure 7.1*:

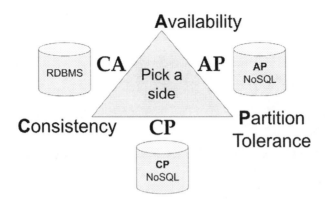

Figure 7.1: *A visualization of the CAP theorem*

Viewing databases in this way leads to the following operational paradigms, sometimes known as *CAP designations*:

- **AP systems:** Distributed systems that support high availability and partition tolerance are AP systems. These databases can serve low-latency results distributed across multiple machines (some may be in a mode of failure) because they elect to be *eventually consistent*. This means it is possible for a query to return results from updated data that may not represent the most recent state. That being said, in most AP databases, the latency between keeping replicas up-to-date is usually a matter of double-digit milliseconds.

- **CP systems:** Systems that support partition tolerance and strong consistency are CP systems. This type of distributed system serves its data in a way that prevents inconsistent data replicas from being returned. This is often achieved through semaphores or other locking mechanisms. Distributed CP systems often support hardware fail over and data sharding to achieve limited availability and horizontal scaling.

- **CA systems:** Systems that support both strong consistency and high availability are CA systems. Most CA databases are RDBMSs that were originally engineered to be deployed on single machines, although now most RDBMSs do have options for distributed deployments.

PostgreSQL

Now that we have introduced databases and some of the theories they are designed around, let us start working with a database. We will practice with PostgreSQL, a commonly used RDBMS.

PostgreSQL, also known as *Postgres*, is a relational database that has been an active open-source project since the late 1980s. Postgres runs on all major operating systems, including

Windows, MacOS, Linux, and others. The current major version of PostgreSQL is 15, with version 16 in beta as of this writing.

> **Note: You can learn more about the PostgreSQL database project at https://www. postgresql.org/about/.**

ElephantSQL

As the focus of this book is Java development and not standing-up database infrastructure, we will not go through the process of downloading, installing, configuring, and running Postgres locally. We will use a cloud-based Postgres **Database as a Service (DBaaS)** called **ElephantSQL**. ElephantSQL has a free tier that should provide enough resources for us to complete the exercises in this book.

Go to **https://www.elephantsql.com/** and create an account. In the signup process, ElephantSQL asks us to create a *team*. The team name can be set to whatever we choose. Inside our new team dashboard, look for the green **Create New Instance** button in the upper right corner. Refer to the following *Figure 7.2*:

Figure 7.2: The "Create New Instance" button on the ElephantSQL dashboard showing the author's "bpb" team.

As with the team name, the database name does not have a technical bearing on our work, so it can be set at the user's discretion. Be sure to select the **Tiny Turtle** plan so that payment information is not needed. The **Tags** field is optional and can be useful for teams containing several databases. Click the green **Select Region** button to continue.

On the next screen, look at the available cloud regions, and select an available region that is geographically close by. When ready, click the green **Review** button. On the final screen, review the database instance to be created and click **Create Instance** when ready. Refer to the following *Figure 7.3*:

Figure 7.3: Reviewing an ElephantSQL database to be created in the cloud

Note: Be sure to record the username and password for the new database and save them somewhere.

Schema

Before we can begin using our new database instance, we need to create our database schema. A database schema is essentially a set of constraints that tells the database how to organize and store our data. To define our schema, we need to use a subset of SQL known as **Data Definition Language (DDL)**.

Most databases have the concept of a **table**, which is the basic organizational structure for storing data. Tables are made up of rows and columns. A **row** is a small group of data stored and often queried together. Data rows in a table are usually related to each other. **Columns** represent the different properties or fields that a row can have.

For example, a table named **product catalog** will have rows of different products. Each product will have a column for properties like the product's name, description, color, and size.

We will create five tables. Each will be designed to store different entity data about the astronauts who flew in the **National Aeronautics and Space Administration**'s (**NASA**) *Project Gemini* (from 1961-1966). Our tables will hold data on the astronauts themselves, where they attended university, which NASA recruiting group they were a part of, and the missions they flew on.

On our **ElephantSQL** dashboard, we will click the **BROWSER** option in the left navigation pane. This will bring up the **SQL Browser** screen, where we will create our tables, run queries, and view our data.

We will start with the **university** table. Type the following into the SQL Query text well:

```
CREATE TABLE university (

    id INT PRIMARY KEY,

    name VARCHAR(100)

);
```

Be sure to click the blue **Execute** button on the right of the text well.

The above DDL SQL instructs Postgres to create a new table with the following two columns:

- **id:** An integer value representing a unique identifier for the table.
- **name:** A variable-length string with a maximum of **100** characters, representing the **name** of the **university**.

The **id** column is also our **primary key**. A table's primary key is a constraint that is made up of a column (or columns) which represents a unique way to identify each entry or row in the table. When designing a primary key, two approaches are available:

- **Natural key:** A natural key is a primary key that is already a part of the table, and known to be unique.
- **Surrogate key:** A surrogate key is a column that is specifically created to be the primary key, and adds little to no value to the actual data stored. This column is often a number.

The **id** column on the **university** table is a surrogate key.

> **Note: In PostgreSQL, tables are not required to have a primary key, but it is highly recommended.**

Next, we will create a similar table for the NASA recruitment groups, named **nasa_group**. Remove the previous command from the **SQL Query** text well and replace it with the following:

```
CREATE TABLE nasa_group (

    id INT PRIMARY KEY,

    year INT

);
```

> **Note: Remember to click Execute after each CREATE TABLE statement has been entered in the ElephantSQL query browser.**

Now, let us create a table to store data for each of the astronauts' missions:

```
CREATE TABLE missions (

    id INT PRIMARY KEY,

    name VARCHAR(50),

    start_date TIMESTAMP,

    end_date TIMESTAMP

);
```

The **missions** table uses a new data type that we have not seen before, known as a **timestamp**. A **timestamp** is essentially a combination of a date and an exact time. As NASA has exact records on the start and end of each mission, our **start_date** and **end_date** columns will use the **timestamp** type to accurately represent the times in question.

Now, we will create a table to hold data on the **astronauts** themselves:

```
CREATE TABLE astronauts (

    name VARCHAR(100) PRIMARY KEY,

    nasa_group_id INT,

    dob DATE,

    birthplace VARCHAR(50),

    university_id INT,

    FOREIGN KEY(nasa_group_id) REFERENCES nasa_group(id),

    FOREIGN KEY(university_id) REFERENCES university(id)

);
```

Let us go through the **astronauts** table one line at a time:

- **name:** The astronaut's full name has a maximum of **100** characters and is the table's primary key. This is a natural key, as the name column is a necessary part of the table data.

- **nasa_group_id:** An integer representing the NASA group that the astronaut was recruited into.

- **dob:** The astronaut's **date of birth** (**DOB**). This uses the date type, as we do not need a time component.

- **birthplace:** A **50-character** string detailing the location where the **astronaut** was born.

- **university_id:** An integer representing a surrogate key on the **university** table, designed to point to the last **university** the **astronaut** attended.

- **FOREIGN KEY:** Constraints have been added to this table to force the **nasa_group_id** and **university_id** columns to reference other tables (**nasa_group** and **university** respectively). If a row written to the **astronaut** table does not provide a valid identifier in those tables, an error will be thrown.

The foreign key constraints on the **astronauts** table help us to maintain relational integrity. As data for each astronaut is spread across all of these tables, they are related.

As many astronauts attended the same universities, the **university** data is stored in its table. This helps eliminate data redundancy and improves the integrity of that data. After all, there is a higher chance to spell a university's name incorrectly when stored with each astronaut. Putting the universities in their table greatly reduces the chance of error. Likewise, correcting the spelling of a university's name once corrects it for all astronauts who reference it.

NASA recruits astronauts in groups. Many astronauts who flew together throughout *Project Gemini* were recruited together. One group has several astronauts. Therefore, the **nasa_group** table has a *many-to-one* relationship with the **astronauts** table. Likewise, the **university** table also has a many-to-one relationship with the **astronauts** table.

Missions are a little different. One astronaut can fly on several (many) missions. However, the Gemini capsule seated two astronauts. The later Apollo missions seated three astronauts. Therefore, the missions table has a many-to-many relationship with the **astronauts** table.

Many-to-many relationships are complicated. One relational data modeling technique is to create a **bridge table** in-between the two tables. A bridge table only has two columns, and they are both a part of the primary key. Its job is to abstract the many-to-many relationship, by hiding two many-to-one relationships underneath. Our last table is a bridge table:

```
CREATE TABLE astronaut_missions (

    astronaut_name VARCHAR(100),
```

```
    mission_id INT,

    PRIMARY KEY (astronaut_name, mission_id)

);
```

This table will end up holding unique pairs of **astronaut_name**s and **mission_id**s. We will talk more about bridge table when we query it.

Normalization

The process of creating database schema with tables based on their data entities is known as **normalization**. A database schema can be rated based on its level of normalization, with what is known as a **normal form**. Here are the most common levels of normalization:

- **First normal form (1NF):** Elimination of redundant data.
- **Second normal form (2NF):** Schema is in 1NF, plus all partial dependencies have been eliminated. This means that all columns in each table are dependent on their primary keys.
- **Third normal form (3NF):** Schema is in 2NF, plus all transitive dependencies have been eliminated. This means that none of the column values in any table are dependent on non-key columns.

Our schema is close to being in the third normal form. To fully get it in 3NF, we would create a surrogate key named **astronaut_id** on the **astronauts** table, and use that as the lone primary key column, instead of the **name** column. Right now, if we wanted to update any of the astronauts' names, we would have to update both the **astronauts** and **astronaut_missions** tables. However, our schema has more value for learning as it is, with both an example of a natural key and discussion around where it could be improved.

While schema normalization to 3NF remains a widely-accepted practice, it is not always followed. RDBMS **database administrators (DBAs)** have learned over time that eliminating **JOIN** operations and duplicating or denormalizing parts of a schema can lead to increases in database performance.

Normalization and basic relational database theory were developed during a time when disk space was very expensive, so it was also seen as a cost saving optimization. Keeping this point in perspective while building a schema is important, although the relative cost of disk space is not nearly as expensive today as it was in prior years.

Loading data

Now, we will get data into our tables. To do this, we are going to use an **INSERT** statement from SQL's **Data Manipulation Language (DML)**. To start with, let us put three rows into the **nasa_group** table:

```
INSERT INTO nasa_group (id, year) VALUES (1, 1959);
```

```
INSERT INTO nasa_group (id, year) VALUES (2, 1962);

INSERT INTO nasa_group (id, year) VALUES (3, 1963);
```

As shown above, the **INSERT** statement uses the **INTO** keyword to specify the table name. Then, we list out the columns we want to provide values for, followed by the **VALUES** keyword with a parameterized list of the values for each row. We can enter all three **INSERT** statements into the SQL Browser text well at once (as long as they are separated by semicolons), and then click **Execute**.

We can do the same for the university table as well:

```
INSERT INTO university (id, name) VALUES (1,'US Military Academy');

INSERT INTO university (id, name) VALUES (2,'Purdue University');

INSERT INTO university (id, name) VALUES (3,'Princeton University');

INSERT INTO university (id, name) VALUES (4,'Air Force Institute of
Technology');

INSERT INTO university (id, name) VALUES (5,'University of Washington');

INSERT INTO university (id, name) VALUES (6,'US Naval Academy');

INSERT INTO university (id, name) VALUES (7,'University of Michigan');

INSERT INTO university (id, name) VALUES (8,'Georgia Institute of Technology');
```

We can do the same to load data into the **missions** table. Here are the **INSERT** statements for the first three Gemini missions:

```
INSERT INTO missions (id, name, start_date, end_date)

VALUES (1, 'Gemini 3', '1965-03-23 14:24:00', '1965-03-23 17:16:31');

INSERT INTO missions (id, name, start_date, end_date)

VALUES (2, 'Gemini 4', '1965-06-03 15:15:59','1965-06-07 17:12:11');

INSERT INTO missions (id, name, start_date, end_date)

VALUES (3, 'Gemini 5', '1965-08-21 13:59:59', '1965-08-29 12:55:13');
```

> **Note: It is perfectly fine for SQL statements to span multiple lines, as long as they are properly ended with a semicolon.**

Do the same for data on the remaining Gemini missions (along with extra mission data for other NASA projects including *Mercury, Apollo,* and others):

```
INSERT INTO astronauts (name, dob, birthplace, nasa_group_id, university_id)
```

```
VALUES ('Buzz Aldrin','1930-01-20','Montclair, NJ', 3, 1);

INSERT INTO astronauts (name, dob, birthplace, nasa_group_id, university_id)

VALUES ('Neil Armstrong','1930-08-05','Wapakoneta, OH', 2, 2);

INSERT INTO astronauts (name, dob, birthplace, nasa_group_id, university_id)

VALUES ('Frank Borman','1928-03-14','Gary, IN', 2, 1);


INSERT INTO astronaut_missions(astronaut_name, mission_id)

VALUES ('Buzz Aldrin',10);

INSERT INTO astronaut_missions(astronaut_name, mission_id)

VALUES ('Buzz Aldrin',14);

INSERT INTO astronaut_missions(astronaut_name, mission_id)

VALUES ('Neil Armstrong',6);

INSERT INTO astronaut_missions(astronaut_name, mission_id)

VALUES ('Neil Armstrong',14);
```

Querying data

If we wanted to view our data to check our progress, we can use the SQL **SELECT** statement:

```
SELECT * FROM university;
```

With a **SELECT** statement, we can specify a comma-delimited list of the individual column names that we want to see. Or, we can specify an asterisk (as shown above). The **FROM** keyword is used with **SELECT** to specify the database and table that we want to query. In our case, **public** is our default database, so we can specify the table name of **university**. This query should return the following data as output:

id	name
1	US Military Academy
2	Purdue University
3	Princeton University
4	Air Force Institute of Technology
5	University of Washington
6	US Naval Academy

7 University of Michigan

8 Georgia Institute of Technology

SQL also allows us to restrict the number of rows that are returned in a result set. This is very useful if a table has many rows. Querying with the **LIMIT** clause of **5** should produce the following output:

```
SELECT * FROM astronauts LIMIT 5;
```

name	nasa_group_id	dob	birthplace	university_id
Buzz Aldrin	3	1930-01-20	Montclair, NJ	1
Neil Armstrong	2	1930-08-05	Wapakoneta, OH	2
Frank Borman	2	1928-03-14	Gary, IN	1
Gene Cernan	3	1934-03-14	Chicago, IL	2
Michael Collins	3	1930-10-31	Rome, Italy	1

In our result set, we can see the column names like **nasa_group_id** and **university_id**. Those column names might mean something to us, but most people do not want to go and look up additional data. To bring in data from the **nasa_group** and **university** tables, we can execute a **JOIN**:

```
SELECT a.name, a.nasa_group_id AS group, a.dob, a.birthplace, u.name as university

FROM astronauts a

INNER JOIN university u ON u.id = a.university_id

LIMIT 5;
```

name	group	dob	birthplace	university
Buzz Aldrin	3	1930-01-20	Montclair, NJ	US Military Academy
Neil Armstrong	2	1930-08-05	Wapakoneta, OH	Purdue University
Frank Borman	2	1928-03-14	Gary, IN	US Military Academy
Gene Cernan	3	1934-03-14	Chicago, IL	Purdue University
Michael Collins	3	1930-10-31	Rome, Italy	US Military Academy

When executing a **JOIN** operation with a **SELECT**, it is always a good idea to explicitly name the columns desired to be returned (instead of using an asterisk), as this can lead to confusion with similarly-named columns. As shown above, the tables specified in the **FROM** and **JOIN** clauses can be denoted with an alias (**a** for astronaut and **u** for university here).

It is also a good idea to use a **WHERE** clause to filter the data that is returned. With this query, we can return all of the *Gemini Astronauts* who attended the *US Naval Academy*:

```
SELECT a.name, g.year, a.dob, a.birthplace, u.name as university

FROM astronauts a

INNER JOIN university u ON u.id = a.university_id

INNER JOIN nasa_group g ON g.id = a.nasa_group_id

WHERE u.name = 'US Naval Academy';
```

name	year	dob	birthplace	university
Jim Lovell	1962	1928-03-25	Cleveland, OH	US Naval Academy
Wally Schirra	1959	1923-03-12	Hackensack, NJ	US Naval Academy
Tom Stafford	1962	1930-09-17	Weatherford, OK	US Naval Academy

In this query, we also added another **JOIN** to pull back the **nasa_group year** column instead of the **id**.

> Note: Running a SELECT query without a WHERE clause can cause widespread performance issues in large relational databases. It is always a good idea to use WHERE or LIMIT to restrict the amount of data returned.

Accessing from Java

With all of that complete, we can return to our Java IDE and work on accessing this data from our Java code.

pom.xml

Open up the **pom.xml** file of our project, and add the following code to the **dependencies** section:

```
<dependency>

    <groupId>org.postgresql</groupId>

    <artifactId>postgresql</artifactId>

    <version>42.6.0</version>

</dependency>
```

This will allow Maven to access the PostgreSQL **Java Database Connectivity (JDBC)** driver. We will use it to connect to our database.

PostgresConn class

We will also build a specific class to handle the connection to our PostgreSQL database. Create a new Java class. Make sure that it is in a packaged named **chapter7** and the name **PostgresConn**. This class will need three **import** statements from the **java.sql** library, as shown below:

```
package chapter7;


import java.sql.Connection;

import java.sql.DriverManager;

import java.sql.SQLException;


public class PostgresConn {


    private Connection conn;
```

Inside our class definition, we will also define a new **Connection** object named **conn**.

First, we will build a new **private** method named **connectToPostgres**. It should accept three string parameters for a **url**, **username**, and **password**:

```
private void connectToPostgres(String url, String username, String password)
{

    try {
        // connects to database
        conn = DriverManager.getConnection(url, username, password);
    } catch (SQLException e) {
        System.out.println(e.getMessage());
    }

}
```

Inside our **connectToPostgres()** method, we set the **conn** object to the result of the **DriverManager.getConnection()** method. As the **getConnection()** method passes-up a **SQLException** for us to handle, we will wrap it inside of a **try**/**catch** statement and output the contents of the exception message.

Above our **connectToPostgres()** method, let us add our constructor. We will build a single constructor, which simply accepts string parameters for **url**, **username**, and **password**; and then calls the **connectToPostgres()** method:

```java
public PostgresConn(String url, String username, String password) {

    connectToPostgres(url, username, password);

}
```

We will also need a **public** method to close our database connection. It is always a good idea to properly close the database connection when we are finished with it. Many database servers have a limit on the number of active connections that can be managed simultaneously. Closing the connection from the application side releases it back into the database's connection pool. Our method for closing the connection is fairly straightforward:

```java
public void closePostgresConnection() {

    try {

        conn.close();

    } catch (SQLException e) {

        System.out.println(e.getMessage());

    }

}
```

Essentially, we are calling the **close()** method on our **conn** object, and trapping for a possible **SQLException**:

Finally, we need to build a **public getter** method for our **conn** object:

```java
public Connection getConn() {

    return this.conn;

}
```

AstronautPostgresDAL

Create another new Java class. Name it **AstronautPostgresDAL**, and make sure that it is inside the **chapter7** package. This class will act as a **data access layer** (DAL) allowing us to abstract our database access code away from the main program code.

> **Note: The idea of creating a DAL to handle database access code is a standard practice. It not only helps abstract the database layer away from the business logic but also makes it easier to change the underlying database, if required at some point.**

Our **AstronautPostgresDAL** class will need **import** statements to help us define collections like **Lists** and **ArrayLists**. We will also need access to the Postgres driver libraries for prepared statements, result sets, SQL statements, and for a potential SQL Exception:

```
package chapter7;

import java.sql.PreparedStatement;

import java.sql.ResultSet;

import java.sql.SQLException;

import java.sql.Statement;


import java.util.ArrayList;

import java.util.List;


public class AstronautPostgresDAL {

    private static PostgresConn postgres;

    protected record AstronautMission(
        String missionName, String startDate,
        String endDate, String astronautName) {};
```

Additionally, we will define a private, local object for our Postgres connection (referencing the class that we wrote) and a protected, local record for our **AstronautMission** data.

Our **AstronautPostgresDAL** class will need a simple constructor. Essentially, we need to ensure our **postgres** object (which manages our connection to the database) is initialized appropriately. Our constructor will accept string parameters for our database **url**, **username**, and **password**. It will then use those parameters to initialize our **PostgresConn** connection object:

```
public AstronautPostgresDAL (String url, String username,
        String password) {

    postgres = new PostgresConn(url, username, password);
}
```

The first task is to pull back the complete roster of Gemini astronauts. To accomplish this, we will write a method named **getGeminiRoster** that will return a **List** of type **String**. We will start by creating a parameterless version of the method, which will technically overload it by calling a default SQL LIMIT of **20**:

```
public List<String> getGeminiRoster() {

  return getGeminiRoster(20);

}
```

Then, we can build the actual method, which has the same name and return type, but accepts an integer named **limit** as a parameter. Inside the method, we will define our return value as a new **ArrayList**. Then, we will build a simple SQL statement to query the **name** column from the **astronauts** table, with our **limit** concatenated on the end. This query should return all of the Gemini Astronauts from the database.

> **Note: Be careful in creating SQL queries this way within code. Doing this with String types can lead to a malicious attack known as a SQL Injection Attack where the attacker inputs a SQL DELETE (or some other malicious code) into a web form in hopes of wiping out or querying sensitive data. It is always better to build variables into a query with a prepared statement. However, for an integer on a LIMIT, our risk here is low.**

```
public List<String> getGeminiRoster(int limit) {

    List<String> returnVal = new ArrayList<>();


    String astronautSQL = "SELECT name FROM astronauts LIMIT "

        + limit;
```

> **Note: It is always a good idea to use WHERE or LIMIT to restrict the amount of data returned. With the small amount of data that we have, this should not be necessary. However, in the interest of building good habits, we will add a LIMIT to our query.**

Next, inside a **try** statement, we will define our **Postgres Statement** object and name it **pgStatement**, by calling the Postgres connection object's **createStatement()** method. We will then create a new Postgres **ResultSet** object named **geminiAstronauts** and set it to the result of our statement's **excuteQuery()** method while passing our **astronautSQL**:

```
    try {

        Statement pgStatement = postgres.getConn().createStatement();

        ResultSet geminiAstronauts =
```

```
        pgStatement.executeQuery(astronautSQL);


    while (geminiAstronauts.next()) {

        returnVal.add(geminiAstronauts.getString("name"));

    }

} catch (SQLException e) {

    System.out.println(e.getMessage());

}


    return returnVal;

}
```

With our query executed and results stored in the **geminiAstronauts** object, we can iterate through the results in a **while** loop, which will continue as long as the **next()** method on our result set is **true**. Inside the **while** loop, we will retrieve the value of the **astronaut name** column for each row, and add it to our **returnVal** list.

You may have noticed above that a **try/catch** is required around most of our Postgres database methods. This is because they pass up a **SQLException** for us to handle. Once we close our **try/catch** by displaying the exception's message, we can return our **returnVal** list to the calling method.

GeminiAstronautsRDBMS class

Next, create a new Java class and name it **GeminiAstronautsRDBMS**. Make sure it is in the **chapter7** package and has a **main** method. Our **GeminiAstronautsRDBMS** class will need the imports **Set**, **HashSet**, and **Random** from the **java.util** library:

```
package chapter7;


import java.util.HashSet;

import java.util.Set;

import java.util.Random;

to

public class GeminiAstronautsRDBMS {


    public static void main(String[] args) {
```

Inside our **main** method, we will access the environment variables for our database credentials. This is necessary because database access credentials should never be inside of code. Therefore, we will set our credentials in the OS environment (later on) and reference them by calling the **System.getenv()** method:

```
String url = System.getenv("POSTGRES_URL");

String username = System.getenv("POSTGRES_USER");

String password = System.getenv("POSTGRES_PASSWORD");


AstronautPostgresDAL astronautDAL =

    new AstronautPostgresDAL(url, username, password);


System.out.println("Project Gemini Astronauts:");
```

We can then use the newly created variables to instantiate our **AstronautPostgresDAL** data access layer. Next, we will call the **getGeminiRoster()** method on our DAL, iterate through the results using a **for** loop, and display the individual astronauts' names:

```
List<String> geminiAstronauts = astronautDAL.getGeminiRoster();


for (String astronaut : geminiAstronauts) {

    System.out.println(astronaut);

}


System.out.println();
```

Try running this code. It should fail with a similar output message:

Exception in thread "main" java.lang.NullPointerException: Cannot invoke "java.sql.Connection.createStatement()" because the return value of "chapter7. PostgresConn.getConn()" is null

   at chapter7.GeminiAstronautsRDBMS.main(GeminiAstronautsRDBMS.java:29)

This exception is happening because we have not defined our database credentials in the environment.

In the **Eclipse IDE**, running our **GeminiAstronautsRDBMS** class should have created a new run configuration for us. We can view the available run configurations by selecting **Run Configurations** from the **Run** menu in **Eclipse**. It should look something like *Figure 7.4*:

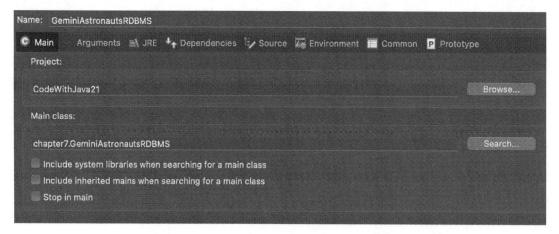

Figure 7.4: The "Main" tab of the GeminiAstronautsRDBMS run configuration.

If run configuration does not exist, then it will need to be created. Next, click on the **Environment** tab. Here, we are going to add three **environment** variables. The information we need to define these variables can be found on the **ElephantSQL Details** page for our database instance, as shown in *Figure 7.5*:

Server	rajje.db.elephantsql.com (rajje-01)
Region	amazon-web-services::us-east-1
Created at	2023-06-27 11:36 UTC+00:00
User & Default database	iubylxio
Password	∗∗∗ ◉ ▣

Figure 7.5: Our database information on the ElephantSQL "Details" page.

Each individual database instance will have its own unique **server**, **username**, and **password**. The following variables we will build are based on the example shown in *Figure 7.5*, so be sure to adjust accordingly:

POSTGRES_URL: jdbc:postgresql://rajje.db.elephantsql.com/iubylxio

POSTGRES_USER: iublxio

POSTGRES_PASSWORD: QYKQfZNgDFShS_EY8lcpAh1yZoi6nbA0

While the **PASSWORD** is obscured by asterisks (*Figure 7.5*), it can be shown by clicking on the *eye* icon, and copied by clicking on the *copy* icon (to the right of the *eye*).

If we were running our Java code from the command line, we would need to set these variables at the OS level. This will vary based on the underlying OS.

Linux/MacOS

```
export POSTGRES_PASSWORD=QYKQfZNgDFShS_EY8lcpAh1yZoi6nbA0

export
    POSTGRES_URL=jdbc:postgresql://rajje.db.elephantsql.com/iubylxio

export POSTGRES_USER=iubylxio
```

Windows

```
set POSTGRES_PASSWORD="QYKQfZNgDFShS_EY8lcpAh1yZoi6nbA0"

set POSTGRES_URL="jdbc:postgresql://rajje.db.elephantsql.com/iubylxio"

set POSTGRES_USER="iubylxio"
```

Note: Showing how to define our environment variables on the command line is meant as an example. If we define them in the run configuration in our IDE, we will not need to do this.

With those variables defined in the **Run Configurations**, running the above code should produce the following result:

```
Project Gemini Astronauts:

Buzz Aldrin

Neil Armstrong

Frank Borman

Gene Cernan

Michael Collins

Pete Conrad

Gordon Cooper

Richard Gordon

Gus Grissom

Jim Lovell

Jim McDivitt

Wally Schirra
```

Dave Scott

Tom Stafford

Ed White

John Young

As we can see above, we have successfully queried the 16 astronauts who participated in **Project Gemini**.

Next, we will show the results of a more complicated query. We will write code to randomly return data on three of the Gemini missions, along with the astronauts who flew on them.

AstronautPostgresDAL class revisited

Before going any further, let us switch back to our **AstronautPostgresDAL** class. Here, we will add a new **public** method of type **List** (of our **AstronautMission** record) and name it **getMissionAstronauts**. The method should accept a single parameter of type **String**, named **missionName**. We will start this method by defining our return value, which is a **List** of **AstronautMission** named **returnVal**:

```
public List<AstronautMission> getMissionAstronauts(String missionName) {


    List<AstronautMission> returnVal = new ArrayList<>();
```

Now, let us build our query. As we discussed earlier in the chapter, our astronauts and missions tables share a many-to-many relationship. To handle that relationship appropriately, we created the **astronaut_missions** bridge table. To query data for astronauts and their missions, we need to **JOIN** on both the **astronaut_missions** and **missions** tables. Take a look at the following code:

```
String missionSQL = "SELECT m.name AS missionname, m.start_date, "

    + "m.end_date, a.name "

    + "FROM astronauts a "

    + "INNER JOIN astronaut_missions am ON am.astronaut_name = a.name "

    + "INNER JOIN missions m ON m.id = am.mission_id "

    + "WHERE m.name = ?;";
```

We will set that query as the value of a **string** variable named **missionSQL**. Notice the **WHERE** clause in the query above. It will filter data based on the name of the mission, represented by a question mark (**?**). To dynamically send this query the name of a new mission at runtime, we are going to use a *prepared statement*.

> **Note: Columns named the same on different tables and returned in the same result set can confuse the ResultSet object. Uniqueness can be ensured using the SQL AS keyword to create an alias for that column inside the result set.**

Prepared statements are database query objects that allow us the flexibility to run the same query several times with different parameters. Prepared statements actually perform better, as their SQL only needs to be parsed once, but can be run many times.

Here, we will create a new prepared statement named **missionStatement**. We will set it to the value of the connection's **prepareStatement()** method and pass our **missionSQL** query as a parameter:

```
try {

    PreparedStatement missionStatement =

        postgres.getConn().prepareStatement(missionSQL);
```

With our statement prepared, we will use our **missionStatement**'s **setString()** method to bind the value of our mission name (at ordinal position 1) to our statement.

> **Note: Bind variable ordinal positions for prepared statements are one-based and not zero-based like the rest of Java is. Therefore, an ordinal position of 1 represents the first question mark found in the prepared statement.**

We will run our query by calling **missionStatement**'s **executeQuery()** method, and set its results to a new **ResultSet** object named **missionAstronauts**:

```
missionStatement.setString(1, missionName);

ResultSet missionAstronauts = missionStatement.executeQuery();
```

At this point, we have run our query bound with **missionName**, and stored the results in our **missionAstronauts** result set. Now, we can iterate through the result set with a **while** loop, instantiate an **AstronautMission** record with the mission's name, date range, and astronaut, and add that record to the **returnVal** list. Take a look at the following code:

```
while (missionAstronauts.next()) {

    AstronautMission astronautMission = new AstronautMission(

        missionAstronauts.getString("missionname"),

        missionAstronauts.getString("start_date"),

        missionAstronauts.getString("end_date"),

        missionAstronauts.getString("name"));
```

```
        returnVal.add(astronautMission);
}
```

With that complete, we can complete our **try**/**catch** while catching for a **SQLException**. Finally, we can **return** our **returnVal** and finish the method. Take a look at the following code:

```
    } catch (SQLException e) {

        e.printStackTrace();

    }


    return returnVal;

}
```

GeminiAstronautsRDBMS class revisited

Back in our **GeminiAstronautsRDBMS** class, inside our **main()** method after our last block of code, we will instantiate a **Set** of integers as well as a **Random** object:

```
Set<Integer> randomMissions = new HashSet<>();

Random random = new Random();

// generate 3 random numbers

while (randomMissions.size() < 3) {

    int missionNumber = random.nextInt(10) + 3;

    randomMissions.add(missionNumber);

}
```

With our **randomMissions** and **random** objects defined, we will iterate through a **while** loop as long as the **randomMissions** set has less than three items. Inside the **while** loop, we will generate a random number from **3** to **12** (inclusive), representing the manned Gemini spaceflights. We will then add the generated number to the **randomMissions** set.

> **Note:** Remember that values within Sets are unique. Therefore, we do not need to worry about the possibility of the same number being generated twice, as any duplicates will be added to randomMissions and promptly ignored.

Now, we will use a **for** loop to iterate through the numbers generated in the **randomMissions** set. We will then build a string with the name **Gemini** (with a space on the end) and concatenate the mission number (**missionNum**) to the end of it. We can then call the **getMissionAstronauts()** method that we wrote above while passing the **mission** with its default **toString()** method:

```
for (Integer missionNum : randomMissions) {

    StringBuilder mission = new StringBuilder("Gemini ");

    mission.append(missionNum.toString());

    List<AstronautMission> missionAstronauts =
        astronautDAL.getMissionAstronauts(mission.toString());

    for (AstronautMission astronautMission : missionAstronauts) {
        System.out.print(astronautMission.missionName() + " ");
        System.out.print(astronautMission.startDate() + " -> ");
        System.out.print(astronautMission.endDate() + " - ");
        System.out.println(astronautMission.astronautName());
    }

    System.out.println();
}
```

We can nest another **for** loop inside of our existing loop to iterate through the **missionAstronauts** list. Inside, we need to display the **missionName**, **startDate**, **endDate**, and **astronautName** for each astronaut on a particular Gemini mission.

Running this code should still show the complete roster of Gemini astronauts, while also producing something similar to this at the end:

```
Gemini 3 1965-03-23 14:24:00 -> 1965-03-23 17:16:31 - Gus Grissom

Gemini 3 1965-03-23 14:24:00 -> 1965-03-23 17:16:31 - John Young


Gemini 4 1965-06-03 15:15:59 -> 1965-06-07 17:12:11 - Jim McDivitt

Gemini 4 1965-06-03 15:15:59 -> 1965-06-07 17:12:11 - Ed White


Gemini 9 1966-06-03 13:39:33 -> 1966-06-06 14:00:23 - Gene Cernan

Gemini 9 1966-06-03 13:39:33 -> 1966-06-06 14:00:23 - Tom Stafford
```

As shown, we have successfully built a RDBMS schema and data set using the PostgreSQL database, and queried it using Java.

Apache Cassandra

Having discussed relational databases and PostgreSQL in particular, we will now shift to a slightly different perspective on data management. We will now discuss Apache Cassandra, a NoSQL database used by many large-scale, big-data-driven enterprises.

Cassandra was originally developed at *Facebook* and released as an open source in 2008. After a brief stint as an *incubator project* in the Apache Software Foundation, it was granted top-level project status in 2010. Since then, Apache Cassandra has been extensively used by enterprises across various industries including video streaming, ride-sharing, financial institutions, and retail. Today, some of the largest deployments of Apache Cassandra are found at companies like *Apple*, *Netflix*, and *Uber*.

Learning about Apache Cassandra is a natural next step for a book about Java programming, as Cassandra is written in Java. Likewise, much of the Cassandra ecosystem of tools is also Java-based. A Java background provides an additional level of understanding when troubleshooting issues in the Cassandra world.

The current version of Apache Cassandra is 4.1, with Cassandra 5.0 projected for the end of 2023.

> **Note: You can learn more about the Apache Cassandra database project at https://cassandra.apache.org/.**

Astra DB

As previously discussed, the focus of this book is Java development and not standing-up distributed database infrastructure. We will use a cloud-based Cassandra DBaaS called **Astra DB**. Astra DB was developed by *DataStax*, the company which has provided enterprise versions of Cassandra since its inception. Astra DB also has a free tier that should provide enough resources for us to complete the exercises in this book.

Go to **https://astra.datastax.com/** and create an account. Once signed-in, the **Astra** dashboard, as shown in *Figure 7.6*, should be visible. In the lower left of the screen, click on the **Create a Database** button:

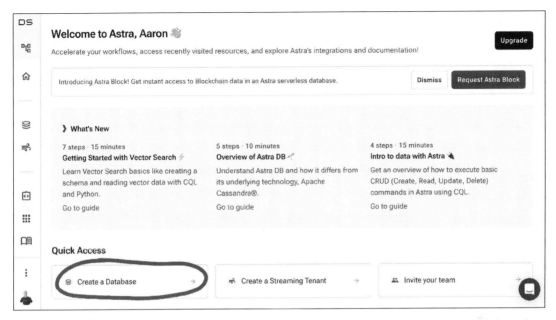

Figure 7.6: *The Astra dashboard after a successful sign-in. The "Create a Database" button is circled in red.*

Note: A new database created in Astra DB will have a *replication factor* of three, by default. This means, every piece of data will be stored three times, and each data replica will be on a different machine instance.

We will specify a name for our database as well as our keyspace on the window that comes up (*Figure 7.7*). A **keyspace** is a logical structure in Cassandra which help keeps our tables separate from others. This is very useful in a large, multi-user database cluster. The database name does not matter, but for the exercises in this book, we should keep the **keyspace name** of `astronaut_data`.

To ensure that we can use Astra DB's free tier, select **Google Cloud Platform** (**GCP**) as the provider. Not all regions will be available on the free tier. In the **Region** drop-down list, select the closest region from the regions listed in bold. For example, those of us in Europe should select the region for **St. Ghislain, Belgium**. Refer to the following figure:

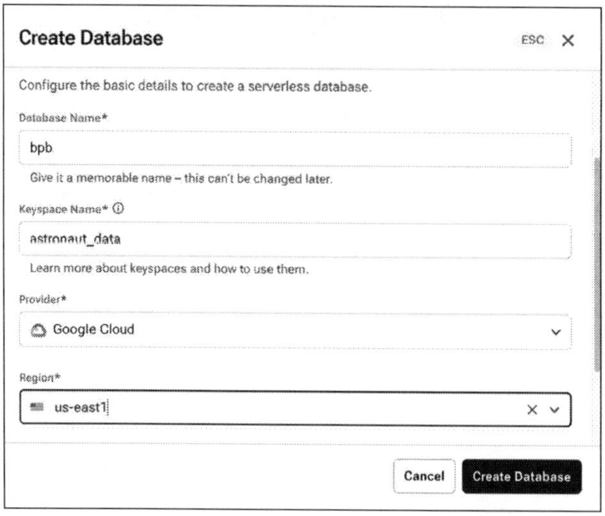

Figure 7.7: *The Create Database window, showing how to configure our database.*

On the next screen, once the database becomes active, we should see the options shown in *Figure 7.8*. Click the **Generate Token** button to get access credentials for the newly created database. There are on-screen options to quickly save and/or copy the generated credentials. Be sure to do one or the other (or both).

Also, be sure to click the **Get Bundle** button. Astra DB keeps almost everything it needs to connect in pre-generated, secure zip files. This includes things like hostnames, port numbers, and **Transport Layer Security** (**TLS**) certificates. This is how data sent over the network between the application and the database is kept secure. Feel free to move the secure bundle to another spot, but make note of it as we will need its directory location later on. Please refer to the following *Figure 7.8*:

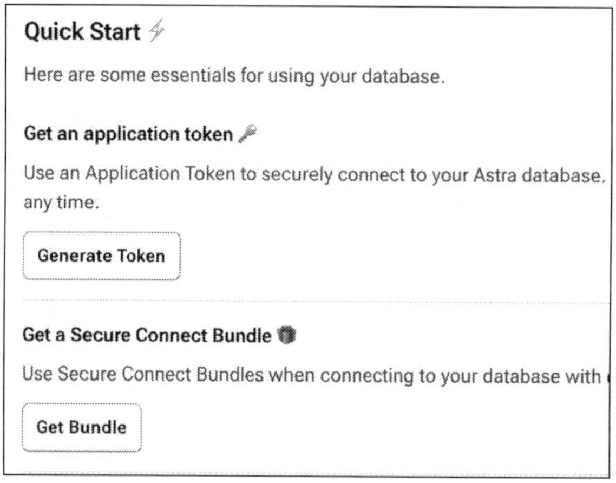

Figure 7.8: *The options for generating token and secure bundle for the new database. Both of these tasks should be completed.*

With our database created, we will move on to creating the schema.

Schema

Similar to what we did with Postgres, we will also create tables to hold our data in Cassandra. However, with Cassandra, we will create tables to support our prospective queries. For example, we will need tables to support the following requests:

- Query for astronauts by name.
- Query for astronauts by NASA recruitment group.
- Query for astronauts by the university that they attended.
- Query for astronauts by the missions that they flew on.

Based on our requirements, we will create four tables. Each of those tables will have a primary key definition built to support our query's **WHERE** clause.

To build our table schema, we first need to use the CQL shell (**cqlsh**) utility. In Astra DB, we can access **cqlsh** by first clicking into **our database details** (see *Figure 7.9*) and then clicking on the **CQL Console** tab. Once inside the **CQL console**, we need to tell Cassandra that we want to access the **astronaut_data** keyspace. We can do that with the **use** command:

```
use astronaut_data;
```

We can now run our **CREATE TABLE** statements. Refer to the following *Figure 7.9*:

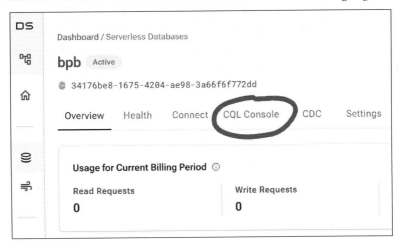

Figure 7.9: The database details page of our "bpb" database, with the CQL Console tab circled.

The first will be the **astronauts** table, and will have a single, primary key of **name**:

```
CREATE TABLE astronauts (

    name TEXT PRIMARY KEY,
```

```
    dob DATE,

    birthplace TEXT,

    nasa_group_id INT,

    nasa_group_year INT,

    university_name TEXT

);
```

Apache Cassandra has its own SQL-like query language known as the **Cassandra Query Language (CQL)**. While similar to SQL in many regards, there are many functionalities of SQL that are absent in CQL. Most of these omissions are because of Cassandra's architectural differences from relational databases. Other differences are around the reuse of certain SQL keywords to provide different functionality. We will highlight these differences as the need arises.

Note: As a general rule, it is important not to make assumptions about how similar commands will work on different systems, databases or otherwise. As with any new system, be sure to read the appropriate documentation on a command or structure before using it in a production environment.

While looking at the CQL code above for the **astronauts** table definition, there are some differences in data types. Instead of a **VARCHAR** with a specified length, Cassandra uses the **VARCHAR** type without requiring a length. **VARCHAR** in Cassandra is also aliased by the **TEXT** datatype, and both map to Java strings upon retrieval.

Casandra's primary keys also behave differently than their RDBMS counterparts. First, Cassandra requires a primary key on all tables. This is because, the primary key helps determine on which database nodes (instances) the data should be stored. Without a primary key, Cassandra would not know where to store the data requested to be written, so it is required.

Secondly, all primary keys are unique in Cassandra. This can have some unintended consequences when multiple writes to the same primary key simply overwrite each other.

The next table will support our query to retrieve astronauts by their NASA recruitment group number:

```
CREATE TABLE astronauts_by_group (

    nasa_group_id INT,

    nasa_group_year INT STATIC,

    astronaut_name TEXT,

    dob DATE,
```

```
    birthplace TEXT,

    university_name TEXT,

    PRIMARY KEY (nasa_group_id, astronaut_name)

) WITH CLUSTERING ORDER BY (astronaut_name ASC);
```

This table has a few new aspects. First, we have specified a **composite primary key**, which means that it is made up of multiple columns. The first part of the primary key is the **partition key**. This key is hashed into a token, and all requests for it are sent to the node or nodes responsible for the range of tokens that it falls into.

The second part of the primary key is known as the **clustering key**. A table's clustering key determines the on-disk sort order within a partition. The clustering key's additional part is shown in the **WITH** clause, as the clustering order is specified along with a sort direction (ascending). If a clustering key is specified in the primary key definition without a **CLUSTERING ORDER BY** clause, the default sort direction will be in **ascending (ASC)** order.

> Note: As ascending order is used by default, all table definitions requiring partition data in descending order must specify a CLUSTERING ORDER BY clause, indicating both the column name and descending (DESC) sort direction.

Finally, the column **nasa_group_year** is designated as a **STATIC** column. This keyword tells Cassandra to store this data at the partition level. Otherwise, each row in a partition will store its own value for that column, which will be the same. In this case, all astronauts from NASA recruitment group 2 will be stored in the same partition and have the same **nasa_group_year** of 1962. Therefore, there is no need to store the same value with every astronaut row.

The next table will support queries for astronauts by the **university** they attended:

```
CREATE TABLE astronauts_by_university (

    university_name TEXT,

    astronaut_name TEXT,

    nasa_group_id INT,

    nasa_group_year INT,

    dob DATE,

    birthplace TEXT,

    PRIMARY KEY (university_name, astronaut_name)

);
```

As previously discussed, the primary key definition indicates that we will be querying by **university_name** and enforcing an ascending sort order on **astronaut_name**. As we have shown, it is standard practice to use natural keys in Cassandra. This is because, the primary key definition defines how the table can be queried, and most users will have a better understanding of **university_name**, as opposed to a (surrogate) **university_id**. The surrogate key approach works better in the RDBMS world because the surrogate keys are usually abstracted behind the scenes (in JOINs), and users usually do not need to understand or know about them.

The **astronauts_by_mission** table will be built in a similar manner:

```
CREATE TABLE astronauts_by_mission (

    mission_name TEXT,

    astronaut_name TEXT,

    mission_start_date TIMESTAMP STATIC,

    mission_end_date TIMESTAMP STATIC,

    university_name TEXT,

    nasa_group_id INT,

    nasa_group_year INT,

    dob DATE,

    birthplace TEXT,

    PRIMARY KEY (mission_name, astronaut_name)

);
```

The main difference here is that the **mission_start_date** and **mission_end_date** are defined as **STATIC**. This way the mission details are stored at the partition level, along with the **mission_name**.

Denormalization

In the last section about RDBMS schema design, we mentioned the idea of denormalization, and how deviating from it in the right scenarios can lead to better performance. With Apache Cassandra and many other NoSQL databases, the approach of data modeling via denormalization is the standard approach. This is because it helps data models work better in a distributed database paradigm.

As with Apache Cassandra and many NoSQL databases, the idea is to build tables to suit our queries. Thus, the practice of denormalization becomes the standard approach rather than an exception to the rule.

Loading data

Next, we will load data into our tables. As we did with loading data into our RDBMS, we will use CQL's **INSERT** statement to write data into our tables.

First, we will write data into our main table. The following CQL will write four rows into the **astronauts** table:

```
INSERT INTO astronauts (name, dob, birthplace, nasa_group_id, nasa_group_
year, university_name)

VALUES ('Buzz Aldrin','1930-01-20','Montclair, NJ', 3, 1963, 'US Military
Academy');

INSERT INTO astronauts (name, dob, birthplace, nasa_group_id, nasa_group_
year, university_name)

VALUES ('Neil Armstrong','1930-08-05','Wapakoneta, OH', 2, 1962, 'Purdue
University');

INSERT INTO astronauts (name, dob, birthplace, nasa_group_id, nasa_group_
year, university_name)

VALUES ('Frank Borman','1928-03-14','Gary, IN', 2, 1962, 'US Military
Academy');

INSERT INTO astronauts (name, dob, birthplace, nasa_group_id, nasa_group_
year, university_name)

VALUES ('Gene Cernan','1934-03-14','Chicago, IL', 3, 1963, 'Purdue
University');
```

Likewise, we can also load a few rows of data into our **astronauts_by_group** table:

```
INSERT INTO astronauts_by_group (astronaut_name, dob, birthplace, nasa_
group_id, nasa_group_year, university_name)

VALUES ('Buzz Aldrin','1930-01-20','Montclair, NJ', 3, 1963, 'US Military
Academy');

INSERT INTO astronauts_by_group (astronaut_name, dob, birthplace, nasa_
group_id, nasa_group_year, university_name)

VALUES ('Neil Armstrong','1930-08-05','Wapakoneta, OH', 2, 1962, 'Purdue
University');

INSERT INTO astronauts_by_group (astronaut_name, dob, birthplace, nasa_
group_id, nasa_group_year, university_name)
```

```
VALUES ('Frank Borman','1928-03-14','Gary, IN', 2, 1962, 'US Military
Academy');

INSERT INTO astronauts_by_group (astronaut_name, dob, birthplace, nasa_
group_id, nasa_group_year, university_name)

VALUES ('Gene Cernan','1934-03-14','Chicago, IL', 3, 1963, 'Purdue
University');

INSERT INTO astronauts_by_group (astronaut_name, dob, birthplace, nasa_
group_id,
```

Loading data into the two remaining tables (**astronauts_by_university** and **astronauts_by_mission**) is almost the same.

Querying data

With our data loaded, we can now run some simple queries.

> Note: Before running a query on the astronaut tables, check that we are *using* the astronaut_data keyspace, as we did above. The current keyspace should be visible in the cqlsh prompt.

As with SQL, data can be queried in CQL using the **SELECT** statement. Let us run a quick query to check for the first five rows in the **astronauts** table:

```
SELECT name, birthplace, dob, university_name

FROM astronauts LIMIT 5;
```

```
         name |      birthplace |        dob |      university_name
--------------+-----------------+------------+---------------------
 Tom Stafford | Weatherford, OK | 1930-09-17 |     US Naval Academy
  Gus Grissom |    Mitchell, IN | 1926-04-03 |     Purdue University
  Gene Cernan |     Chicago, IL | 1934-03-14 |     Purdue University
 Frank Borman |        Gary, IN | 1928-03-14 | US Military Academy
  Buzz Aldrin |   Montclair, NJ | 1930-01-20 | US Military Academy

(5 rows)
```

It looks like we have successfully loaded data into our **astronauts** table. Now, let us try querying the table in a different way. Instead of pulling back the columns above, we will **SELECT** only **name**, and then call CQL's **token()** function on the name column, as well:

```
SELECT name, token(name)
FROM astronauts LIMIT 10;
```

```
 name          | system.token(name)
---------------+----------------------
 Tom Stafford  | -8607991424493416553
 Gus Grissom   | -8176206291262860019
 Gene Cernan   | -7356385580624371974
 Frank Borman  | -6869292563996231224
 Buzz Aldrin   | -6706969656915434294
 John Young    | -6312120392268580847
 Jim Lovell    | -1248849440530769199
 Ed White      |   977776247299278927
 Pete Conrad   |  1176349381245339423
 Jim McDivitt  |  2355184077141388896
```

(10 rows)

The primary key for the **astronauts** table is the **name** column. By adding the **token()** function to our query and passing name as a parameter, we are able to see the tokens that are used to determine placement inside the database cluster.

Cassandra uses the **Murmur3** hash algorithm, which will hash partition key values into the same tokens across different system. Running the above query should get the same results from each row's call to the **token()** function.

Now, let us rerun a query similar to what we ran on Postgres. We will pull back data about astronauts and their universities. Several of the Gemini astronauts attended the **US Military Academy**, so we will start from there:

```
SELECT astronaut_name, dob, birthplace, university_name as university
FROM astronauts_by_university
```

```
WHERE university_name = 'US Military Academy';
```

```
 astronaut_name  | dob         | birthplace       | university
-----------------+-------------+------------------+--------------------
     Buzz Aldrin | 1930-01-20 |     Montclair, NJ | US Military Academy
      Dave Scott | 1932-06-06 | San Antonio, TX | US Military Academy
        Ed White | 1930-11-14 | San Antonio, TX | US Military Academy
     Frank Borman | 1928-03-14 |        Gary, IN | US Military Academy
  Michael Collins | 1930-10-31 |      Rome, Italy | US Military Academy
```

(5 rows)

As you can see, we have five astronauts who attended the **US Military Academy**. If we examine the rows closely, we can see that the rows are in order by the **astronaut_name** column.

Likewise, we can query for the three Gemini astronauts who attended the **US Naval Academy**:

```
SELECT astronaut_name, dob, birthplace, university_name as university
FROM astronauts_by_university
WHERE university_name = 'US Naval Academy';
```

```
 astronaut_name | dob         | birthplace       | university
-----------------+-------------+------------------+------------------
    Jim Lovell | 1928-03-25 |    Cleveland, OH | US Naval Academy
   Tom Stafford | 1930-09-17 | Weatherford, OK | US Naval Academy
  Wally Schirra | 1923-03-12 |   Hackensack, NJ | US Naval Academy
```

(3 rows)

> **Note: As with Postgres, we should not run queries in Cassandra without a WHERE or LIMIT clause. Queries like this in Cassandra can overwhelm nodes in the cluster, and potentially lead to query timeouts or even node crashes.**

Accessing from Java

With our data loaded, let us return to our Java IDE.

pom.xml

To access Cassandra from Java, we first need to pull down the **DataStax** open-source Java driver for Apache Cassandra. Open up our project's **pom.xml** file, and add the following **dependency**:

```
<dependency>

    <groupId>com.datastax.oss</groupId>

    <artifactId>java-driver-core</artifactId>

    <version>4.16.0</version>

</dependency>
```

This will allow Maven to access the Java driver for Cassandra.

CassandraConn class

Next, we will create a new Java class named **CassandraConn** inside the **chapter7** package. It will not have a **main** method, but we will need to define imports to use a **List** and locate a file on-disk:

```
package chapter7;


import java.nio.file.Paths;

import java.util.List;


import com.datastax.oss.driver.api.core.CqlSession;


public class CassandraConn {


    private CqlSession cqlSession;
```

We will also build a **private CqlSession** object named **cqlSession** to manage our connection to Cassandra. We will then build a constructor to accept four parameters of type **String**:

- A **username**.
- A **password**.

- A **secureBundleFileLocation** to hold the name of the file and its directory location.

- A **keyspace** variable to hold the name of the default **keyspace** to use (unless otherwise specified).

As we did with our PostgreSQL connector class, we will wrap our connection attempt inside of a **try/catch**. The Cassandra Java driver has a **builder** for its **CqlSession** object, which will allow us to define and execute our connection with one single, multi-line command:

```
public CassandraConn(String username, String pwd,

        String secureBundleLocation, String keyspace) {


    try {

        cqlSession = CqlSession.builder()

            .withCloudSecureConnectBundle

                (Paths.get(secureBundleLocation))

            .withAuthCredentials(username, pwd)

            .withKeyspace(keyspace)

            .build();


        System.out.printf("[OK] Welcome to Astra DB! "

    "Connected to Keyspace %s\n",

        cqlSession.getKeyspace().get());

    } catch (Exception ex) {

        System.out.println(ex.getMessage());

    }

}
```

Usually, the **CQLSession builder** accepts parameters for SSL/TLS security context and a list of IP addresses. With Astra DB, our secure bundle takes care of all that for us, so we need to set the location using the **withCloudSecureConnectBundle()** method. We can set our credentials and default **keyspace** using the similar methods of **withAuthCredentials()** and **withKeyspace()**, respectively. We can then execute the connection process by invoking the **build()** method. Once the connection succeeds, we can display a welcome message with the default **keyspace** name that we have connected to using the **CqlSession** **getKeyspace()** method.

Our main program will need access to our connection, so let us quickly build a getter method for it:

```
public CqlSession getCqlSession() {

    return cqlSession;

}
```

We will also build a **finalize()** method on our class. In Java, the **finalize()** method is automatically called when an object is determined to be out of scope and picked up by the JVM garbage collector, prior to its destruction. For our **finalize()** method, we will make sure to call the **close()** method on our connection:

```
protected void finalize() {

    cqlSession.close();

    System.out.println("[shutdown_driver] Closing connection");

    System.out.println();

}
```

AstronautCassandraDAL class

As we did with Postgres, we will use a DAL as a level of abstraction between our main code and the database access code. Create a new Java class named **AstronautCassandraDAL** and make sure that it is in the **chapter7** package. This new class should not have a **main** method.

Our new class will require imports for a **List**, **ArrayList**, and the **time** type **Instant**. We will also require four objects from the Cassandra driver for **BoundStatement**, **PreparedStatement**, **ResultSet**, and **Row**:

```
package chapter7;


import java.time.Instant;

import java.util.ArrayList;

import java.util.List;


import com.datastax.oss.driver.api.core.cql.BoundStatement;

import com.datastax.oss.driver.api.core.cql.PreparedStatement;
```

```
import com.datastax.oss.driver.api.core.cql.ResultSet;

import com.datastax.oss.driver.api.core.cql.Row;


public class AstronautCassandraDAL {

    private CassandraConn cassandra;


    protected record AstronautMission(

        String missionName, Instant startDate,

        Instant endDate, String astronautName) {};
```

As shown above, we will also define a **private** variable for our **CassandraConn** class, as well as our **AstronautMission** record. This **AstronautMission** record will be slightly different from the one we built for Postgres, as it uses the **Instant time** type for the mission start and end dates.

Now, let us build our constructor. Our constructor will accept string parameters for our **username** and **password** credentials, along with the on-disk location of the secure connect bundle file and the name of our **keyspace**. It will then use those parameters to initialize our **CassandraConn** connection object:

```
public AstronautCassandraDAL(String username, String password,

        String bundleLoc, String keyspace) {


    cassandra = new CassandraConn(username, password, bundleLoc, keyspace);

}
```

With our constructor complete, we will now look at building the **getGeminiRoster()** methods, similar to what we previously built for our **PostgresDAL**. We will take the same approach again, overloading the methods to allow both a specified limit and a parameterless version. This way the first, parameterless version of the **getGeminiRoster()** method simply calls the other with a default limit of **20**:

```
public List<String> getGeminiRoster() {

    return getGeminiRoster(20);

}
```

The other method accepts an integer named **limit**. It begins by defining the return value as a **List** of **String** named **returnVal**. We then define our query to pull the **name** column back from the **astronauts** table, while specifying the **LIMIT** that was passed-in to the method as a parameter:

```
public List<String> getGeminiRoster(int limit) {

    List<String> returnVal = new ArrayList<>();


    String astronautCQL = "SELECT name FROM astronauts LIMIT "
        + limit;


    try {

        ResultSet astronauts =

            cassandra.getCqlSession().execute(astronautCQL);


        for (Row astronaut: astronauts) {

            returnVal.add(astronaut.getString("name"));

        }

    } catch (Exception e) {

        System.out.println(e.getMessage());

    }


    return returnVal;

}
```

We then build a **try**/**catch** around our database access call. We initialize a new **ResultSet** object named **astronauts** to the result of our executed query. Finally, we will iterate through each CQL row in the result set and add the value of the **name** column to our **returnVal** list. Once we **catch** for a possible exception, we can return our **returnVal** to the calling method.

GeminiAstronautsNoSQL class

Next, we will create a new Java class. It should be named **GeminiAstronautsNoSQL**, located inside the **chapter7** package, and have a **main** method. Our **GeminiAstronautsNoSQL** class will need imports for a **Set** and a **HashSet**, a **List** and a **Random** number generator from the **java.util** library. We will also import the **AstronautMission** record from the **AstronautCassandraDAL** class:

```
package chapter7;
```

```
import java.util.HashSet;

import java.util.List;

import java.util.Random;

import java.util.Set;


import chapter7.AstronautCassandraDAL.AstronautMission;


public class GeminiAstronautsNoSQL {


    public static void main(String[] args) {
```

With that complete, let us define local variables for our environment variables and use them to instantiate our **AstronautCassandraDAL** class as an object named **astronautDAL**:

```
String bundleLoc = System.getenv("ASTRA_DB_BUNDLE");

String username = System.getenv("ASTRA_DB_USER");

String password = System.getenv("ASTRA_DB_PASSWORD");

String keyspace = System.getenv("ASTRA_DB_KEYSPACE");


AstronautCassandraDAL astronautDAL =

        new AstronautCassandraDAL(username, password, bundleLoc, keyspace);
```

Next, we will define a new **List** of type **String** named **geminiAstronauts** and set it to the result from our **getGeminiRoster()** method call. We will then iterate through each name returned in the **geminiAstronauts** list, and display it:

```
System.out.println("Project Gemini Astronauts:");


List<String> geminiAstronauts = astronautDAL.getGeminiRoster();


for (String astronaut : geminiAstronauts) {

    System.out.println(astronaut);

}


System.out.println();
```

Running our code should produce an output similar to this:

```
null

Project Gemini Astronauts:

Cannot invoke "com.datastax.oss.driver.api.core.CqlSession.execute(String)"
because the return value of "chapter7.CassandraConn.getCqlSession()" is null


Exception in thread "main" java.lang.NullPointerException: Cannot invoke
"com.datastax.oss.driver.api.core.CqlSession.prepare(String)" because the
return value of "chapter7.CassandraConn.getCqlSession()" is null
        at chapter7.AstronautCassandraDAL.
        getMissionAstronauts(AstronautCassandraDAL.java:54)

        at chapter7.GeminiAstronautsNoSQL.main(GeminiAstronautsNoSQL.
        java:45)
```

This exception is happening because we have not defined our environment variables as a part of our IDE's run configuration. We need four for this class, and their values are fairly easy to find. First, we are going to have a look at the Astra DB credentials file that we downloaded when generating a new token at database creation time. By default, that file should go into the **Downloads** directory:

```
cat ~/Downloads/bpb-token.json
```

```json
{

  "clientId": "JuPplXTOxsdfOeZRUZKIX",

  "secret": "iZLo0nus_cS_9vPTejpPH2+MDXdZh1IfGq0Z6Tn3jmqkNKzT-EZj,ACj8olji_
  DZH8YQZayjLGZX.PCHSALwfCMH.Lpfs89d7doS1rWAoqEkf1cFxwyqt.I-nLiZf",

  "token": "AstraCS:JuPplXTOxLBxZgmOeZRUZKIX:2f1da723f14cdfa03605d3"

}
```

Note that each ***token.json** file that is generated and downloaded will be unique. The file shown above is an example. But the part that we need is the **"token" json** property at the bottom. Make a note of this property, as we will need it in a moment.

The four environment variables that we need are shown here, along with sample values:

ASTRA_DB_BUNDLE: /Users/aaronploetz/Downloads/secure-connect-bpb.zip

ASTRA_DB_KEYSPACE: astronaut_data

ASTRA_DB_PASSWORD: AstraCS:JuPplXTOxLBxZgmOeZRUZKIX:2f1da723f14cdfa03605d3

`ASTRA_DB_USER: token`

Here is some guidance on how they should be set:

- **ASTRA_DB_BUNDLE:** This should be the directory location and file name of the secure connect zip bundle that was downloaded from **astra.datastax.com** earlier. This will vary based on the operating system, system user name, and default browser settings.

- **ASTRA_DB_KEYSPACE:** As we mentioned above, this should be set to **astronaut_data**, or to whatever the **KEYSPACE** was named.

- **ASTRA_DB_PASSWORD:** This should be the **"token"** value from the ***token.json** file shown above.

- **ASTRA_DB_USER:** This should always be the literal word **"token."**

If we are setting these variables inside of a **Run Configurations** in our **Eclipse IDE**, they should be defined similar to what is shown in *Figure 7.10*:

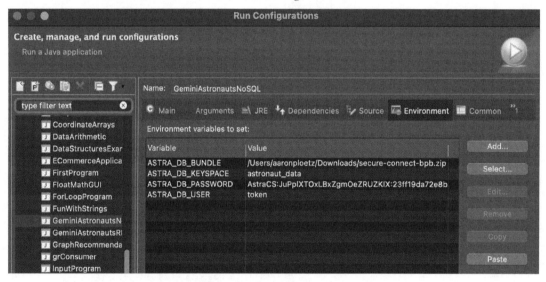

Figure 7.10: *Our run configuration for the GeminiAstronautsNoSQL class, showing the "Environment" tab.*

Now, running our **GeminiAstronautsNoSQL** class should produce the following output:

`[OK] Success`

`[OK] Welcome to Astra DB! Connected to Keyspace astronaut_data`

`Project Gemini Astronauts:`

`Tom Stafford`

`Gus Grissom`

`Gene Cernan`

Frank Borman

Buzz Aldrin

John Young

Jim Lovell

Ed White

Pete Conrad

Jim McDivitt

Neil Armstrong

Richard Gordon

Michael Collins

Gordon Cooper

Dave Scott

Wally Schirra

With this complete, we can move on to our next query to show the astronauts who flew on three random Gemini missions.

AstronautCassandraDAL class revisited

To start with this, we will go back to our **AstronautCassandraDAL** class, and create a new method named **getMissionAstronauts**. It will return a value of a **List** of our **AstronautMission** record, and accept the **missionName** as a string parameter.

We will start by defining our return value (**returnVal**), our CQL query (**missionCQL**), our prepared statement (**missionStatement**), bound statement (**boundCQLMission**, and result set (**missionAstronauts**):

```
public List<AstronautMission> getMissionAstronauts(String missionName) {

    List<AstronautMission> returnVal = new ArrayList<>();

    String missionCQL = "SELECT mission_name, mission_start_date, "
            + "mission_end_date, astronaut_name "
            + "FROM astronauts_by_mission "
            + "WHERE mission_name = ?;";

    PreparedStatement missionStatement =
```

```
        cassandra.getCqlSession().prepare(missionCQL);


    BoundStatement boundCQLMission =

            missionStatement.bind(missionName);

    ResultSet missionAstronauts =

            cassandra.getCqlSession().execute(boundCQLMission);
```

Then, we finish the method by building a **for** loop to iterate through the rows in the result set. Inside the loop, we build a new **AstronautMission** record and add it to **returnVal**. When the loop is finished, we return the following results:

```
for (Row amRow : missionAstronauts) {

    AstronautMission astronautMission = new AstronautMission(

        amRow.getString("mission_name"),

        amRow.getInstant("mission_start_date"),

        amRow.getInstant("mission_end_date"),

        amRow.getString("astronaut_name"));


    returnVal.add(astronautMission);

}


return returnVal;
```

GeminiAstronautsNoSQL class revisited

Back in our **GeminiAstronautsNoSQL** class, our code to pull back astronauts by mission is going to look very similar to what we did in our **GeminiAstronautsRDBMS** class. We will instantiate a **Set** of integers as well as a **Random** object to generate our three Gemini missions:

```
Set<Integer> randomMissions = new HashSet<>();

Random random = new Random();

// generate 3 random numbers

while (randomMissions.size() < 3) {

    int missionNumber = random.nextInt(10) + 3;
```

```
randomMissions.add(missionNumber);
```

}

With our **randomMissions** and **random** objects defined, we will iterate through a **while** loop if the **randomMissions** set has less than three items. Inside the **while** loop, we will generate a random number from **3** to **12** (inclusive), representing the manned Gemini spaceflights. We will then add the generated number to the **randomMissions** set.

Now, we will use a **for** loop to iterate through the numbers generated in the **randomMissions** set. We will then build a string with the name **"Gemini"** (with a space on the end) and concatenate the mission number (**missionNum**) to the end of it. We can then call the **getMissionAstronauts()** method on our DAL while passing the **mission** with its default **toString()** method:

```
for (Integer missionNum : randomMissions) {

    StringBuilder mission = new StringBuilder("Gemini ");

    mission.append(missionNum.toString());

    List<AstronautMission> missionAstronauts =
        astronautDAL.getMissionAstronauts(mission.toString());
```

Finally, we will build a nested **for** loop (inside the loop shown above) which will iterate through the **AstronautMission** records and display their contents:

```
    for (AstronautMission astronautMission : missionAstronauts) {

        System.out.print(astronautMission.missionName() + " ");

        System.out.print(astronautMission.startDate() + " -> ");

        System.out.print(astronautMission.endDate() + " - ");

        System.out.println(astronautMission.astronautName());

    }


    System.out.println();

}
```

Running our code should produce an output (after our complete Gemini astronaut roster) similar to this:

```
Gemini 3 1965-03-23T14:24:00Z -> 1965-03-23T17:16:31Z - Gus Grissom

Gemini 3 1965-03-23T14:24:00Z -> 1965-03-23T17:16:31Z - John Young
```

```
Gemini 7 1965-12-04T19:30:03Z -> 1965-12-18T14:05:04Z - Frank Borman

Gemini 7 1965-12-04T19:30:03Z -> 1965-12-18T14:05:04Z - Jim Lovell


Gemini 10 1966-07-18T22:20:26Z -> 1966-07-21T21:07:05Z - John Young

Gemini 10 1966-07-18T22:20:26Z -> 1966-07-21T21:07:05Z - Michael Collins
```

`[shutdown_driver]` `Closing connection`

As shown, we have successfully built a distributed database schema and data set using the Apache Cassandra database and queried it with Java.

Choosing the right database

This is a topic of much debate and certainly one with many answers. The key is to understand the requirements of the application being built. In fact, we could take any application design and talk through its requirements in terms of the CAP theorem (from earlier in this chapter), and we should be able to arrive at a database to support its desired behaviors.

In simpler terms, a relational database should be used if a dynamic query model is required and performance is not a concern. Applications that serve data in an **online analytical processing (OLAP)** system paradigm would benefit more from a RDBMS. On the other hand, if performance across a large geographic region is required, a NoSQL database is probably a better fit. Ultimately, it is all about the data and how it needs to be served.

Conclusion

In this chapter, we briefly discussed the history of databases and the computer science theory behind them. We then talked through different types of databases, and took a closer look at how to use two of them. More information on working with PostgreSQL and Apache Cassandra can be found on their respective project websites, as well as in the appendices of this book.

One point that this chapter should make clear, is that good DBaaS platforms will offer a free tier with enough resources to appropriately test and determine long term use. In today's world, developers do not want to have to think about the underlying data storage technologies that back their applications. Utilizing a DBaaS in the cloud eliminates the need for developers to run and maintain infrastructure components.

However, it is important for developers to understand how to architect data models and build levels of data abstraction into their applications. The concept of coding a DAL was explained in this chapter, as well as how loosely-coupling an application with its data layer makes changing the underlying database a much easier task. The concepts explained in this chapter can become powerful tools for Java developers to wield.

In the next chapter, we will discuss building web applications in Java. We will be utilizing the database knowledge that we acquired in this chapter, while exploring how to build web services and even simple web page front ends.

Points to remember

- Relational databases were designed to store data efficiently.
- NoSQL databases were designed to serve data efficiently.
- Open-source databases (like PostgreSQL and Apache Cassandra) are widely used across many industries.
- One way to inject credentials into an application is to use environment variables.
- Database credentials should not be hard-coded into an application.
- A **SELECT** query should always have either a **WHERE** or a **LIMIT** clause.
- Prepared statements are a great way to increase the performance of queries that are often run. This is because the database will not need to parse them on each use.
- When using prepared statements with a loop, prepare the query outside of the loop and execute the query inside of the loop.
- Prepared statements can also lower the risk of a SQL Injection Attack.
- A DAL is an important concept to understand when building a data-intensive application.
- Database connection objects should be created once and reused. It is not recommended to open a new connection for each operation.
- Every database was designed to solve a specific problem. Usually, a problem that its predecessors could not solve well.

Join our book's Discord space

Join the book's Discord Workspace for Latest updates, Offers, Tech happenings around the world, New Release and Sessions with the Authors:

https://discord.bpbonline.com

CHAPTER 8

Web Applications

Introduction

In this chapter, we will talk about web architecture and building web-based applications. This is an area in which we have seen a significant shift over the last couple of decades. Before this, each application would ship with its **user interface (UI)**, its data access points, and its way of rendering information.

Today, most applications run through a web browser, including many developer tools. Applications like infrastructure control platforms, source control, word processing, spreadsheets, and presentation tools can all run inside of a web browser. There are even IDEs that run inside of a browser, like *GitPod*. In the previous chapter, we deployed databases and operated on them within command shells, all done through a browser.

Structure

In this chapter, we will discuss RESTful calls. We will build small web services. Following that, we will build a GUI on top to make a complete application. To start on this path, we will cover the following topics:

- Restful operations
- Web services with Spring Boot
- Building web UIs

Objectives

The learning goals for this chapter are to build a foundational understanding of how to build web applications in Java. By the end of this chapter, we will:

- Learn what a web service does, and how to build them.
- Understand the properties of RESTful web service endpoints.
- Learn how to build web services in Java using Spring Boot.
- Learn how to build data-intensive web applications with Spring Data.
- Learn how to build a GUI using the **Vaadin** framework.

Restful operations

In web programming, **Representational State Transfer (REST)** outlines specific operations and ways to work with data in a web application. Previously, the abbreviation for **REST** was capitalized, but is now simply known as **Rest**.

A service is considered restful if it conforms to certain standards or principles. The idea is that Restful services should be:

- **Lightweight**: Consume as few resources as possible.
- **Purposeful**: Perform as few functions (preferably one) as possible.
- **Scalable**: Designed to benefit from multiple copies of themselves running in parallel.
- **Stateless**: While they may transfer or work with persistent data, nothing about the service require persistence.
- **Loosely-coupled**: Not dependent on other services for successful operation.

When building Restful services, there are specific types of base **Hypertext Transfer Protocol (HTTP)** operations that they can perform:

- **GET**: Easily the most-common Restful operation used for retrieving data. Parameters are specified in the (uniform resource identifier) URI of the request, and a response is returned.
- **POST**: Used for creating a new stateful entry. Parameters can be specified in the URI or the body of the request, and a response is returned.
- **PUT**: Functions similarly to POST, but is intended to be used for updating existing data.
- **DELETE**: As implied by the name, it is meant to remove existing data by parameters in the URI.

Note: There are additional Restful operations, but we are only going to concern ourselves with these four.

All web requests and responses have a header and a body. Restful services typically need data from one or the other (or both). This will be discussed in detail.

Restful URIs

It is worth discussing that Restful operations have their own structure for URIs. Typically, it is a version and service name followed by a combination of plural nouns. For example:

https://www.bigboxco.com/storeapi/v1/stores/{store_number}/details

In this case, a fictitious company named **Big Box Company** is exposing a service known as their **storeapi**. It is the first version of this service, as evidenced by the **v1**. The **stores** endpoint accepts a store number and then offers additional endpoints, including **details**.

It is an accepted best practice to **version** our service endpoint URIs. This way, if we need to make breaking changes to one or more service endpoints, our users can still use our old version until they are ready to switch. For example, consider if we made a code to change the **stores** service for Big Box Company's **storeapi**. The best way to implement that change is as a new service, updating the version to **v2**.

Note: Unfortunately, there is a lot of discussion in various web forums about the *right* way to build and name *true Restful* services. Much of this is subjective, so experienced web developers may want to build their service endpoints differently than shown in this book. This will not affect the underlying service functionality. Also, readers are encouraged not to engage in such dogmatic discussions online, as they typically do not result in a meaningful resolution.

Simple operations

One way we can quickly practice consuming (using) a Restful web service is by using the public API hosted by the **United States' National Weather Service** (**NWS**). We can use this service to get weather data from any of the weather stations listed here: **https://forecast.weather.gov/stations.php?foo=2**.

For example, let us use the station defined for the **Minneapolis/St. Paul International Airport**, with station ID **KMSP**.

Enter the following address in your browser: **https://api.weather.gov/stations/kmsp/observations/latest**.

Running this request yields a bit of raw data. If we do a **find** on the page for the text `temperature`, we should see this block of data:

```
"temperature": {

    "unitCode": "wmoUnit:degC",

    "value": 21.100000000000001,

    "qualityControl": "V"

},
```

This data is in the **JavaScript Object Notation (JSON)** format. In JSON, each block of data is enclosed inside a pair of curly braces **{}**. These blocks can also be embedded or nested within each other. For example, if we go out from **temperature**, we can see that it is enclosed inside the properties block:

```
"properties": {

    "@id": "https://api.weather.gov/stations/KMSP/observations/2023-07-
    09T14:53:00+00:00",

    "@type": "wx:ObservationStation",

    "elevation": {

        "unitCode": "wmoUnit:m",

        "value": 255

    },

    "station": "https://api.weather.gov/stations/KMSP",

    "timestamp": "2023-07-09T14:53:00+00:00",

    "rawMessage": "KMSP 091453Z 23011G19KT 10SM SCT100 BKN110 21/09
    A2993 RMK AO2 SLP130 T02110094 58002",

    "textDescription": "Mostly Cloudy",

    "icon": "https://api.weather.gov/icons/land/day/bkn?size=medium",

    "presentWeather": [],

    "temperature": {

        "unitCode": "wmoUnit:degC",

        "value": 21.100000000000001,

        "qualityControl": "V"

    },
```

We can also run Restful web calls from a terminal or command line interface using the cURL application. cURL is a command line tool for working with data from the web. Originally built in 1996 as a small project by Swedish developer (and **Polhem Prize** recipient) *Daniel Stenberg*, cURL is now widely used as the main tool for system-level web requests. It has become quite prolific, as cURL ships with Linux, MacOS, Windows 11, and later versions of Windows 10. It is even found in many other types of embedded systems, as many appliances and automobiles made today also run cURL natively.

> **Note: For more information on cURL, visit https://www.curl.se.**

To verify our installation of cURL, we can run the **curl --version** command from our own terminal:

```
curl --version
```

```
curl 7.81.0 (x86_64-pc-linux-gnu) libcurl/7.81.0 OpenSSL/3.0.2 zlib/1.2.11
brotli/1.0.9  zstd/1.4.8  libidn2/2.3.2  libpsl/0.21.0  (+libidn2/2.3.2)
libssh/0.9.6/openssl/zlib nghttp2/1.43.0 librtmp/2.3 OpenLDAP/2.5.14

Release-Date: 2022-01-05

Protocols: dict file ftp ftps gopher gophers http https imap imaps ldap ldaps
mqtt pop3 pop3s rtmp rtsp scp sftp smb smbs smtp smtps telnet tftp

Features: alt-svc AsynchDNS brotli GSS-API HSTS HTTP2 HTTPS-proxy IDN IPv6
Kerberos Largefile libz NTLM NTLM_WB PSL SPNEGO SSL TLS-SRP UnixSockets zstd
```

To run the same request above (for weather station data) from **curl**, we would do this:

```
curl -X GET https://api.weather.gov/stations/kmsp/observations/latest
-H "Content-Type: application/json"
-H "Accept: application/json"
```

First, we are using the **-X** option to specify that we are running a **GET** request. Then, we specify our URI, followed by our header options, using the **-H** option twice.

In this case, we are specifying a **Content-Type** of **application/json**, which means that we are telling cURL that our request body will be in the JSON format. This request does not have a request body, so we do not need it. Next, we are also specifying the **Accept** property in our header, also with a value of **application/json**. This is our way of telling the web server that we would like to receive our data in the JSON format.

> **Note: As Accept properties are about telling the web server how we would like our data formatted in the response, they are typically not used in response headers.**

Before moving on, let us run one more cURL **GET** request. If it has been a few days since we last worked on the previous chapter, our Astra DB cloud instance may have entered a **hibernated** state. We will need to reactivate it, as it will be required for some of the services we are going to build as we progress through this chapter. Fortunately, Astra DB operations are exposed as a Restful API, and it can be **awakened** by querying the **keyspaces** endpoint on our database:

```
curl -X GET https://34176be8-1675-4204-ae98-3a66f6f772dd-us-east1.apps.
astra.datastax.com/api/rest/v2/schemas/keyspaces/
-H "X-Cassandra-Token:
AstraCS:JuPplXTOxLBxZgmOeZRUZKIX:2f1da723f14cdfa03605d3"
-H "Content-Type: application/json"
-H "Accept: application/json"

{"message":"Resuming your database, please try again shortly."}
```

Our database URI consists of our database ID and region. We are also passing along values in the request header for **Content-Type**, **Accept**, and **X-Cassandra-Token**. Do note that each endpoint and token will be different for each and every Astra DB instance.

> Note: Be careful not to pass sensitive data in an unsecured (http) web request. All web sites and services should be secured with a TLS certificate.

Web services with Spring Boot

Now, we will progress toward building web services with Java. Web services are essentially methods that are exposed to and run on the web without a GUI, making them headless. A single web service typically performs a single function, either writing or retrieving data. A group of web services can be called a **service layer.**

Typically, building and running a web service layer involves standing up a web server locally and deploying code to it. However, we will take the easy path and use Spring Boot.

Spring Boot is a web service framework that allows us to quickly build and deploy standalone Java web applications for testing or production. Spring Boot allows the developer to embed the web server along with the compiled Java binaries, which makes deploying the application much easier.

Spring has developed an online tool to quickly build and configure starting project files. All it takes is a few buttons click, and we will be ready to go. To get to the **spring initializr**, simply browse to: **https://start.spring.io/**. We should see a screen that shows *Figure 8.1* and *Figure 8.2*.

For our Weather Application, we will configure it as shown in *Figure 8.1* with data from the following properties:

- **Project**: Maven
- **Language**: Java

- **Spring Boot version: 3.1.1**
- **Group: `com.codewithjava21`**
- **Artifact and name: weatherapp**
- **Description: Consumes and displays weather data**
- **Package name: `com.codewithjava21.weatherapp`**
- **Packaging: Jar**
- **Java version: 21**

Figure 8.1: The left side of the Spring Initializr, allowing specification of dependency management and other points of project configuration.

With that complete, let us have a look at the right side of the screen, shown in *Figure 8.2*. We will add three dependencies. We only need to click the **ADD DEPENDENCIES** button, and then search for each of the following dependencies individually:

- **Spring Web**
- **Vaadin**
- **Spring Data for Apache Cassandra**

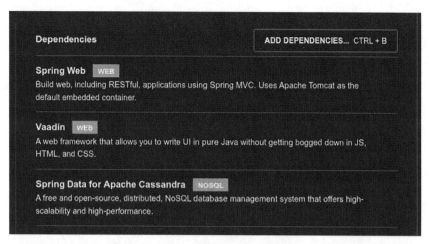

Figure 8.2: The right side of the Spring Initializr. This is where the initial project dependencies are added.

With both sides of the **Spring Initializr** screen addressed, we can then click the **Generate** button. This will cause our web browser to download a file that should be named **weatherapp.zip**.

To import the file into our IDE, we will first move the ZIP file into our workspace directory and unzip/uncompress/expand it. Then inside Eclipse, we can click on the **File** menu, followed by the **Import** option. In the next dialog, we will indicate that we are importing **Existing Maven Projects** (as shown in *Figure 8.3*) and click **Next**. From there, we will browse to the directory location of our new **weatherapp** folder and click into it, ensuring that the **pom.xml** file is present. From there, we can click the **Finish** button to complete the process.

> **Note: As long as we are in the directory containing the pom.xml file, the IDE should find the project for import.**

We have now imported the new project into our IDE. With that complete, we should now see the **weatherapp** in the project explorer on the left side of our IDE. Refer to the following *Figure 8.3:*

Figure 8.3: The "Import" dialog option to indicate that our zip file will be an existing Maven project.

pom.xml

Have a look at our **pom.xml** file, which has been generated by the **Spring Boot Initializr**. When building an application, this certainly helps speed-up the initial development cycles, quickly getting programmers to the point where they can start writing code.

That being said, we are going to make some adjustments. First, if an option for Java 21 was not available in the **Spring Boot Initializr**, we need to adjust that. Look for the **properties** section, and make sure that the **java.version** property is set appropriately:

```
<properties>

    <java.version>21</java.version>
```

Next, we should comment out the **dependencies** for Spring Data Cassandra and Vaadin. These will not be needed right away, and can sometimes cause issues if not properly configured. Be sure to use the HTML/XML style of comment characters (<!-- -->). Our **dependencies** section should now look like this:

```
<dependencies>

<!-- <dependency>

        <groupId>org.springframework.boot</groupId>
```

```
        <artifactId>spring-boot-starter-data-cassandra</artifactId>

    </dependency> -->

    <dependency>

        <groupId>org.springframework.boot</groupId>

        <artifactId>spring-boot-starter-web</artifactId>

    </dependency>

<!--    <dependency>

        <groupId>com.vaadin</groupId>

        <artifactId>vaadin-spring-boot-starter</artifactId>

    </dependency> -->

    <dependency>

        <groupId>org.springframework.boot</groupId>

        <artifactId>spring-boot-starter-test</artifactId>

        <scope>test</scope>

    </dependency>

</dependencies>
```

MVC

Many software products are built on widely known design patterns. These design patterns are essentially standard ways of architecting software components. We will make use of the more common design patterns for web applications known as the **Model, View, Controller (MVC)** pattern.

With MVC, the components of a web application are broken up into three parts:

- **Model**: The structure of the data and how it goes into the underlying data store.
- **View**: The UI, which handles user interactions and how the data is displayed to the user.
- **Controller**: The middle layer which abstracts the model from the view. It handles data requests from the UI, and can sometimes function as a standalone service endpoint provider.

We will build our weather application using the MVC pattern, starting with the controller.

Weather application controller

Create a new Java class named **WeatherAppController** inside the **com.codewithjava21. weatherapp** package. This class should not have a **main** method. We will need imports from the Spring Framework for the following classes: **ResponseEntity**, **GetMapping**, **RequestMapping**, and **RestController**:

```
package com.codewithjava21.weatherapp;

import org.springframework.http.ResponseEntity;

import org.springframework.web.bind.annotation.GetMapping;

import org.springframework.web.bind.annotation.RequestMapping;

import org.springframework.web.bind.annotation.RestController;

@RequestMapping("/weather")

@RestController

public class WeatherAppController {
```

The **RequestMapping** and **RestController** classes are annotations. With these annotations, Spring Boot knows how to quickly wire up our application to be served. We just have to use them to tell Spring Boot what each component is. Our class defines a Restful controller, so we need the **@RestController** annotation. The base service name for this controller is **weather**, so we will need to specify that with the **@RequestMapping** annotation, as shown above.

Hello world service endpoint

Now we will build a simple service endpoint on our weather service. We will build a method named **getHello**. It will be prefaced with a **@GetMapping** annotation, specifying the service endpoint name of **helloworld**. It will have a return type of **ResponseEntity** of type **String**:

```
@GetMapping("/helloworld")

public ResponseEntity<String> getHello() {

    return ResponseEntity.ok("Hello world!\n");

}
```

The method itself is fairly straightforward. We will return the result of the **ResponseEntity. ok()** method, with the message **Hello world!** as its lone parameter. If everything works, this should return the HTTP response code of 200 (ok).

Note: A short reference of HTTP Response Codes can be found in the Appendices.

We can now execute a **Maven Install** via the IDE, and then run our application. When first trying to run this application, we might be prompted to select our application. Refer to the following *Figure 8.4:*

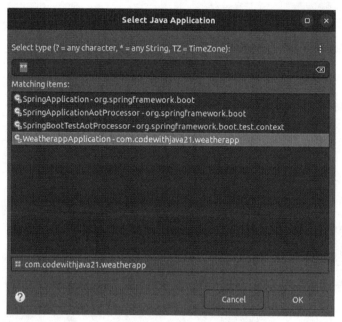

Figure 8.4: Make sure to select our "WeatherApplication" from the list.

When running our application from our IDE, the console window should display a message log similar to this:

```
  .   ____          _            __ _ _
 /\\ / ___'_ __ _ _(_)_ __  __ _ \ \ \ \
( ( )\___ | '_ | '_| | '_ \/ _` | \ \ \ \
 \\/  ___)| |_)| | | | | || (_| |  ) ) ) )
  '  |____| .__|_| |_|_| |_\__, | / / / /
 =========|_|==============|___/=/_/_/_/
```

```
 :: Spring Boot ::                (v3.1.1)
```

```
2023-07-13T07:00:57.366-05:00  INFO 8481 --- [          main] c.c.weatherapp.
WeatherappApplication      : Starting WeatherappApplication using Java 21-ea
with PID 8481
```

There will be some additional lines to follow. The last two are important:

```
2023-07-13T07:00:59.444-05:00  INFO 8481 --- [        main] o.s.b.w.embedded.
tomcat.TomcatWebServer  : Tomcat started on port(s): 8080 (http) with context
path ''
```

```
2023-07-13T07:00:59.457-05:00  INFO 8481 --- [        main] c.c.weatherapp.
WeatherappApplication     : Started WeatherappApplication in 2.592 seconds
(process running for 3.124)
```

The last line indicates that our application is indeed running. The second to last line shows that the embedded **Apache Tomcat**® is running on port **8080** via (**http**).

With this running, let us go to a terminal to test our **Hello World** service with cURL. Be sure to specify the following:

- We are performing a **Get** operation.
- Prefix the URI with **http**.
- Use the local, home address followed by a colon and port (**127.0.0.1:8080**).
- Specify the service name of **weather** and the service endpoint of **helloworld**, delimited by a slash (**/weather/helloworld**).

```
curl -X GET http://127.0.0.1:8080/weather/helloworld
```

```
Hello world!
```

We now have a simple, working web service endpoint that we can call from the command line or from a web browser. Now let us progress to a more complicated example.

Weather Application model

Now we will build the services for our weather application. Before we can add new service endpoints for our application, we first need to create our data model.

Spring gives us a toolset to manage our model, based on the underlying database that we are using. This toolset is known as **Spring Data**. For our project, we are going to use the subset of Spring Data, known as **Spring Data Cassandra**.

Define a new keyspace

As we have resumed our Astra DB database, let us go to our Astra **Dashboard** and click on the **Add Keyspace** button, as shown in *Figure 8.5*. Name this new keyspace **weatherapp**. Next, click on the **CQL Console** tab and **use** our new keyspace:

```
use weatherapp;
```

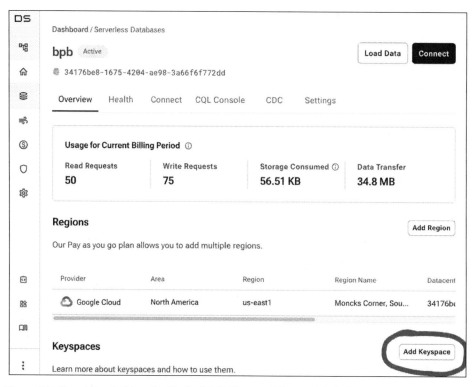

Figure 8.5: Our Astra dashboard with the "Add Keyspace" button (circled) in the lower right corner.

Define a new table

To store weather data in our database, we first need to build a new table. Our new table will be named **weather_by_station_by_month**, and its CQL definition will look like this:

```
CREATE TABLE weather_by_station_by_month (

    station_id TEXT,

    month_bucket INT,

    reading_timestamp TIMESTAMP,

    reading_icon TEXT,

    station_coordinates_lat FLOAT,

    station_coordinates_lon FLOAT,

    temperature_c FLOAT,

    wind_direction_deg INT,

    wind_speed_kmh FLOAT,
```

```
    wind_gust_kmh FLOAT,

    visibility_m INT,

    precipitation_last_hour FLOAT,

    cloud_cover MAP<INT,TEXT>,

    PRIMARY KEY ((station_id,month_bucket),reading_timestamp)
) WITH CLUSTERING ORDER BY (reading_timestamp DESC);
```

This should be a straightforward way to organize and store the data as it comes back from the NWS.

The idea behind our primary key definition is to create a compound partition key of **station_id** and **month_bucket**. First, we will only store the relevant station data. But we could store multiple stations if we wanted to. While Cassandra will do a great job of hosting our data in a distributed database, if we were to partition based on **station_id**, we would end up with **hot** partitions.

Hot partitions are partitions that are read from or written to much more than the others. This can lead to uneven data distribution and access patterns. Therefore, we need to use more than the **station_id** for our partition key.

Time-based data is sometimes called **time series** data. The other problem with having only **station_id** as our partition key is that it would grow unbound. Over time as we continue writing data for each new **timestamp**, the partition would grow too large. Therefore, we need to create a time component to add to our partition key to ensure that our partition will only grow to a finite amount.

This is a data modeling technique known as **bucketing**. For our use case, a time bucket based on the month will be fine. If we were to store an entry in our partition for each station by the hour, we would never exceed 744 rows in a partition (24 hours per day, max of 31 days per month). Therefore, each row will store a **month_bucket**, which will be a combined value of the year and numeric month (For example: 202307 for July of 2023).

Within each partition, we need something to uniquely identify each row. The **timestamp** property fits this requirement. However, **timestamp** is not a great name for a database column, as many databases (Cassandra included) have a **timestamp** data type. Therefore, we will name it **reading_timestamp**, inferring that it is the **timestamp** of the current weather reading.

Generate a new token

Unfortunately, our database access token that was automatically generated by Astra in the last chapter does not have sufficient privileges for this application. Therefore, we will need to generate a new one. On the Astra dashboard, go to **databases**. On the next screen, as shown in *Figure 8.6*, go to our **bpb** database and look for the **three dots** menu icon on the far right. Click on it to see the option to **Generate a Token**.

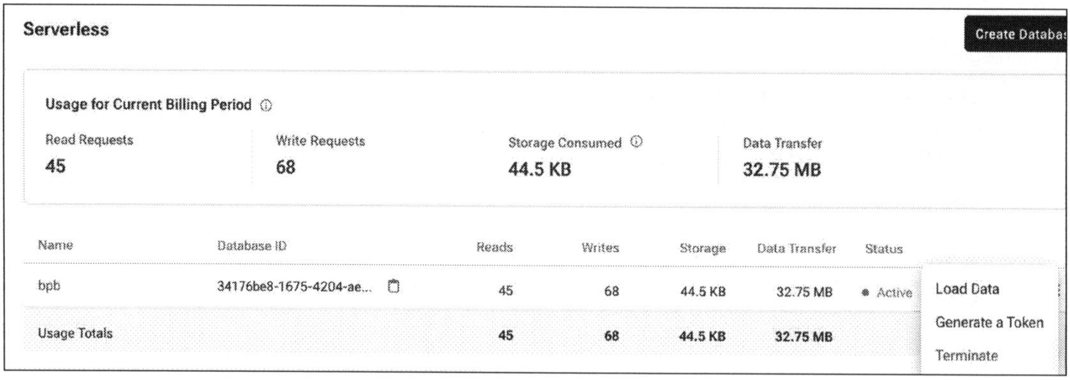

| Serverless | | | | | | | Create Databa |

Usage for Current Billing Period ⓘ				
Read Requests	Write Requests	Storage Consumed ⓘ	Data Transfer	
45	68	44.5 KB	32.75 MB	

Name	Database ID		Reads	Writes	Storage	Data Transfer	Status	
bpb	34176be8-1675-4204-ae...	⬜	45	68	44.5 KB	32.75 MB	● Active	Load Data
Usage Totals			45	68	44.5 KB	32.75 MB		Generate a Token
								Terminate

Figure 8.6: The details for the "bpb" database showing how to generate a new access token.

Projects using the Spring Data framework are capable of recreating database schema if it does not exist. They will need table creation and other schema level privileges to run. Therefore, we must create a new token for the **Database Administrator** role.

Set application properties and environment variables

Once we have the new token, we will need to set our environment variables as we did in the last chapter. Our application will need the following environment variables defined:

- **ASTRA_DB_KEYSPACE**
- **ASTRA_DB_APP_TOKEN**
- **ASTRA_DB_ID**
- **ASTRA_DB_REGION**

> **Note: Remember, in the Eclipse IDE environment, variables can be set as a part of the run configuration. See the previous chapter for more information.**

Inside our project, we should see a file named **application.properties** located under the **src/main/resources** directory. Start by renaming this file to **application.yml** so that we can use the **Yet Another Markup Language** (**YAML**) format for our application configuration. Our **application.yml** file should look like this:

```
server:

  port: 8080

  error:

    include-stacktrace: always
```

```yaml
spring:
  application:
    name: WeatherApp
  profiles:
    active: default
  data:
    cassandra:
      schema-action: NONE

astra:
  api:
    application-token: ${ASTRA_DB_APP_TOKEN}
    database-id: ${ASTRA_DB_ID}
    database-region: ${ASTRA_DB_REGION}
    cross-region-failback: false
  cql:
    enabled: true
    download-scb:
      enabled: true
    driver-config:
      basic:
        session-keyspace: ${ASTRA_DB_KEYSPACE}
        request:
          timeout: 8s
          consistency: LOCAL_QUORUM
          page-size: 5000
      advanced:
        connection:
```

```
        init-query-timeout: 10s

        set-keyspace-timeout: 10s

    control-connection:

        timeout: 10s
```

> **Note: The specification of the environment variables under the astra section, as the Spring framework can pull them in from the OS.**

pom.xml redux

At this point, it is time to revisit the **pom.xml** file, and uncomment the **dependency** for Spring Data Cassandra. We should also add another **dependency** for the Astra Spring Boot Starter:

```xml
<dependency>

    <groupId>org.springframework.boot</groupId>

    <artifactId>spring-boot-starter-data-cassandra</artifactId>

</dependency>

<dependency>

    <groupId>com.datastax.astra</groupId>

    <artifactId>astra-spring-boot-3x-starter</artifactId>

    <version>0.6.4</version>

</dependency>
```

WeatherPrimaryKey class

Create a new class named **WeatherPrimaryKey** inside of the **com.codewithjava21. weatherapp** package. It should not have a **main** method.

```java
package com.codewithjava21.weatherapp;


import java.time.Instant;


import org.springframework.data.cassandra.core.cql.PrimaryKeyType;

import org.springframework.data.cassandra.core.mapping.PrimaryKeyClass;

import org.springframework.data.cassandra.core.mapping.PrimaryKeyColumn;
```

```
@PrimaryKeyClass
public class WeatherPrimaryKey {
```

Our class will have four imports. We will want to import the **Instant** class from Java's time library. Then, from our Spring Data Cassandra library, we will import the **PrimaryKeyType**, **PrimaryKeyClass**, and **PrimaryKeyColumn** classes. We will use the **PrimaryKeyClass** as the annotation which precedes our class definition (as shown in the code above).

Next, we will define three privately-scoped properties on our **WeatherPrimaryKey** class:

```
@PrimaryKeyColumn(name = "station_id",
                  ordinal = 0,
                  type = PrimaryKeyType.PARTITIONED)
private String stationId;


@PrimaryKeyColumn(name = "month_bucket",
                  ordinal = 1,
                  type = PrimaryKeyType.PARTITIONED)
private int monthBucket;


@PrimaryKeyColumn(name = "reading_timestamp",
                  ordinal = 2,
                  type = PrimaryKeyType.CLUSTERED)
private Instant timestamp;
```

These properties will be for our **station_id**, **month_bucket**, and **timestamp** properties. Note that we will precede these property definitions with the **@PrimaryKeyColumn** annotation. We will use this annotation to help our Java repository to better understand how our primary key columns are defined in Cassandra. Make sure that:

- The **name** properties match the column names from the table.
- The **ordinal** property matches their order in the primary key definition.
- The **type** of the primary key component matches (either partitioned or clustered).

Next, we will build a simple, three-argument constructor to help us instantiate new **WeatherPrimaryKey** objects:

```
public WeatherPrimaryKey(String stationId, int monthBucket,
```

```
        Instant timestamp) {
    this.stationId = stationId;

    this.monthBucket = monthBucket;

    this.timestamp = timestamp;

}
```

Finally, the last thing that our class needs is the **getter** and **setter** methods for each property:

```
public String getStationId() {

    return stationId;

}


public void setStationId(String stationId) {

    this.stationId = stationId;

}


public int getMonthBucket() {

    return monthBucket;

}


public void setMonthBucket(int monthBucket) {

    this.monthBucket = monthBucket;

}


public Instant getTimestamp() {

    return timestamp;

}


public void setTimestamp(Instant timestamp) {

    this.timestamp = timestamp;

}
```

WeatherEntity class

With that class finished, let us create a new class named **WeatherEntity** and make sure that it is a part of the **com.codewithjava21.weatherapp** package. It should have four imports, including the **Map type**, and the **Column**, **PrimaryKey**, and **Table** classes from the Spring Data Cassandra library:

```
package com.codewithjava21.weatherapp;


import java.util.Map;


import org.springframework.data.cassandra.core.mapping.Column;

import org.springframework.data.cassandra.core.mapping.PrimaryKey;

import org.springframework.data.cassandra.core.mapping.Table;


@Table("weather_by_station_by_month")

public class WeatherEntity {
```

In Spring Data, our entity classes directly map to database tables. Therefore, we will use the **@Table** annotation (with our table name) to indicate which table this class maps to. We will create properties for our primary key (using the **WeatherPrimaryKey** class) and each of our individual columns. The columns will be marked with the **@column** annotation, which will indicate their matching column name in Cassandra:

```
@PrimaryKey

private WeatherPrimaryKey primaryKey;


@Column("reading_icon")

private String readingIcon;


@Column("station_coordinates_lat")

private float stationCoordinatesLatitude;


@Column("station_coordinates_lon")

private float stationCoordinatesLongitude;


@Column("temperature_c")
```

```
private float temperatureCelsius;

@Column("wind_direction_deg")
private int windDirectionDegrees;

@Column("wind_speed_kmh")
private float windSpeedKMH;

@Column("wind_gust_kmh")
private float windGustKMH;

@Column("visibility_m")
private int visibilityM;

@Column("precipitation_last_hour")
private float precipitationLastHour;

@Column("cloud_cover")
private Map<Integer,String> cloudCover;
```

We will also need to create getters and setters for each of our properties, including the **primary key**.

> **Note: In the interest of brevity, we will not show the getter and setter definitions for this class, as there are several of them. At this point, we should know how to create getters and setters. For more information, refer the companion GitHub repository for the book.**

WeatherReading class

Next, we need to create a new class named **WeatherReading** inside the **com.codewithjava21. weatherapp** package. This is a simple **POJO** class that we will use for returning our weather data to the calling services:

```
package com.codewithjava21.weatherapp;


import java.time.Instant;
```

```
import java.util.Map;

public class WeatherReading {

    private String stationId;

    private int monthBucket;

    private Instant timestamp;

    private String readingIcon;

    private float stationCoordinatesLatitude;

    private float stationCoordinatesLongitude;

    private float temperatureCelsius;

    private int windDirectionDegrees;

    private float windSpeedKMH;

    private float windGustKMH;

    private int visibilityM;

    private float precipitationLastHour;

    private Map<Integer,String> cloudCover;
```

Similar to the **WeatherEntity** class, we will not list the getters and setters.

WeatherAppRepository interface

Next, we will create a new interface named **WeatherAppRepository** inside the **com.codewithjava21.weatherapp** package. Our interface will need two imports from the Spring Data framework, including the **CassandraRepository** and **Repository** classes:

```
package com.codewithjava21.weatherapp;

import org.springframework.data.cassandra.repository.CassandraRepository;

import org.springframework.stereotype.Repository;

@Repository

public interface WeatherAppRepository extends

        CassandraRepository<WeatherEntity,WeatherPrimaryKey> {
```

```
@Query("SELECT * FROM weather_by_station_by_month WHERE station_id=?0
AND month_bucket=?1 LIMIT 1")

List<WeatherEntity> findByStationIdAndMonthBucket(String stationId, int
monthBucket);

}
```

First, we will mark our interface with the **@Repository** annotation. Then, we will extend our interface to use the **CassandraRepository** class while passing our **WeatherEntity** and **WeatherPrimaryKey** classes as **type** arguments.

We are also going to define a custom **SELECT** query. Spring Data provides a default retrieval by the complete primary key. However, we only want to query with two parts of our primary key and restrict our results with **LIMIT**. Therefore, we will define a query method named **findByStationIdAndMonthBucket**, pass **stationId**, and **monthBucket** as parameters, and specify our exact query with the **@Query** annotation.

Building our response JSON objects

For the next parts of the application, we will go back to our **WeatherAppController** and its supporting classes. First we need to build a Java class to help us serialize the output from the NWS' latest weather JSON response into a POJO. If we recall the output from the service endpoint of **https://api.weather.gov/stations/kmsp/observations/latest**, it becomes apparent that we will need a few different types of object classes nested inside of each other.

Measurement class

If we examine the JSON returned from the service above, many of the measurements in the **properties** section have a standard format of **unitCode**, **value**, and **qualityControl**. We will skip the **qualityControl** property as it is not useful (to us). But we will need a **Measurement** class with properties for **unitCode** and **value**.

Create a new class named **Measurement** inside of the **com.codewithjava21.weatherapp** package. Our class will only have privately-scoped properties for **unitCode** and **value**, along with getters and setters for each:

```
package com.codewithjava21.weatherapp;


public class CloudLayer {

    private Measurement base;

    private String amount;
```

```
    public Measurement getBase() {

        return base;

    }


    public void setBase(Measurement base) {

        this.base = base;

    }


    public String getAmount() {

        return amount;

    }


    public void setAmount(String amount) {

        this.amount = amount;

    }

}
```

CloudLayer class

One of the more unique data structures under the **properties** section is the **CloudLayer** section. The **CloudLayer** section looks similar to the **Measurement** class, but it is named **base**. Between this and the **amount** property, we could build a class using our **Measurement** class.

Create a new class named **CloudLayer** inside of the **com.codewithjava21.weatherapp** package. It will have two **private** properties; a **Measurement** object named **base** and a **String** property named **amount**:

```
package com.codewithjava21.weatherapp;


public class CloudLayer {

    private Measurement base;

    private String amount;
```

```
    public Measurement getBase() {

        return base;

    }


    public void setBase(Measurement base) {

        this.base = base;

    }


    public String getAmount() {

        return amount;

    }


    public void setAmount(String amount) {

        this.amount = amount;

    }

}
```

Properties class

Now we should be able to build the **Properties** class. Create a new class named **Properties** inside the **com.codewithjava21.weatherapp** package. It will need a single import of **Instant** from Java's **time** library. We will build several privately-scoped properties on it, matching the **properties** JSON section from the web service call, including an array of **CloudLayer**:

```
package com.codewithjava21.weatherapp;


import java.time.Instant;


public class Properties {

    private String station;

    private Instant timestamp;

    private String icon;
```

```
private Measurement temperature;

private Measurement windDirection;

private Measurement windSpeed;

private Measurement windGust;

private Measurement visibility;

private Measurement precipitationLastHour;

private CloudLayer[] cloudLayers;
```

Similar to our **WeatherEntity** class, we will not show the definitions for the getter and setter methods for this class. But they need to be built.

Geometry class

One section of the NWS response JSON was named **Geometry**, and it had some information about our weather station. It had a **String** type named **type**, as well as a floating point array to hold the latitude and longitudinal coordinates of the station. We will build a new class named **Geometry** inside of the **com.codewithjava21.weatherapp** package with appropriate properties to match:

```
package com.codewithjava21.weatherapp;

public class Geometry {

    private String type;
    private float[] coordinates;

    public String getType() {
        return type;
    }

    public void setType(String type) {
        this.type = type;
    }

    public float[] getCoordinates() {
```

```
        return coordinates;
    }

    public void setCoordinates(float[] coordinates) {
        this.coordinates = coordinates;
    }
}
```

LatestWeather class

Finally, we have all the parts in place for us to build the main, root object class for the response JSON. Create a new class named **LatestWeather** inside of the **com.codewithjava21. weatherapp** package. It will have three privately-scoped properties for the station **id**, the station **geometry**, and the **properties**:

```
package com.codewithjava21.weatherapp;

public class LatestWeather {

    private String id;

    private Geometry geometry;

    private Properties properties;

    public String getId() {
        return id;
    }

    public void setId(String id) {
        this.id = id;
    }

    public Geometry getGeometry() {
        return geometry;
    }
}
```

```java
public void setGeometry(Geometry geometryCoordinates) {

    this.geometry = geometryCoordinates;

}


public Properties getProperties() {

    return properties;

}


public void setProperties(Properties properties) {

    this.properties = properties;

}

}
```

Weather application controller redux

And now, we can move back into our **WeatherApplicationController** class. First, we will build three methods. This first method will be scoped as **protected**, named **getBucket** and will return an **int** type. This method will generate our **month bucket** from the **timestamp** that we read in from the NWS.

Our method will essentially define a new **ZonedDateTime** object (new import required from **java.time**) from the **String timestamp** that we read in. We will then pull the **year** and **month** from it, build a string from that, and return it as an integer:

```java
protected int getBucket(Instant timestamp) {


    ZonedDateTime date = ZonedDateTime.parse(timestamp.toString());

    // parse date into year and month to create the month bucket

    Integer year = date.getYear();

    Integer month = date.getMonthValue();

    StringBuilder bucket = new StringBuilder(year.toString());


    if (month < 10) {

        bucket.append("0");
```

```
}
bucket.append(month);


return Integer.parseInt(bucket.toString());
}
```

One possible bug that can happen here, is that building an integer of **202307** (for July of 2023) could appear as **20237**. We will need to make sure that it is padded with a leading zero. After all, that is how we represent our dates. So, we have an if statement to check if month is less than **10**, and **append** a leading zero for us.

> Note: While we do want to protect our accessor methods (getters) from outside access, we will need to call the getBucket() method from our UI. Therefore, we will scope it as protected so that it is accessible from within our package.

The next method will need to map our **LatestWeather** object to the **WeatherEntity** class for the database. It will be a **private** method named **mapLatestWeatherToWeatherEntity** and accept parameters for a **weather** object of type **LatestWeather** and the **stationId** string. The method will begin by defining a **WeatherEntity** object **returnVal**, serializing our **timestamp**, and generating our bucket:

```
private WeatherEntity mapLatestWeatherToWeatherEntity(
        LatestWeather weather, String stationId) {

    WeatherEntity returnVal = new WeatherEntity();

    // use timestamp from response to create date
    Instant timestamp = weather.getProperties().getTimestamp();
    int bucket = getBucket(timestamp);

    // gen PK
    WeatherPrimaryKey key = new WeatherPrimaryKey(stationId,
            bucket, timestamp);

    returnVal.setPrimaryKey(key);
    returnVal.setReadingIcon(weather.getProperties().getIcon());
    returnVal.setStationCoordinatesLatitude(
```

```
        weather.getGeometry().getCoordinates()[0]);

    returnVal.setStationCoordinatesLongitude(

        weather.getGeometry().getCoordinates()[1]);

    returnVal.setTemperatureCelsius(

        weather.getProperties().getTemperature().getValue());

    returnVal.setWindDirectionDegrees((int)

        weather.getProperties().getWindDirection().getValue());

    returnVal.setWindGustKMH(

        weather.getProperties().getWindGust().getValue());

    returnVal.setPrecipitationLastHour(

        weather.getProperties().getPrecipitationLastHour()

        .getValue());
```

We will instantiate our **WeatherPrimaryKey** as key, and set that on **returnVal**, along with all the other properties. Finally, we will iterate through the cloud layers and build them into a map, set the **cloudMap** to **returnVal**, and return it:

```
    // process cloud layers

    CloudLayer[] clouds = weather.getProperties().getCloudLayers();

    Map<Integer,String> cloudMap = new HashMap<>();


    for (CloudLayer layer : clouds) {

        // measurements come back as floats, but we need ints

        cloudMap.put((int)layer.getBase().getValue(),

            layer.getAmount());

    }


    returnVal.setCloudCover(cloudMap);


    return returnVal;

}
```

For the last method, we will build a **private** method named **mapWeatherEntityToWeatherReading**. While our last method maps the raw response from the NWS endpoint to a Spring Data entity, this one maps the entity class to a POJO. This way, we can return **WeatherReading** class objects and prevent the calling application or user from having to know anything about our **WeatherPrimaryKey** class:

```
private WeatherReading mapWeatherEntityToWeatherReading(
        WeatherEntity entity) {

    WeatherReading returnVal = new WeatherReading();

    returnVal.setStationId(entity.getPrimaryKey().getStationId());
    returnVal.setMonthBucket(entity.getPrimaryKey().getMonthBucket());
    returnVal.setStationCoordinatesLatitude(
            entity.getStationCoordinatesLatitude());
    returnVal.setStationCoordinatesLongitude(
            entity.getStationCoordinatesLongitude());
    returnVal.setTimestamp(entity.getPrimaryKey().getTimestamp());
    returnVal.setTemperatureCelsius(entity.getTemperatureCelsius());
    returnVal.setWindSpeedKMH(entity.getWindSpeedKMH());
    returnVal.setWindDirectionDegrees(
            entity.getWindDirectionDegrees());
    returnVal.setWindGustKMH(entity.getWindGustKMH());
    returnVal.setReadingIcon(entity.getReadingIcon());
    returnVal.setVisibilityM(entity.getVisibilityM());
    returnVal.setPrecipitationLastHour(
            entity.getPrecipitationLastHour());
    returnVal.setCloudCover(entity.getCloudCover());

    return returnVal;

}
```

The **mapWeatherEntityToWeatherReading()** method is simple, as all it needs to do is a one-to-one property mapping between the two object classes.

With all the methods and object classes built and assembled, we can finally write our service endpoint method:

```
@PutMapping("/latest/station/{stationid}")

public ResponseEntity<WeatherReading> putLatestData(

    @PathVariable(value="stationid") String stationId) {


    LatestWeather response = restTemplate.getForObject(

            "https://api.weather.gov/stations/" + stationId

            + "/observations/latest",

            LatestWeather.class);


    // map latest reading to a WeatherEntity

    WeatherEntity weatherEntity =

            mapLatestWeatherToWeatherEntity(response, stationId);


    // save weather reading

    weatherRepo.save(weatherEntity);


    WeatherReading currentReading = mapWeatherEntityToWeatherReading(

            weatherEntity);


    return ResponseEntity.ok(currentReading);

}
```

Now, we will execute a **mvn clean install** on either the command line or from within our IDE.

> **Note: There may be an issue found during a mvn clean install with the autogenerated test in the project. As we are not using it, feel free to delete the src/test/java/com/codewithjava21/weatherapp/WeatherappApplicationTests.java file.**

To run our application, we should be able to click the **Run** button in our IDE (assuming that our run configuration is defined). It can also be run from the command line with Maven:

```
mvn spring-boot:run
```

Once the service comes up and runs, we can test it with our **helloworld** endpoint like we did before. Or, we can run a **PUT** operation with **curl**:

```
curl -X PUT http://127.0.0.1:8080/weather/latest/station/kmsp
```

```
{"primaryKey":{"stationId":"kmsp","monthBucket":202307,"timestamp":"202
3-07-17T22:53:00Z"},"readingIcon":"https://api.weather.gov/icons/land/
day/bkn?size=medium","stationCoordinatesLatitude":-93.22,"stationCo-
ordinatesLongitude":44.88,"temperatureCelsius":23.3,"windDirectionDe-
grees":330,"windSpeedKMH":0.0,"windGustKMH":0.0,"visibilityM":0,"precipi-
tationLastHour":0.0,"cloudCover":{"1520":"FEW","2130":"BKN"}}
```

By calling this service endpoint, a weather reading was:

- Produced by the latest data read from the NWS for the **kmsp** station.
- Saved into our Astra database.

If we go to the **CQL session** tab in Astra, we should be able to query the row that was just written:

```
token@cqlsh> use weatherapp ;
```

```
token@cqlsh:weatherapp> SELECT station_id, reading_timestamp, temperature_c
FROM weather_by_station_by_month ;
```

```
 station_id | reading_timestamp              | temperature_c

------------+--------------------------------+---------------

       kmsp | 2023-07-17 22:53:00.000000+0000 |          23.3
```

We will also write an endpoint to retrieve the latest weather entry by **stationId** and **monthBucket**. Our method will be named **getLatestData** and served on the service endpoint of **/latest/station{stationid}/month/{month}** as indicated by the **@GetMapping** annotation. The method will simply call the custom query method in our **WeatherRepository**, check for null, and return the result:

```
@GetMapping("/latest/station/{stationid}/month/{month}")

public ResponseEntity<WeatherReading> getLatestData(

        @PathVariable(value="stationid") String stationId,

        @PathVariable(value="month") int monthBucket) {
```

```
WeatherEntity recentWeather =

        weatherRepo.findByStationIdAndMonthBucket(

            stationId, monthBucket);


WeatherReading currentReading = mapWeatherEntityToWeatherReading(

        recentWeather);


if (currentReading != null) {

    return ResponseEntity.ok(currentReading);

} else {

    return ResponseEntity.notFound().build();

}

}
```

When running our service, we can call this endpoint using **curl** with a **GET** operation:

```
curl -X GET http://127.0.0.1:8080/weather/latest/station/kmsp/month/202307
```

```
{"primaryKey":{"stationId":"kmsp","monthBucket":202307,"timestamp":"202
3-07-18T00:53:00Z"},"readingIcon":"https://api.weather.gov/icons/land/
night/sct?size=medium","stationCoordinatesLatitude":-93.22,"stationCo-
ordinatesLongitude":44.88,"temperatureCelsius":21.7,"windDirectionDe-
grees":310,"windSpeedKMH":0.0,"windGustKMH":0.0,"visibilityM":0,"precipi-
tationLastHour":0.0,"cloudCover":{"1520":"FEW","2130":"SCT"}}
```

With our latest weather service working, we can now move on to building a simple front end.

Building web user interfaces

Designing and building web user interfaces can be an arduous task. The final result is often a combination of many languages and frameworks, including JavaScript, React. js, and CSS. Fortunately, the Vaadin framework allows Java developers to quickly build simple and functional user interfaces.

pom.xml redux

At this point, it is time to revisit the **pom.xml** file, and uncomment the **dependency** for the **vaadin-spring-boot-starter**:

```
<dependency>

    <groupId>com.vaadin</groupId>

    <artifactId>vaadin-spring-boot-starter</artifactId>

</dependency>
```

Weather application view

We will now create the UI for our weather application. To do this, we can create a new class named **WeatherMainView** inside of the **com.codewithjava21.weatherapp** package. Our class is going to have several imports, including ten from the Vaadin framework:

```
package com.codewithjava21.weatherapp;


import com.vaadin.flow.component.button.Button;

import com.vaadin.flow.component.button.ButtonVariant;

import com.vaadin.flow.component.Component;

import com.vaadin.flow.component.html.Image;

import com.vaadin.flow.component.orderedlayout.HorizontalLayout;

import com.vaadin.flow.component.orderedlayout.VerticalLayout;

import com.vaadin.flow.component.radiobutton.RadioButtonGroup;

import com.vaadin.flow.component.textfield.TextField;

import com.vaadin.flow.component.grid.Grid;

import com.vaadin.flow.router.Route;


import java.time.Instant;

import java.util.ArrayList;

import java.util.List;


import org.springframework.http.ResponseEntity;
```

```
@Route("")
```

```
public class WeatherMainView extends VerticalLayout {
```

After our imports are defined, we need to add the **@Route** annotation with an empty string as a parameter. It tells our web server that the page defined by this class is at the relative **root** of our web URL. Once the application is running, we simply need to browse to **http://127.0.0.1:8080/** and we should see our page.

Our class will also need to inherit the **VerticalLayout** class from Vaadin. Therefore, we should add it at the end of our class definition with the extends keyword.

Next, we have several privately-scoped properties that we need to define in our class. Most of the properties are Vaadin components that we will build into our UI. Text fields, radio buttons, images, and data grids will certainly help to round out the visual functionality of our application:

```
private Image iconImage = new Image();
```

```
private TextField stationId = new TextField("Station ID");
```

```
private TextField month = new TextField("Year/Month");
```

```
private TextField dateTime = new TextField("Date/Time");
```

```
private TextField temperature = new TextField("Temperature");
```

```
private TextField windSpeed = new TextField("Wind Speed");
```

```
private TextField windDirection = new TextField("Wind Direction");
```

```
private TextField visibility = new TextField("Visibility");
```

```
private TextField precipitationLastHour = new TextField(
        "Precipitation 1 hour");
```

```
private RadioButtonGroup<String> unitSelector =
        new RadioButtonGroup<>();
```

```
private Grid<Cloud> cloudGrid = new Grid<>(Cloud.class);
```

```
private WeatherAppController controller;
```

```
private record Cloud(int elevation, String desc) {
}
```

We will also define a **private** property for our **WeatherAppController**, as we will need to call its services. Additionally, we will create a record named **Cloud** to have an easier way to work with our cloud layer data.

Next, we will build our class constructor. Its lone parameter will be our **WeatherAppRepository**, as we need it to declare an instance of our controller. We will also set default values for the station **kmsp** and generate a **monthBucket** for the current date. With that complete, we can configure our **cloudGrid**, be sure to set appropriate sizes for the columns and the grid. We can also directly map our **elevation** and **desc** properties from our **Cloud** record:

```
public WeatherMainView(WeatherAppRepository repo) {

    controller = new WeatherAppController(repo);


    // set default values

    Integer monthBucket = controller.getBucket(Instant.now());

    month.setValue(monthBucket.toString());

    stationId.setValue("kmsp");


    // configure grid

    cloudGrid.addColumn(Cloud::elevation)

        .setWidth("100px")

        .setHeader("Elevation");

    cloudGrid.addColumn(Cloud::desc)

        .setWidth("150px")

        .setHeader("Description");

    cloudGrid.setWidth("250px");

    cloudGrid.setHeight("250px");


    // compose layout

    add(buildControls());

    add(buildStationDataView());

    add(buildTempPrecipView());
```

```
    add(buildCloudVisibilityView());

}
```

At the end of the constructor, we will assemble our page layout. As our class is inheriting the **Vaadin's VerticalLayout** class by default, any calls to the **add()** method will **stack** the returned components vertically. This means that any horizontal design needs to be done in the **buildControls()**, **buildStationDataView()**, **buildTempPrecipView()**, and **buildCloudVisibilityView()** methods, which we will build next.

Horizontal build methods

First, we will build a privately-scoped method named **buildControls** It will not have any parameters and will return a type of the **Component** class. In each of our **build** methods, we will start by instantiating a new **HorizontalLayout** object named **layout** We will use the layout object and return with our horizontally-placed components:

```
private Component buildControls() {

    HorizontalLayout layout = new HorizontalLayout();


    Button queryButton = new Button("Refresh");

    queryButton.addThemeVariants(ButtonVariant.LUMO_PRIMARY);

    layout.add(queryButton, buildUnitRadio());


    queryButton.addClickListener(click -> {

        refreshData();

    });


    return layout;

}
```

For this particular method, we are creating the **controls** for our UI. This includes a **Refresh** button which will call our **getLatestData()** method/endpoint on our controller (and ultimately executes a query on our database). In addition to assigning one of Vaadin's button themes, we will also create a **listener**. The **addClickListener()** method essentially tells Vaadin that any time the button is clicked, it should call the **refreshData()** method (which we will build later on). The layout **add()** method is where we add our **queryButton** to our layout, as well as the result of our **buildUnitRadio()** method (which we will build next).

The **buildUnitRadio** method builds a selector or **radio** button This particular radio button will allow us to switch our display between **Metric** and **Imperial** units of measure. Essentially, we will label it **Units** and define its items as **Celsius/Metric** and **Fahrenheit/Imperial**. We will also set the initial, default value to **Cesius/Metric**:

```java
private Component buildUnitRadio() {

    HorizontalLayout layout = new HorizontalLayout();


    unitSelector.setLabel("Units");

    unitSelector.setItems("Celsius/Metric", "Fahrenheit/Imperial");

    unitSelector.setValue("Celsius/Metric");


    unitSelector.addValueChangeListener(click -> {

        refreshData();

    });


    layout.add(unitSelector);


    return layout;

}
```

Our **unitSelector** button will also have a listener defined. Essentially, any time it is clicked (regardless of what the final value is), we want our **refreshData()** method to be called.

Next, we will build the **buildStationView** method. This method will assemble the data for our weather station, as well as the current icon image and time components. It is relatively simple, compared to most of the others. Essentially, we are going to add our **private stationId**, **month**, **iconImage**, and **dateTime** components to this **HorizontalLayout**, and return it:

```java
private Component buildStationDataView() {

    HorizontalLayout layout = new HorizontalLayout();


    layout.add(stationId, month, iconImage, dateTime);


    return layout;

}
```

Next, we can build our **buildTempPrecipView** method. This method will construct the visual elements for the current temperature, wind, and precipitation data:

```
private Component buildTempPrecipView() {

    HorizontalLayout layout = new HorizontalLayout();


    layout.add(temperature, precipitationLastHour,
            windSpeed, windDirection);


    return layout;

}
```

Our final **build** method is the **buildCloudLayerView** method. It is simply adding our **cloudGrid** and **visibility** text field to its **HorizontalLayout**:

```
private Component buildCloudVisibilityView() {

    HorizontalLayout layout = new HorizontalLayout();

    layout.add(cloudGrid, visibility);

    return layout;

}
```

Before we get further, we need a few **private** methods to compute our unit conversions between **Metric** and **Imperial** units:

```
private float computeFahrenheit(float celsius) {

    return (celsius * 9 / 5) + 32;

}


private float computeMiles(float kilometers) {

    return (kilometers * 1.609F);

}


private int computeFeet(int meters) {

    return (int)(meters * 3.281F);

}
```

```
private float computeInches(float millimeters) {

    return millimeters / 25.4F;

}
```

We also need a method to convert our wind direction from degrees into a string. This will assign our **windDirection** text field a compass direction based on its value on a **360** degree spectrum:

```
private String convertWindDirection(Integer degrees) {

    StringBuilder returnVal = new StringBuilder();

    if ((degrees > 338 && degrees <= 360) ||
            degrees >= 0 && degrees < 23) {

        returnVal.append("North");
    } else if (degrees > 22 && degrees < 68) {

        returnVal.append("Northeast");
    } else if (degrees > 67 && degrees < 113) {

        returnVal.append("East");
    } else if (degrees > 112 && degrees < 158) {

        returnVal.append("Southeast");
    } else if (degrees > 157 && degrees < 203) {

        returnVal.append("South");
    } else if (degrees > 202 && degrees < 248) {

        returnVal.append("Southwest");
    } else if (degrees > 247 && degrees < 293) {

        returnVal.append("West");
    } else {

        returnVal.append("Northwest");
    }


    return returnVal.toString();
```

```
}
```

Finally, we can build our **refreshData** method. This method will make the call to our service layer, map the response data to the UI, and implement any additional logic that we need. First, we will call the **getLatestData()** method on our **controller**. We will then set the data to a **WeatherReading** object named **latestWeather**, and then assign many of its properties to local variables (this way, they are easier to work with):

```
private void refreshData() {

    ResponseEntity<WeatherReading> latest = controller.getLatestData(

            stationId.getValue(), Integer.parseInt(month.getValue()));

    WeatherReading latestWeather = latest.getBody();


    Instant time = latestWeather.getTimestamp();

    Float temp = latestWeather.getTemperatureCelsius();

    Float windSpd = latestWeather.getWindSpeedKMH();

    String iconURL = latestWeather.getReadingIcon();

    Integer windDir = latestWeather.getWindDirectionDegrees();

    Integer visib = latestWeather.getVisibilityM();

    Float precip = latestWeather.getPrecipitationLastHour();
```

Next, we will check the value of our **unit** radio button. If it is not equal to **Celsius/Metric**, we will convert our **temperature**, **wind speed**, **visibility**, and **precipitation** into Imperial units. After that, we will set values for most of the individual components on the UI:

```
if (!unitSelector.getValue().equals("Celsius/Metric")) {

    temp = computeFahrenheit(temp);

    windSpd = computeMiles(windSpd);

    visib = computeFeet(visib);

    precip = computeInches(precip);

}


temperature.setValue(temp.toString());

windSpeed.setValue(windSpd.toString());
```

```
precipitationLastHour.setValue(precip.toString());

dateTime.setValue(time.toString());

iconImage.setSrc(iconURL);
```

Next, we will check if our wind speed and **visibility** are greater than zero. If our weather data indicates that visibility is zero, we will display the text **Unlimited**. Additionally, we need to show the wind direction only if the wind speed is greater than zero. We also do not need to convert degrees to a compass direction if wind is zero:

```
if (visib > 0) {

    visibility.setValue(visib.toString());

} else {

    visibility.setValue("Unlimited");

}


if (windSpd > 0) {

    windDirection.setValue(convertWindDirection(windDir));

    windDirection.setVisible(true);

} else {

    windDirection.setVisible(false);

}
```

Finally, we will process our cloud layers. We will iterate through them and (after checking if we need to convert to Imperial units) build a list using the **Cloud** record. The resulting list clouds is then easily **set** to populate the grid:

```
    List<Cloud> clouds = new ArrayList<>();


    for (int key : latestWeather.getCloudCover().keySet()) {


        String description = latestWeather.getCloudCover().get(key);

        if (!unitSelector.getValue().equals("Celsius/Metric")) {

            key = computeFeet(key);

        }
```

```
        Cloud cloud = new Cloud(key,description);

        clouds.add(cloud);

    }


    cloudGrid.setItems(clouds);

}
```

Running the weather application

With all of that complete, we should be able to run our application. Click the **Run** button inside our IDE, or execute a `mvn spring-boot:run` from the command line.

Once the application is running, navigate in a browser to **http://127.0.0.1:8080/**. Once there, our web page should be visible with most of its data empty. Click on the **Refresh** button and see the output as shown in *Figure 8.7*.

If nothing happens when the **Refresh** button is clicked, check the table to ensure it has data. We might have to run a **PUT** operation (from the command line) to get a recent weather data row into the table:

```
curl -X PUT http://127.0.0.1:8080/weather/latest/station/kmsp
```

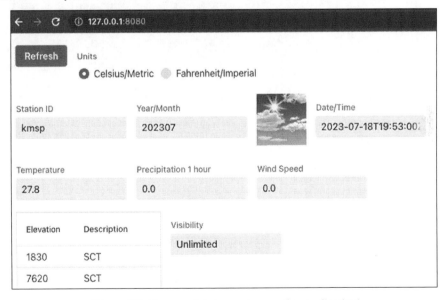

Figure 8.7: *Our completed, running weather application!*

The point of this section was to show how to build a simple front end user interface for an application using only Java. For our requirements of displaying our weather data, Vaadin worked perfectly.

Conclusion

In this chapter, we discussed many aspects of building web-based applications. We utilized three frameworks, Spring Boot, Spring Data, and Vaadin to make this easier. In the end, we could set up a functioning web-based Weather Application. We also put the ideas behind loose coupling into practice. Instead of building a giant, interdependent, monolithic application, we followed the MVC design pattern, which kept the functional parts of our application separate from each other.

The point to understand is that a web front-end view should really only care about interacting with and displaying data to the user. The data model or DAL should only care about storing and retrieving data. Those two layers should not have to know anything about each other. This is how applications can be built without their components being interdependent on each other. Keeping those application layers independent also allows their underlying infrastructure to be scaled independently.

In the next chapter, we will explore working with graphics in Java. We will cover simple approaches to drawing simple shapes, such as lines, squares, and circles. We will also show techniques to animate shapes as well.

Points to remember

- Restful services are lightweight, purposeful, scalable, stateless, and loosely-coupled.
- Common restful HTTP operations are **GET**, **POST**, **PUT**, and **DELETE**.
- Restful requests and responses have individual components, such as a body and a header.
- Designing an application with the MVC pattern is a great way to keep your model, view, and controller separate from each other.
- Many databases have different permission levels for different functions. Remember that Spring Data usually needs permission to modify the database schema.
- With Apache Cassandra, modeling your partitions with a time component or **bucket** is a great strategy to keep them from growing too big.
- It is often a good idea to build a **Plain Old Java Object** (**POJO**) along with a Spring Data entity class. This way, the POJO can be returned to calling services and users, and not expose the underlying data model.
- Vaadin classes typically extend the **VerticalLayout** class and assemble the remaining components in multiple **HorizontalLayout** classes.
- Some Vaadin components can be configured with **listeners** which will perform certain functions when a user input action (mouse click or key press) is detected.

CHAPTER 9
Graphics in Java

Introduction

In this chapter, we will learn how to program **graphics** with Java. Graphics programming is simultaneously one of the most fun and difficult areas of computing. Many people study graphics programming because they want to get into video games. However, it is heavily steeped in logic and mathematics, making it a great teaching tool!

Here, we get to be creative and have fun while learning. We will start with some simple lines and shapes and advance to some animation. At the end of the chapter, we will build the clone of a classic **Atari** game from the late 1970s.

Structure

In this chapter, we will cover the following topics:

- Simple graphics with AWT and Swing
- Animation
- Java Breakout

Objectives

The aim of this chapter is to build an introductory level of knowledge around using simple graphics techniques. To reach that goal, our objectives for this chapter are:

- Learn how to draw simple graphics elements.
- Understand how to animate visible objects.
- Learn how to control the pace and flow of an application using a virtual thread.
- Learn how to build logic to handle shape collisions and user input.

Simple graphics with AWT and Swing

To implement graphics in Java, we are going to use classes from the **Abstract Window Toolkit (AWT)** and Swing libraries. The AWT library has been around for a while; the Swing library has improved upon it and also offers some additional functionalities.

> **Note: The JavaFX library was created to improve upon the capabilities of both AWT and Swing. However, readers will benefit from exposure to AWT and Swing, as many enterprises today still rely on code from those libraries.**

SimpleDraw class

Let us create a new Java class named **SimpleDraw**. Make sure that it is in a package named **chapter9** and that it has a **main** method. This class will need a single **import**, known as Swing's **JFrame** class:

```
package chapter9;


import javax.swing.JFrame;


public class SimpleDraw {


    public static void main(String[] args) {
```

Inside our **main()** method, we will instantiate a **new JFrame()** named **frame**. We will then set some initial properties on our **frame** object:

```
JFrame frame = new JFrame();


frame.setDefaultCloseOperation(JFrame.EXIT_ON_CLOSE);

frame.setTitle("Simple Drawings");
```

These properties are fairly simple. We want our application to stop when the window is closed, and we want to set the title to **"Simple Drawings"**.

MyPanel class

Next, we will create a new class named **MyPanel** inside the **chapter9** package. It should not have a **main** method. Our class will have several imports, including the **JPanel** class from Swing, the **ImageIO** class from the **ImageIO** library, as well as the **BufferedImage**, **Color**, **Dimension**, **Graphics**, and **Graphics2D** classes from AWT. Our class should also extend the **JPanel** class, and it should start out by generating a **serialVersionUID**:

```
package chapter9;


import java.awt.Color;

import java.awt.Dimension;

import java.awt.Graphics;

import java.awt.Graphics2D;

import java.awt.image.BufferedImage;


import java.io.File;

import java.io.IOException;


import javax.imageio.ImageIO;


import javax.swing.JPanel;


public class MyPanel extends JPanel {

    private static final long serialVersionUID =

            5433149762760327082L;


    private BufferedImage logo;
```

We also want a **private** class variable named **logo** of type **BufferedImage**. This will be used for drawing a PNG image on our panel.

Next, we need to create a constructor for the **MyPanel** class. This constructor will perform some necessary tasks to build our **JPanel**. This includes setting the size of our window and the background color, allowing our window to accept modal focus (be selected):

```java
public MyPanel() {

    this.setPreferredSize(new Dimension(800, 600));

    this.setBackground(Color.black);

    this.setFocusable(true);


    logo = loadImage("data/bpb.png", 100, 100);

}
```

> **Note: For the loadImage() method to work, the bpb.png image file needs to be in the main project's data/ directory. This file can be downloaded from the online assets available for this book.**

We will have an example in this program that displays a pre-built PNG image. To do that, we need to create a **private** method named **loadImage** (referenced in the code above). The **loadImage()** method should take a (**String**) directory path to the file, as well as parameters for the **width** and **height** to **scale** the **image** to:

```java
private BufferedImage loadImage(String imagePath, int width,

        int height) {

BufferedImage scaledImage = null;


    try {

        // load image

        File imgFile = new File(imagePath);

        BufferedImage image = ImageIO.read(imgFile);

        // scale image

        scaledImage = new BufferedImage(width, height,

                image.getType());

        Graphics2D g2 = scaledImage.createGraphics();
```

```
        g2.drawImage(image, 0, 0, width, height, null);

        g2.dispose();


    } catch (IOException ex) {

        ex.printStackTrace();

    }


    return scaledImage;

}
```

Note: Scaling the image is important because we want to ensure it will fit on our panel with the other graphics elements.

Essentially, the **loadImage()** method uses a **try**/**catch** to handle the case where the image file cannot be located. The image is read from the disk into a **BufferedImage** object named **image**. It is then scaled by being set to a new **BufferedImage** named **scaledImage**, which is used to create a local **Graphics2D** object named **g2**. We then call **g2**'s **drawImage()** method to **draw image** onto **scaledImage**. We then return **scaledImage** so that it is saved in the **logo** variable and can easily be drawn onto our panel later.

With our constructor and image loader complete, we can now build a publicly-scoped method named **paintComponent** with alone parameter of a **Graphics** object. The **paintComponent()** method is inherited, so we are overriding it here. We will start by calling the same method in our superclass. This will make sure that the options we set in the constructor are enforced:

```
public void paintComponent(Graphics g) {

    super.paintComponent(g);

    Graphics2D g2 = (Graphics2D)g;
```

We will also cast our **Graphics** object into a **Graphics2D** object named **g2**. The **g2** library has most of the drawing tools that we will be using. Let us start by drawing a single, cyan-colored line:

```
g2.setColor(Color.CYAN);

g2.drawLine(100, 100, 700, 500);
```

The **setColor()** method allows you to create a new color or use any of the twelve predefined colors, as shown in *Table 9.1*:

Black
Blue
Cyan
Dark Gray
Green
Light Gray
Magenta
Orange
Pink
Red
White
Yellow

Table 9.1: List of predefined colors in the AWT Color class.

We can then draw a line. Our line will be drawn from coordinates **100,100** to **700,500**. It is important to note that the panel's coordinates start at **0,0** in the upper-left corner of the window. Therefore, our line will start at **100** pixels to the right and **100** pixels down. It will continue in a right-downward direction until it has reached **700** pixels to the right and **500** pixels downward, as shown in *Figure 9.1*:

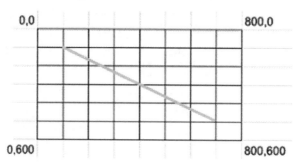

Figure 9.1: A visual depiction of the frame coordinates and our cyan-colored line.

Now, let us go back to our **SimpleDraw** class. Add the following to the end of our **main()** method code:

```
MyPanel panel = new MyPanel();

frame.add(panel);

frame.pack();

frame.setVisible(true);
```

Here, we are instantiating our **MyPanel** class as an object named **panel**. We are then adding **panel** to our **frame** object. Additionally, we will call the **pack()** method on **frame**, as this will help ensure that all of the contents within the **frame** are sized appropriately. Finally, we will instruct the **frame** to be visible.

At this point, if we run our code, we should see an *800x600* pixel window appear with a black background. Our cyan line should start in the upper left corner and run toward the lower right corner. We can stop our program simply by closing the window.

Let us return to the **MyPanel** class. After drawing the cyan line, we will draw a magenta line that is parallel to it:

```
g2.setColor(Color.MAGENTA);

g2.drawLine(100, 200, 700, 600);
```

> **Note: A frame can support draw operations at coordinates that are up to and beyond its maximum size definition. However, even though the results are *out of frame* and not viewable, they still consume memory.**

Additionally, we can draw squares and rectangles using the **drawRect()** method. The parameters are the x-coordinate, y-coordinate, and then the desired width and height of the shape. Let us draw a green, *100x100* pixel square:

```
g2.setColor(Color.GREEN);

g2.drawRect(600, 100, 100, 100);
```

This method should draw the outline of a green square. If we wanted that square to be filled in, we could replace it with a call to the **fillRect()** method:

```
g2.fillRect(600, 100, 100, 100);
```

We can also draw a square or rectangle with rounded corners. The parameters of the **fillRoundRect()** method are the same, except for two new parameters that indicate the **width** and **height** of the **arc**:

```
g2.setColor(Color.BLUE);

g2.fillRoundRect(400, 100, 100, 100, 50, 50);
```

> **Note: Setting height, width, arc height and arc width to the same value for the fillRoundRect() method will draw a circle!**

As indicated in the note above, the **fillRoundRect()** method can draw a circle. However, it is much easier to draw circles using the **drawOval()** and **fillOval()** methods. Both methods take four parameters: the x-coordinate (**coordX**), y-coordinate (**coordY**), **width**, and **height**. To draw a circle (instead of an oval) the **width** and **height** should be set to the desired pixel diameter of the circle. Now, we will draw a purple circle with a diameter of **100** pixels at coordinates **100,400**:

```
g2.setColor(new Color(128,0,192));
```

```
g2.drawOval(100, 400, 100, 100);
```

To draw a filled-in circle, we can replace **drawOval()** with the **fillOval()** method:

```
g2.fillOval(100, 400, 100, 100);
```

Note that purple is not one of the predefined colors, so we had to create it by instantiating a new object of the **Color** class. It has a few different constructors available, but we used the constructor with three integer parameters for values of **0** to **255** for the colors red, green, and blue, respectively. For our shade purple, we used the following values:

- **Red: 128**
- **Green: 0**
- **Blue: 192**

> **Note: If a project requires something other than one of the twelve predefined colors, generating a new RGB color with a value of 0 to 255 for red, green, and blue yields more than 16.5 million possible colors.**

A list of common colors and their RGB codes can be found in the appendices.

Next, consider the image that we loaded and scaled earlier. We will now use it to demonstrate how to draw a PNG or JPG image on to our panel:

```
g2.drawImage(logo, 250, 400, null);
```

The **Graphics2D drawImage()** method accepts a **BufferedImage** object, X-coordinate (**coordX**), Y-coordinate (**coordY**), and an **ImageObserver** as parameters. We will not use an **ImageObserver** object, so we will just set that to **null**.

Running our completed code should produce something similar to what is shown in *Figure 9.2*:

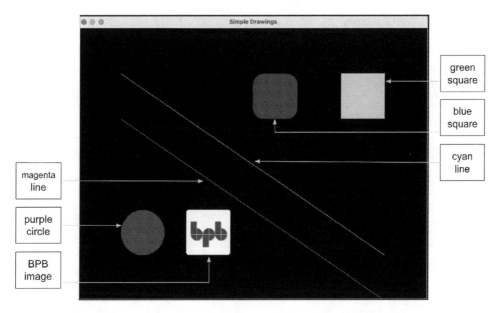

Figure 9.2: A screenshot of the output generated by our SimpleDraw program.

Animation

Now that we understand the basics of drawing simple shapes on a **JPanel**, we will now learn how to animate them. Here, we will build a simple animation of the inner planets of our solar system orbiting around the Sun.

Planet class

To start, we first create a new Java POJO class named **Planet**. This class should be inside the **chapter9** package and should not have a **main** method. Our **Planet** class is going to require the **Color** class from the AWT library to be imported, and it will have the following privately-scoped properties:

- **int coordX**
- **int coordY**
- **int degree**
- **int diameter**
- **int distance**
- **int speed**
- **Color color**

Let us create the **Planet** class:

```
package chapter9;

import java.awt.Color;

public class Planet {

    private int coordX;

    private int coordY;

    private int degree;

    private int diameter;

    private int distance;

    private int speed;


    private Color color;
```

Next, we can build the **Planet** constructor. It should accept four parameters: An AWT Color, and three integers for **diameter**, **orbit**, and **speed** respectively:

```
public Planet(Color color, int diameter, int orbit, int speed) {

    this.color = color;

    this.diameter = diameter;

    this.speed = speed;

    this.distance = orbit * 100;

    this.degree = 0;

}
```

We will use **color**, **diameter**, and **speed** to set the like-named class properties. All planets will start at **0** degree (out of **360** for a complete orbit). The **orbit** parameter will be a whole number representing a sequential index of **orbit** tracks around the Sun, with possible values of **1** to **4**. The lower the orbit, the closer the planet is to the Sun. We will use **orbit** to compute the **distance** from the Sun by multiplying it times **100** pixels.

We will need a new, **private** method to compute the planet's next X,Y coordinates based on its current degree in its circular **orbit**. We will name this method **computeNewXY**. First, we will convert degrees into radians by multiplying the **degree** property by *Pi/180*. Then, we can easily compute our new X,Y coordinates by multiplying either the Cosine (for X) or Sine (for Y) of our radians by our **distance** property:

```java
private void computeNewXY() {

    double radians = degree * Math.PI / 180;

    coordX = (int) (distance * Math.cos(radians));

    coordY = (int) (distance * Math.sin(radians));

}
```

Note that we are computing our X,Y coordinates relative to another position, which will be addressed in the method **computeNewXY()**. Next, we also need a **private** method to compute the radius of the planet. This is easily accomplished as we have the planet's diameter:

```java
private int getRadius() {

    return diameter / 2;

}
```

Our first **public** method will be the **update** method. This method does not accept any parameters, and will be called to compute our planet's next movement along its **orbit**:

```java
public void update() {

    degree -= speed;

    if (degree < 0) {

        degree += 360;

    }

    computeNewXY();

}
```

Essentially, our planet will be moving in a counter-clockwise motion. Hence we will be subtracting the **speed** property from the current value of **degree**. The **update()** method ensures that our **degree** property always has a valid value between **0** and **359**. Once our new **degree** is computed, it then calls the **computeNewXY()** method we wrote above.

Finally, we have the getters for our properties. We do not need to build setter methods, as we should not need to modify any of our properties from outside of the class. The only getters worth noting are the **getCoordX()** and **getCoordY()** methods. This is because we adjusted our X,Y coordinates to account for the point of drawing being different from the center. Therefore, we need to subtract the radius from both X and Y to center the **orbit** properly:

```java
public int getCoordX() {

    return coordX - getRadius();

}


public int getCoordY() {

    return coordY - getRadius();

}
```

With the remaining properties, getter methods will simply return the property, and we are finished with the **Planet** class.

SolarSystem class

Create a new Java class named **SolarSystem**. It should be inside the **chapter9** package, and it should not have a **main** class. The **SolarSystem** class will have seven imports including **JPanel** from the Swing library, **List** and **ArrayList** from the **util** library, and then **Color**, **Dimension**, **Graphics**, and **Graphics2D** from the AWT library. The **SolarSystem** class will also extend the **JPanel** class, and it will implement the **Runnable** interface:

```java
package chapter9;


import java.awt.Color;

import java.awt.Dimension;

import java.awt.Graphics;

import java.awt.Graphics2D;


import java.util.ArrayList;

import java.util.List;


import javax.swing.JPanel;


public class SolarSystem extends JPanel implements Runnable {
```

Implementing the **Runnable** class will enable our **SolarSystem** class objects to run as threads. Threads can be of big help in games or graphics applications, as they give the developer more control over application behavior, including setting how fast the panel is refreshed.

After generating a **serialVersionUID**, we will define several properties. First, we will limit our animation to **60 frames per second**. The variable is named **fPS** and instantiated as a constant (using the **final** keyword) integer with a value of **60**. We will also define properties for the size and middle of the panel, as well as a **List<Planet>** and a **panelThread** of type **Thread**:

```java
private static final long serialVersionUID = -6923126786235441890L;


private final int fPS = 60; // frames per second


private int panelWidth;

private int panelHeight;

private int middleWidth;

private int middleHeight;


private List<Planet> planetList;


private Thread panelThread;
```

Note: Both platform threads and virtual threads are operated by the Thread class.

We will now build two constructors for our **SolarSystem** class. One constructor will accept a **width** and **height** (as integers) to indicate the size of the panel. The other will be a no-argument constructor which simply calls the other:

```java
public SolarSystem() {
    this(1024,1024);
}


public SolarSystem(int width, int height) {
    panelWidth = width;
    panelHeight = height;
    middleWidth = panelWidth / 2;
```

```
        middleHeight = panelHeight / 2;

        panelThread = Thread.ofVirtual()
                .name("solarSystemThread")
                .unstarted(this);

        this.setPreferredSize(new Dimension(panelWidth, panelHeight));
        this.setBackground(Color.black);
        this.setFocusable(true);

        this.planetList = new ArrayList<>();
        // mercury
        planetList.add(new Planet(Color.DARK_GRAY, 20, 1, 5));
        // venus
        planetList.add(new Planet(Color.GRAY, 48, 2, 4));
        // earth
        planetList.add(new Planet(Color.BLUE, 50, 3, 3));
        // mars
        planetList.add(new Planet(Color.RED, 25, 4, 2));
}
```

Our **main** constructor will start by setting properties for the panel dimensions, including the middle. Then, it instantiates **panelThread** as a virtual thread with the name **solarSystemThread**, and sets it to use this class as **unstarted**. Next, it sets the panel size and background color and allows it to achieve modal window focus. Finally, it instantiates the **planetList**, and adds new **Planets** for **mercury**, **venus**, **earth**, and **mars**.

Next, we will define the **run** method. This method is inherited from the **Thread** class, and we are required to override it. Our **run()** method is fairly simple. We will check if **panelThread** is alive (with the **isAlive()** method), and then call our **update()** and **repaint()** methods. Finally, we will invoke the **sleep()** method from the **Thread** class, to pause the application for a short time (one-sixtieth of a second).

```
@Override
public void run() {
```

```
    while (panelThread.isAlive()) {

        update();

        repaint();

        try {

            Thread.sleep(1000/fPS);

        } catch (InterruptedException e) {

            e.printStackTrace();

        }

    }

}
```

We will then build the privately-scoped **update()** method. The **update()** method iterates through the **Planet** objects in **planetList** and calls their **public update()** methods. This recomputes each planet's position before they are repainted on the panel:

```
private void update() {

    for (Planet planet : planetList) {

        planet.update();

    }

}
```

Next, we will build a new, **public** method named **paintComponent**. This method is called when the AWT Component **repaint()** method is called (from the **run()** method above). Similar to what we did in the **MyPanel** class, this method does the actual drawing and coloring. Once we call the same method in our superclass and instantiate a **Graphics2D** object, we start by drawing the Sun:

```
public void paintComponent(Graphics g) {

    super.paintComponent(g);

    Graphics2D g2 = (Graphics2D)g;

    // draw sun
```

```
int diameter = 48;

int radius = diameter / 2;


g2.setColor(Color.YELLOW);

g2.fillOval(middleWidth - radius, middleHeight - radius,

        diameter, diameter);


// draw planets

for (Planet planet : planetList) {

    g2.setColor(planet.getColor());

    g2.fillOval(middleWidth + planet.getCoordX(),

            middleHeight + planet.getCoordY(),

            planet.getDiameter(), planet.getDiameter());

}


g2.dispose();

}
```

After drawing the Sun, we iterate through **planetList** and use the data on each **planet** object to draw them in their new position. Finally, we dispose of the **Graphics2D g2** object.

Before moving on to our **main** class, we need to build one last method. The **start()** method will allow **panelThread** to start, thus initiating the loop that we built in the **run()** method above:

```
public void start() {

    panelThread.start();

}
```

Our code for the **SolarSystem** class is now complete, and we can move on to the **DrawPlanets** class.

DrawPlanets class

We can put all of this together by building a new Java class named **DrawPlanets**. This class will be in the **chapter9** package and should have a **main** method. The **DrawPlanets** class will have a single import of the **JFrame** from the **Swing** library:

```
package chapter9;


import javax.swing.JFrame;


public class DrawPlanets {
```

Our **main** method will instantiate a **JFrame** object named **frame**. Similar to what we did with the **SimpleDrawClass**, we will set our **frame** properties to ensure that it closes properly and has the name **"Planet Orbits"**:

```
public static void main(String[] args) {

    JFrame frame = new JFrame();

    frame.setDefaultCloseOperation(JFrame.EXIT_ON_CLOSE);

    frame.setTitle("Planet Orbits");

    SolarSystem panel = new SolarSystem();

    frame.add(panel);

    frame.pack();

    frame.setVisible(true);

    panel.start();

}
```

We will then instantiate a **SolarSystem** object named **panel**, add **panel** to **frame**, call the **pack()** method, and ensure it is visible. Finally, we will call the panel's **start()** method to trigger the virtual thread to begin.

Running the **DrawPlanets** class should produce a window with planets rotating around the Sun, similar to *Figure 9.3*:

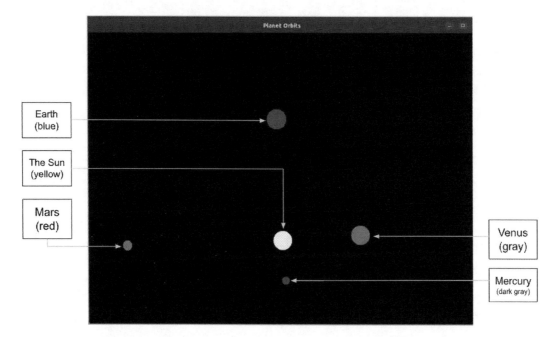

Figure 9.3: *The DrawPlanets class running, showing Earth, Mars, Venus, and Mercury orbiting around the Sun.*

Java Breakout

The period of the late 1970s and early 1980s was certainly an interesting time for the video games industry. Arcade games came along first, and soon afterward, early video game consoles appeared in homes. The foundation of the video game boom of the time was built on classic titles such as Atari's **Breakout**.

> **History of Breakout**
>
> Breakout was first built as an arcade game by Atari in 1976. The project was given to a young game designer named *Steve Jobs*. Jobs described the game to his friend, *Steve Wozniak*, and contracted him to engineer the game. They completed it in just four days (*Hanson 2015*), and legend is that the pair did not sleep during the project. A few months later, *Steve Jobs* and *Steve Wozniak* co-founded a company that we all know as *Apple Inc*.

We will build a clone of Breakout called **Java Breakout**. Java Breakout is a one-player game where the player controls a paddle to redirect a ball at an array of multi-colored bricks. The object of the game is for the player to break all of the bricks.

pom.xml

We will create a new, simple **Maven** project. The project should have the following **properties**:

- **Group ID: com.codewithjava21**
- **Artifact ID: javabreakout**
- **Name: JavaBreakout**

Once the project is created, edit the resulting **pom.xml** file and add the following **properties**:

```
<properties>

    <java.version>21</java.version>

    <maven.compiler.source>21</maven.compiler.source>

    <maven.compiler.target>21</maven.compiler.target>

</properties>
```

> Note: The <properties> section is a first-level element just inside the <project> element.

Once the project is created, we can start building the application classes.

Ball class

We need a class to govern the behavior of the ball. To that end, we will create a new Java class named **Ball**, inside the **javabreakout** package. This class should not have a **main** method. The **Ball** class will need to import the **Random** class, and create a few object properties:

```
package javabreakout;

import java.util.Random;

public class Ball {

    private final int maxSpeed = 8;

    private final int oneThird = maxSpeed / 3;


    private boolean movingUp;
```

```java
    private boolean movingLeft;

    private int ballSizeOffset;

    private int ballX;

    private int ballY;

    private int ballSize;

    private int hSpeed;

    private int vSpeed;
```

We will need integer properties to store the ball's size, coordinates, and speed. It will also be important to know which direction the ball is traveling in, so we will create two **boolean** properties of **movingUp** and **movingLeft**. We will also need a constant integer of **maxSpeed** which we will set to a value of **8**. Likewise, we will need a constant integer for one-third of **maxSpeed**, which is computed as **maxSpeed** divided by a value of **3**.

> Note: The idea of reducing the speed by one-third was implemented before the optimal value for maxSpeed was determined to be 8. Technically, in this scenario, the variable oneThird will actually hold a value equal to one-quarter of the maxSpeed.

Our constructor for the **Ball** class will accept parameters for **size**, the **width** of the panel, the **height** of the bricks, as well as the **height** of the space above the bricks. The last three parameters help determine the starting position of the ball. Its starting location should be in the middle of the screen, and below the bricks. We will take care of these computations in the constructor:

```java
public Ball(int size, int panelWidth, int brickHeightx8,
        int brickBuffer) {
    ballSize = size;
    ballSizeOffset = (size / 2) + 1;

    ballX = panelWidth / 2;
    ballY = brickHeightx8 + brickBuffer + 10;

    // starting speed and set angle (45 degrees)
    hSpeed = maxSpeed;
    vSpeed = maxSpeed;
```

```
    // starting direction

    Random leftRightDirection = new Random();

    movingLeft = leftRightDirection.nextBoolean();

    movingUp = false;

}
```

Likewise, we will also set the starting angle for the ball to be **45** degrees. We can control this by setting both the ball's horizontal and vertical speed to the **maxSpeed**. We will also randomly determine whether or not the ball is initially moving left or right.

Next, we will build the **update()** method. This method will simply move the ball by the ball's speed. Additionally, it will add or subtract the speed depending on whether or not the ball is moving in a specific direction:

```
public void update() {

    if (movingLeft) {

        ballX -= hSpeed;

    } else {

        ballX += hSpeed;

    }

    if (movingUp) {

        ballY -= hSpeed;

    } else {

        ballY += vSpeed;

    }

}
```

The angle of the ball can change. Therefore, we have two methods for controlling the angle of the ball. Essentially, we will add or subtract the computed value of the **oneThird** property to increase or decrease the angle:

```
public void increaseAngle() {

    if (vSpeed - oneThird > 1) {
```

```
        // don't want it to get too low (flat)

        hSpeed += oneThird;

        vSpeed -= oneThird;

    }

}


public void decreaseAngle() {

    if (hSpeed - oneThird > 1) {

        // don't want it to get too low (vertical)

        hSpeed -= oneThird;

        vSpeed += oneThird;

    }

}
```

When the ball hits the ceiling, a paddle, or a brick, we will need to reverse its vertical direction. To that end, we will build a short method to handle it:

```
public void flipVerticalDirection() {

    if (movingUp) {

        movingUp = false;

    } else {

        movingUp = true;

    }

}
```

To finish up the **Ball** class, we will build getters and setters for the following properties:

- **movingUp**
- **movingLeft**
- **ballX**
- **ballY**

We should also create getters for **ballSize** and **ballSizeOffset** (these two properties do not need setters).

Brick class

Create a new Java class named **Brick** inside of the **javabreakout** package. This class will have one **import**, which will be the **Color** class from the AWT library. It will have properties to maintain the coordinates and color of the current brick, and whether or not it is broken:

```java
package javabreakout;


import java.awt.Color;


public class Brick {

    private int brickX;

    private int brickY;

    private int brickMaxX;

    private int brickMaxY;


    private Color color;

    private boolean broken;
```

Our constructor will take parameters for coordinates, size, and color:

```java
public Brick(int brickX, int brickY, int width, int height,
        Color color) {

    this.color = color;

    this.brickX = brickX;

    this.brickY = brickY;

    this.brickMaxX = brickX + width;

    this.brickMaxY = brickY + height;

    this.broken = false;

}
```

We will need getters for all of our properties, but we only need setters for **color** and **broken**. This is because our bricks do not move, but once they are broken we will set the **broken** property to true and **color** is set to black.

Paddle class

We will also need a class to define and control our paddle. Create a new Java class named **Paddle** inside of the **javabreakout** package:

```
package javabreakout;

public class Paddle {

    private int paddleX;

    private int paddleY;

    private int paddleHeight;

    private int paddleWidth;

    private int paddleSpeed;
```

The **Paddle** class needs properties for the paddle's location, size, and speed. These are all set by the constructor:

```
public Paddle(int paddleX, int paddleY, int paddleWidth,
        int paddleHeight, int paddleSpeed) {

    this.paddleX = paddleX;

    this.paddleY = paddleY;

    this.paddleHeight = paddleHeight;

    this.paddleWidth = paddleWidth;

    this.paddleSpeed = paddleSpeed;

}
```

The paddle is only allowed to move left or right. We will build two methods to account for that:

```
public void moveLeft() {

    paddleX -= paddleSpeed;

}

public void moveRight() {

    paddleX += paddleSpeed;
```

}

To finish this class, we will simply add getter methods for all of the properties.

KeyHandler class

For our Breakout application, the paddle is controlled by the keyboard. Therefore, we must build a class to handle input from specific keys. Create a new Java class named **KeyHandler** inside the **javabreakout** package. The **KeyHandler** class has two imports, the **KeyEvent** class and the **KeyListener** interface from the AWT library. Our **KeyHandler** class will also implement the **KeyListener** interface:

```
package javabreakout;


import java.awt.event.KeyEvent;

import java.awt.event.KeyListener;


public class KeyHandler implements KeyListener {

    private BreakoutPanel panel;

    private boolean leftPressed = false;

    private boolean rightPressed = false;
```

Our class also has properties for whether or not the *left* and *right* keys have been pressed. Additionally, we have a property for our **BreakoutPanel** class, which we have not created yet.

It is important to note, that our **KeyHandler** class will be instantiated into an object and also set as a property inside our **BreakoutPanel** class. This is known as a **circular reference** in Java. In general, circular references have a tendency to lead to complex issues with dependency and deadlock issues that are difficult to solve. Use of a circular reference prevents us from having to:

- write additional complex logic around releasing a new ball.
- pass an additional property along with every key press event.

Note: The accepted wisdom on circular references is to avoid their use. They are usually more prone to trouble than they are worth. However, they can be useful in the right situation.

Our constructor requires the **BreakoutPanel** to pass a reference to itself as the lone parameter:

```
public KeyHandler(BreakoutPanel breakoutPanel) {

    this.panel = breakoutPanel;

}
```

Implementing the **KeyListener** interface requires us to override three publicly-scoped, voided methods: **keyPressed**, **keyReleased**, and **keyTyped**.

We will not use the **keyTyped()** method, so it can remain empty:

```
@Override

public void keyTyped(KeyEvent e) {


}
```

Our **keyPressed()** method is where we handle whether or not the player is moving the paddle left or right, as well as if they are trying to release a new ball. It accepts a **KeyEvent** object, which is quickly set to the local **code** integer. We can then use that code to determine which key was pressed:

```
@Override

public void keyPressed(KeyEvent keyPress) {

    int code = keyPress.getKeyCode();

    if (code == KeyEvent.VK_A) {

        leftPressed = true;

    }
    if (code == KeyEvent.VK_D) {

        rightPressed = true;

    }
    if (panel.getBallIsDead()) {

        if (code == KeyEvent.VK_ENTER) {

            panel.releaseBall();

        }
```

```
        }

}
```

Players will use the *A* and *D* keys to move left and right, respectively. These keys were chosen from the standard WASD layout commonly used in gaming. In these if checks, we are setting either the **leftPressed** or **rightPressed boolean** property to **true**.

This method is also where our circular reference back to the **BreakoutPanel** comes into play. The *enter* key is used to release a new ball, but it is only valid if there is currently no other ball in play. The if check for this uses the result of the Breakout Panel's **getBallIsDead()** method. Otherwise, key presses from the *Enter* key are ignored. The method to release a new ball (**releaseBall()**) is also on the **BreakoutPanel**, and is called in this instance.

The last method required to be written is the **keyReleased()** method. Similar to the **keyPressed()** method, it accepts a **KeyEvent** to determine if a previously pressed key was released. If so, we simply set either the **leftPressed** or **rightPressed boolean** property to **false**:

```
@Override

public void keyReleased(KeyEvent keyRelease) {


    int code = keyRelease.getKeyCode();


    if (code == KeyEvent.VK_A) {

        leftPressed = false;

    }

    if (code == KeyEvent.VK_D) {

        rightPressed = false;

    }

}
```

Finally, the **KeyHandler** class needs getters for **leftPressed** and **rightPressed**. We also need to build two getter and setter methods or this class:

```
public boolean isLeftPressed() {

    return leftPressed;

}


public boolean isRightPressed() {
```

```
        return rightPressed;

}
```

BreakoutPanel class

The **BreakoutPanel** class is where the magic happens for this application. Create a new Java class named **BreakoutPanel** inside of the **javabreakout** package. This class will extend the **JPanel** class and implement the **Runnable** interface. The **BreakoutPanel** class will require imports from the following libraries:

- **AWT: Color**, **Dimension**, **Font**, **Graphics**, **Graphics2D**
- **Util: ArrayList**, **List**
- **Swing: JPanel**

Let us create the **BreakoutPanel** class:

```
package javabreakout;


import java.awt.Color;

import java.awt.Dimension;

import java.awt.Font;

import java.awt.Graphics;

import java.awt.Graphics2D;


import java.util.ArrayList;

import java.util.List;


import javax.swing.JPanel;


public class BreakoutPanel extends JPanel implements Runnable {

    private static final long serialVersionUID =
            -7279076888542180135L;

    private final int fPS = 60; // frames per second

    private final int brickWidth = 64;
```

```java
private final int brickHeight = 32;

private final int brickBuffer = 128;

private final int ballSize = 11;
```

Our class will require a generated **serialVersionUID**. We will also define five constants with the **final** keyword, and set their values. These constants are for fundamental aspects of our game, such as the frames per second, the size of the bricks and the ball, and how many pixels are above the bricks.

The **BreakoutPanel** class also has four simple properties. Two **booleans** for tracking whether or not the **ballIsDead** and whether or not the **ballIsPlayable** (these are not mutually-exclusive). We also will have properties to store the **height** and **width** of the **JPanel** itself, as well as a couple of other things:

```java
private boolean ballIsDead;

private boolean ballIsPlayable;


private int panelHeight;

private int panelWidth;

private int score = 0;

private int ballsRemaining = 3;
```

We also require properties on the class for keeping track of the list of bricks and available colors (in the order that they should be used). There is a limited amount of text we want to show on the panel, so we will instantiate a **Font** object named **arial40** for that:

```java
private Font arial40 = new Font("Arial", Font.PLAIN, 40);


private List<Brick> bricks;

private List<Color> colorList;
```

Additionally, we need properties for objects of the **Ball**, **KeyHandler**, and **Paddle** classes. Similar to the **SolarSystem** class (from the previous section), we also need a property for the thread:

```java
private Ball ball;

private KeyHandler keyHandler;

private Paddle paddle;

private Thread panelThread;
```

For the constructors, we will take the same approach we took with the **SolarSystem** class and build two constructors. One accepts arguments for the size of the panel, and another, no-argument constructor simply calls the first:

```
public BreakoutPanel() {

    this(1024,1024);

}


public BreakoutPanel(int width, int height) {

    panelWidth = width;

    panelHeight = height;


    this.setPreferredSize(new Dimension(panelWidth, panelHeight));

    this.setBackground(Color.black);

    this.setFocusable(true);


    keyHandler = new KeyHandler(this);

    this.addKeyListener(keyHandler);


    bricks = generateBricks();

    paddle = new Paddle((panelWidth / 2) - 64,

            panelHeight - 200, 128, 16, 16);

    ballIsDead = true;

    ballIsPlayable = false;

    panelThread = Thread.ofVirtual()

            .name("Breakout")

            .unstarted(this);

}
```

Our primary constructor will set the **height** and **width** of the panel, as well as the background color (**black**), and allow the panel to obtain modal focus on the desktop. Next, we will instantiate our **KeyHandler** object and name it **keyHandler**, and pass **this** as (a reference to the current class) the only parameter. We will then generate the bricks and instantiate a new **Paddle** object named **paddle**. We will also set the initial states for the **boolean** properties of **ballisDead** and **ballIsPlayable**. Finally, the constructor will instantiate **panelThread** as a new virtual thread in a **unstarted** state.

Before we can generate the bricks, we need a list of colors. Typically, the bricks in Breakout are built in a different color for each row. As we will have eight rows of bricks, we will build a method to compose a list of eight colors and store them in the **colorList** property:

```java
private void generateColors() {

    colorList = new ArrayList<>();

    colorList.add(Color.RED);

    colorList.add(Color.MAGENTA);

    colorList.add(Color.PINK);

    colorList.add(Color.GRAY);

    colorList.add(Color.YELLOW);

    colorList.add(Color.CYAN);

    colorList.add(Color.GREEN);

    colorList.add(Color.BLUE);

}
```

Next, we will build the **generateBricks()** method. After initializing our return value and the brick row/column numbers, we will draw the bricks from top-to-bottom and left-to-right. The nested **while** loops will ensure that we build a column of **8** bricks **16** times. Each time, we are creating a new **Brick** object, saving its parameters, and adding it to the list:

```java
private List<Brick> generateBricks() {

    generateColors();
    List<Brick> returnVal = new ArrayList<>();
    int brickRow = 0;
    int brickCol = 0;

    while (brickCol < 16) {
        while (brickRow < 8) {
            Brick newBrick = new Brick(brickCol * brickWidth,
```

```
            (brickRow * brickHeight) + brickBuffer,

        brickCol + brickWidth, brickRow + brickHeight,

        colorList.get(brickRow));

    returnVal.add(newBrick);

    brickRow++;

  }

  brickRow = 0;

  brickCol++;

}

return returnVal;

}
```

Once we have completed building a column of **8** bricks, we set the **brickRow** (counter) back to zero and increment **brickCol**. The loop completes once the 16th column has been built. Notice that the value of **brickRow** is used to set the color of the brick.

In our brick height calculations, we also include a **brickBuffer** value of **128**. This is because we want a **128** pixel open area between the top of the panel and the top row of bricks.

Since the Breakout game will run as a virtual thread, we will override the **run()** method. Essentially, our game will continue to run as long as panel thread's method **isAlive()** and continues to return a value of true. Inside the loop, we will call our **update()** method as well as the panel's **repaint()** method, and then force the thread to sleep (pause) for *16 ⅔* seconds:

```
@Override

public void run() {

    while (panelThread.isAlive()) {

        update();

        repaint();

        // compute pauses based on frames per second

        try {

            Thread.sleep(1000 / fPS);
```

```
        } catch (InterruptedException e) {

            e.printStackTrace();

        }

    }

}
```

There is one possible issue that our code could have regarding the amount of frames being processed per second. Currently, the code will run and then be paused for a short time. The pause time is equal to one second divided by the value of **fPS**, which is **60**. The assumption is that we are not accounting for the CPU time taken for the **update()** and **repaint()** methods to run.

During the development of this code, the time required for those two methods to complete was measured as being less than a single millisecond while running on an **AMD A8-5500** processor from 2012. Therefore, while the compute time taken to run both **update()** and **repaint()** is not zero, it is trivial, considering the modern CPU architecture. However, for optimum efficiency, a developer could certainly redo this method to record the times before **update()** was run and after **repaint()** was run and subtract the difference from the value used in the **Thread.sleep()** method.

Next, we will build the **update()** method. Here, we account for the new positions of **paddle** and **ball**. Fortunately, the bricks do not move, so we do not need to recompute anything for them. For the paddle, we also need to check with **keyHandler** to see if either the left or right keys have been pressed, and if they are, adjust their movement using the **moveLeft()** and **moveRight()** methods. We will also check that the paddle does not move off of the visible portion of the screen:

```
private void update() {

    // paddle

    if (keyHandler.isLeftPressed() || keyHandler.isRightPressed()) {

        if (keyHandler.isLeftPressed()) {

            if (paddle.getPaddleX() - paddle.getPaddleSpeed() > 0) {

                paddle.moveLeft();

            }

        } else {

            if (paddle.getPaddleX() + paddle.getPaddleSpeed()

                    < panelWidth) {
```

```
            paddle.moveRight();

        }

    }

}


// ball

if (!ballIsDead) {

    checkCollision();

    if (ballIsPlayable) {

        // checkCollision method could render the ball unplayable

        ball.update();

    }

}

}
```

For the ball, we only need to update if the ball is both alive and playable. We will also call the **checkCollision()** method to see if the ball is currently touching a brick, a wall, or the **paddle**.

The **checkCollision()** method is fairly complex and is written to account for various possibilities. First, there are variables instantiated to help us know the coordinates for both the **ball** and the **paddle**, as well as the size dimensions of the **paddle**.

The first if check is to see if the ball's Y coordinate has exceeded the bottom of the viewable playing space on the panel. Remember that the point **0,0** is in the upper-left corner, so checking the value of **panelHeight** is at the **bottom** of the screen. If it has exceeded the bottom limit, we declare the ball both dead and not playable, before destroying it and decrementing **ballsRemaining**:

```
private void checkCollision() {

    int ballX = ball.getBallX();

    int ballY = ball.getBallY();

    int paddleX = paddle.getPaddleX();

    int paddleY = paddle.getPaddleY();
```

```
int paddleWidth = paddle.getPaddleWidth();

int paddleHeight = paddle.getPaddleHeight();


if (ballY  > panelHeight) {

    // bottom "pit"

    ballIsDead = true;

    ballIsPlayable = false;

    // destroy ball

    ball = null;

    ballsRemaining--;
```

Next, we need to check if the ball is both moving downward and has contacted the **paddle**. If this is **true**, then we reverse the vertical direction with ball's **setMovingUp()** method. We will also check to see if the player is actively pressing either directional key during the point of collision, and we will adjust the angle of the ball accordingly:

```
} else if (ballY >= paddleY && !ball.isMovingUp()) {

    // paddle

    // bottom Y axis and check X axis

    if (ballY < paddleY + paddleHeight &&

            ballX >= paddleX &&

            ballX <= paddleX + paddleWidth) {


        ball.setMovingUp(true);


        // check for ball angle adjustment

        if (keyHandler.isLeftPressed()) {

            if (ball.isMovingLeft()) {

                ball.increaseAngle();

            } else {

                ball.decreaseAngle();

            }
```

```
        } else if (keyHandler.isRightPressed()) {

            if (ball.isMovingLeft()) {

                ball.decreaseAngle();

            } else {

                ball.increaseAngle();

            }

        }

    }
```

In the next two if checks, we are looking to see if the ball has contacted either side wall. If so, we reverse the horizontal direction by calling the ball's **setMovingLeft()** method:

```
} else if (ballX <= 0 && ball.isMovingLeft()) {

    // left wall

    ball.setMovingLeft(false);

} else if (ballX >= panelWidth && !ball.isMovingLeft()) {

    // right wall

    ball.setMovingLeft(true);
```

Here, we check to see if the ball has collided with any of the bricks. The if check looks to see if the ball's coordinates are equal to or between the top, bottom, left, and rightmost coordinates of the complete **brick** area. If it is, then we iterate through all of the bricks to see which specific, unbroken **brick** has a collision with the **ball**:

```
} else if (ballY <= (brickHeight * 8) + brickBuffer + brickHeight

        && ballY > brickBuffer) {

    // bricks

    for (Brick brick : bricks) {

        if (!brick.isBroken()) {

            // only check for collision if it is not broken

            int brickX = brick.getBrickX();

            int brickY = brick.getBrickY();

            int brickMaxX = brick.getBrickMaxX();

            int brickMaxY = brick.getBrickMaxY();
```

```
            if (ballX >= brickX && ballX <= brickMaxX

                    && ballY >= brickY && ballY <= brickMaxY) {

                // break brick!

                brick.setBroken(true);

                brick.setColor(Color.BLACK);

                score++;


                // for now, just flip the ball's direction

                // on a brick break

                ball.flipVerticalDirection();

            }

        }

    }
```

If a collision has occurred with an intact **brick**, we then call the brick's **setBroken()** method with a value of **true**, set the brick's color to black with the **setColor()** method, and increment **score**. This way, we do a soft delete on the broken bricks. They are still there but will not trigger collisions or be visible (because they match the background color).

Here, we are checking if the ball has reached the uppermost portion of the screen. If it has, we want it to bounce back down and call the ball's **setMovingUp()** method to reverse its vertical direction. If our program flow makes it through this check without triggering any additional logic, then the ball has not collided with anything. Let us look at the following code:

```
    } else if (ball.getBallY() <= 1) {

        // top wall

        ball.setMovingUp(false);

    }


    // otherwise, no collision

}
```

The last big method we need to build is our override of the **paintComponent()** method, which is called on a call to the **repaint()** method. First, we need to call the same method on our **JPanel** superclass and create a new, local **Graphics2D** object named **g2**. Then, we can iterate through the bricks and draw each one:

```java
public void paintComponent(Graphics g) {

    super.paintComponent(g);

    Graphics2D g2 = (Graphics2D)g;

    // bricks

    for (Brick brick : bricks) {
        int brickX = brick.getBrickX();

        int brickY = brick.getBrickY();

        g2.setColor(brick.getColor());

        g2.fillRect(brickX, brickY, brickWidth, brickHeight);

    }
```

Once we have drawn the bricks, we move on to the paddle:

```java
    // paddle

    g2.setColor(Color.WHITE);

    g2.fillRect(paddle.getPaddleX(), paddle.getPaddleY(),

            paddle.getPaddleWidth(), paddle.getPaddleHeight());
```

Next, we draw the ball. The ball is a very small square, and we use the **centerOffset** variable to ensure that we draw the ball from its center instead of its upper-left corner. This lowers the complexity of our collision detection. Let us look at the following code:

```java
    // ball

    if (ball != null) {
        // SILVER

        g2.setColor(new Color(192,192,192));

        int centerOffset = ball.getBallSizeOffset();

        g2.fillRect(ball.getBallX() - centerOffset,

            ball.getBallY() - centerOffset, ball.getBallSize(),

            ball.getBallSize());
```

```
    }
```

Finally, we display the current values of **score** and **ballsRemaining** at the top of the screen. Technically, we are displaying the text in the playable area, but it will not induce any collisions and is up too high so as to impede the player:

```
    // score and balls remaining

    StringBuilder scoreBuilder = new StringBuilder("Score: ");

    scoreBuilder.append(score);

    StringBuilder currentBallBuilder =

            new StringBuilder("Current Ball: ");

    currentBallBuilder.append(ballsRemaining);


    g2.setColor(Color.white);

    g2.setFont(arial40);

    g2.drawString(scoreBuilder.toString(), 50, 50);

    g2.drawString(currentBallBuilder.toString(), 700, 50);


    g2.dispose();

}
```

The final methods that we need to build are very small. We need a method to start the game, which invokes the **start()** method on the **panelThread**:

```
public void start() {

    panelThread.start();

}
```

We need a method to generate a new ball and put it into play. The **releaseBall()** method will do this, so long as the value of **ballsRemaining** is greater than zero:

```
public void releaseBall() {

    if (ballsRemaining > 0) {

        ball = new Ball(ballSize, panelWidth, brickHeight * 8,

                brickBuffer);

        ballIsDead = false;
```

```
        ballIsPlayable = true;

    }

}
```

Finally, we need a getter for the **ballIsDead** property:

```
public boolean getBallIsDead() {

    return this.ballIsDead;

}
```

BreakoutGame class

With all of that complete, we can move on to the final class. Create a new Java class with the name **BreakoutGame** and make sure that it is inside the **javabreakout** package. This class will have one **import** (**JFrame** from Swing) and should have a **main** method:

```
package javabreakout;

import javax.swing.JFrame;

public class BreakoutGame {

    public static void main(String[] args) {

        JFrame frame = new JFrame();

        frame.setDefaultCloseOperation(JFrame.EXIT_ON_CLOSE);

        frame.setTitle("Java Breakout");

        BreakoutPanel panel = new BreakoutPanel();

        frame.add(panel);

        frame.pack();

        frame.setVisible(true);

        panel.start();

    }
```

}

Breakout Game's **main()** method builds a new **JFrame** object named **frame**. We then configure the **frame** to set our desired close behavior, the title of **frame** to **"Java Breakout"**, and we indicate that we want the **frame** to be visible.

> **Note: It was observed on a Mac that calling JFrame's setVisible() method too early could result in the KeyListener not functioning properly. Therefore, it is advised to call setVisible(true) as the last action performed on the JFrame.**

We then instantiate a new object of **BreakoutPanel** named **panel**. Finally, we add **panel** to **frame**, pack the frame, set it to be visible, and invoke the **start()** method on **panel** to begin the game.

Running **BreakoutGame** in the IDE should begin our game and allow us to play it. Try moving the **paddle** back and forth with the *A* and *D* keys, and press the *Enter* key when ready to play! We should see something similar to *Figure 9.4*:

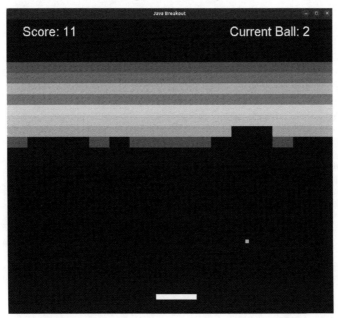

Figure 9.4: *The completed, running game of Java Breakout.*

To play Java Breakout outside of the IDE, open a terminal and change to its project directory. As we have built Java Breakout using Maven as a dependency manager, we can invoke a build with the following command:

```
mvn clean install
```

Once that completes, the **jar-with-dependencies** JAR file should be in the **target/** directory. The game can then be run by executing:

```
java -jar target/javabreakout-0.0.1-SNAPSHOT-jar-with-dependencies.jar
```

Conclusion

In this chapter, we learned how to program graphics in Java. We started with some simple shapes and eventually progressed into some simple animation. After exploring how to construct visual elements, we built a near-complete arcade game! We will continue practicing what we have learned in the next chapter, where we will build a full Java web application.

Java Breakout was designed to help teach the lessons in this chapter. However, it is not a complete game. Additional development could be done to include additional features such as:

- a menu
- an **ending** screen (when the player has used their last ball)
- a **win** screen when the player has broken all of the bricks
- sounds
- a way to restart the game
- increasing levels of difficulty (more bricks, the ball moves faster, and so on)
- proper physics when breaking a **brick** from the side

In the next chapter, we will build our final project. This project will be a web application with a database back end that will draw from all the knowledge we have gained from the preceding chapters.

Points to remember

- Programming graphics with the AWT and Swing libraries in Java support drawing on a **JPanel** that has been added to a **JFrame**.
- Coordinates on a **JPanel** begin with the X,Y coordinate of **0,0** in the upper-left corner. Increasing X coordinates progress to the right, and increasing Y coordinates progress downward.
- The AWT **Graphics2D** methods must have a color set before execution.
- The AWT **Graphics2D** library has twelve predefined colors.
- The AWT **draw** method will draw the outline of the specified shape in the color that was previously set.
- The AWT **fill** method will draw the outline of the specified shape and fill it in with the color that was previously set.

- If a class is to be run as a thread, it must extend the **Runnable** class, and the **run()** method must be overridden.

- The **Thread** class is valid for implementing platform threads and virtual threads.

- Circular references can be helpful in the right context but are best avoided.

- Be sure to load things like images and fonts ahead of time (in the constructor) so they can be quickly called at runtime.

Join our book's Discord space

Join the book's Discord Workspace for Latest updates, Offers, Tech happenings around the world, New Release and Sessions with the Authors:

https://discord.bpbonline.com

CHAPTER 10
Final Java Project

Introduction

Welcome to the final chapter! Here we are going to work on a final project, which will utilize much of the skills and knowledge that we have acquired throughout the preceding chapters.

Structure

In this chapter, we will cover the following topics while working on our project:

- Introducing movie application
- Database
- Data loader
- Querying the data
- Creating the movie application project
- Model
- Controller
- Querying the service
- View

Objectives

The main objective of this chapter is to practice many of the lessons learned from the prior chapters. We will also show how to use the knowledge from those lessons to build an application. The learning objectives are as follows:

- Build a data layer for our application with useful, real-world examples.
- Understand some of the trade-offs made in database and application design.
- Learn how to leverage the **Optional** type to prevent null pointer errors.
- Learn how to precisely configure visual elements in **Vaadin**.

Introducing movie application

We will build an application that catalogs movies and stores information about them in a database. Our application will be web-based (for now) and store data about different movies. The movie data in our database will be quarriable by an ID, the complete title, or a vector query (vector search will be introduced later in this chapter).

Architecture

Similar to what we did in *Chapter 8, Web Applications*, we are going to use the **Model View Controller** (**MVC**) design pattern. If this were an actual application for a real company, we might be asked to build a mobile application in the future. Therefore, it makes sense to keep the front end, service layer, and **Data Access Layer** (**DAL**) decoupled as much as possible.

Given these requirements, building a web application with Spring Boot seems like the correct approach. With Spring Boot, we can easily expose our controller's service endpoints for use by other applications. We can also add libraries to use a database of our choosing with Spring Data. And we also know that we can pull in the **Vaadin** libraries to build a front-end user interface.

Database

For the design of our data layer, let us start by discussing what our application has to do to be functional. If we have used a site or application such as the *Internet Movie Database* (**https://imdb.com**) or *The Movie Database* (**https://www.themoviedb.org/**) before, we should have a fair understanding of what our application needs to do:

- Look up a movie
- Add/update an image for a movie.
- Suggest similar movies based on the current movie.

Based on those functional requirements, our model needs to support the following queries:

- Query movie data by ID and title.
- Store our own images for a movie.
- Query for similar movies.

Database selection

Websites like **IMDB.com** support (**IMDB 2023**) over 200 million unique visitors each month. Hypothetically, it would take a while for our new site to see that traffic. That being said, the use case suggests that we should use a distributed database on the backend. Additionally, we should use one capable of scaling and growing as our data and traffic needs are likely to grow over time. Therefore, we will build our site to use Apache Cassandra as its database.

Create a new vector database

In the **vector** database world, vectors are numeric representations (often an array of floats) of data in multidimensional space. Vector databases are data stores that support searching by data embedded as a **vector**. The vector embeddings themselves are often created by a generative **artificial intelligence (AI)** process known as a **transformation**, resulting in data expressed as text, image, or sound to be tokenized into an array of numbers.

Vector searches are typically built on cosine-based similarity algorithms, such as **K-Nearest Neighbor (KNN)** or **Approximate Nearest Neighbor (ANN)**. To support the above query for similar movies, we will require a database capable of supporting a query by ANN. This will allow us to provide relevant suggestions about which movies our users should consider watching next.

From prior chapters, we should still have our free **Astra DB account**, so we will use that for our **Cassandra** database. To begin, we will want to create a new database. In a browser, head to **https://astra.datastax.com**, sign in and create a new **Vector** database.

> **Note: For this application, we should create a new Vector database (instead of Serverless). The serverless database that we created on Astra before is not vector-enabled, and cannot be used for this application.**

We should set up the new database with the following parameters:

- **Database name: bpbMovies**
- **Keyspace name: movieapp**
- **Provider: Google Cloud**
- **Region:** (pick the closest **free** region)

While the token we used in *Chapter 7, Working with Databases* should still be fine, we will need to download our new database's **secure connect bundle** (**SCB**). Feel free to copy the SCB to a different location (other than the **Downloads** directory).

> **Note: If a new token is required, return to** *Chapter 7, Working with Databases* **for instructions on generating a new token for Astra DB.**

Table design

To support our proposed query patterns, we will need two tables created inside of our **movieapp** keyspace. The first will be a table named **movies**, with a lone primary key of **movie_id**. This table will contain all the data we will keep about each movie in the database. The final column in the database will be our vector embedding, which will be stored as a seven-dimensional float.

To create our new tables, go to the Astra DB dashboard, click on the **bpbMovies** database, and then on the **CQL Console** tab. We will first want to use our keyspace:

```
use movieapp;
```

Then, we can enter our table definition:

```
CREATE TABLE movies (

    movie_id INT PRIMARY KEY,

    imdb_id TEXT,

    original_language TEXT,

    genres MAP<INT,TEXT>,

    website TEXT,

    title TEXT,

    description TEXT,

    release_date DATE,

    year INT,

    budget BIGINT,

    revenue BIGINT,

    runtime float,

    movie_vector vector<float,7>

);
```

Additionally, we will need to create an index on this table. Secondary indexes are far more common (and useful) in the relational database world. They are not used often in NoSQL databases (like Apache Cassandra) because distributed indexes are problematic at larger scales. However, we need to have one to make our **vector** search query possible. It will not be as problematic as a regular index-based query, as we will limit the results (and thus the resource consumption):

```
CREATE CUSTOM INDEX ON movieapp.movies (movie_vector) USING
'StorageAttachedIndex';
```

Our second table will be named **movies_by_title** and it will support the query for movies by their exact title. With **title** as the primary key, **movie_id** is the only non-key column present in the table:

```
CREATE TABLE movies_by_title (

    title TEXT PRIMARY KEY,

    movie_id INT

);
```

This modeling technique is known as a **manual index** in Cassandra. Essentially, we will make two queries when querying by title. The first will query our **movies_by_title** table by **title**. The second query will be on the **movies** table with the **movie_id** obtained from the first query. This technique prevents us from having to use a secondary index.

While the manual index approach may seem counterintuitive, it will perform faster and more efficiently than if we used a secondary index. As mentioned earlier, a query with a secondary index built on the **title** column would consume a high level of compute and network resources, as shown in *Figure 10.1*:

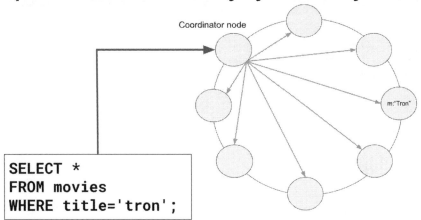

Apache Cassandra - Query by secondary index

Figure 10.1: *A visual representation of the network path of a secondary index query in Cassandra.*

Let us assume that we are trying to query the movie **'tron'** by a secondary index on the **title** column. As **title** is not the partition key, the cluster node(s) responsible for its data cannot be determined by performing a **Murmur3** hash of the value. Therefore, the application (driver) will select a node as the query coordinator.

The **Coordinator node** will poll all of the nodes in the cluster in an attempt to find a match on the indexed value for the **title** column. The coordinator will then collect responses from all nodes, build the result set, and return it to the application. That is a lot for a single node to do. This problem is exacerbated as the cluster and data footprint grow larger.

However, if we build a separate table to support queries by title, this query can be completed in a much smaller number of network hops. Essentially, querying by the partition keys allows the application to pull data directly from the nodes responsible for it, as demonstrated in *Figure 10.2*:

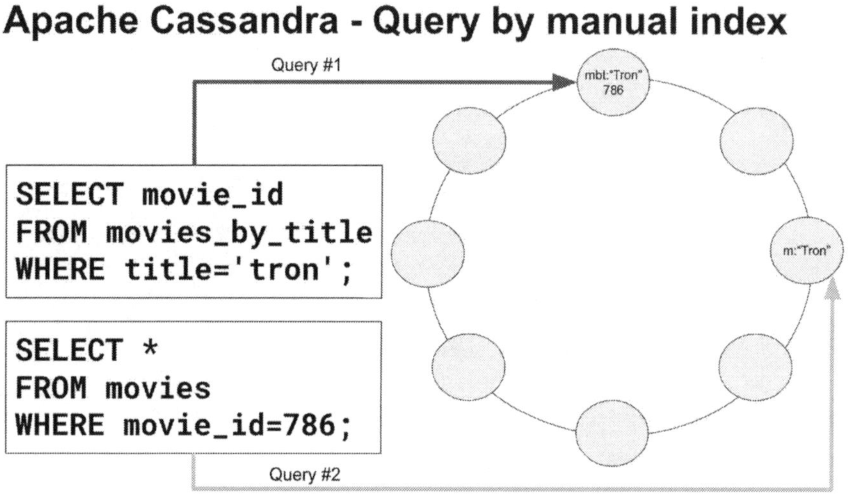

Apache Cassandra - Query by manual index

```
SELECT movie_id
FROM movies_by_title
WHERE title='tron';
```

```
SELECT *
FROM movies
WHERE movie_id=786;
```

Figure 10.2: Manual index query in Cassandra, illustrating two partition key queries more efficient than a single secondary index query.

> Note: Sending queries directly to the nodes responsible for the requested data requires the application to connect to Apache Cassandra using a token-aware load-balancing policy. Astra DB is designed to utilize an optimized coordinator node approach, but it will still consume fewer resources than a similar query driven on a secondary index.

Data loader

For our dataset, we will utilize a shortened version of the **movies_metadata.csv** file from **Kaggle**. Kaggle is a collaboration site for data scientists, data engineers, and other data enthusiasts to share and work on different public-domain datasets.

Our version of the file will only contain around 1000 rows. This should be enough for us to have a diverse dataset without waiting for the data to load.

> **Note: The full version of the movies_metadata.csv contains over 45000 movies and can be found here https://www.kaggle.com/datasets/rounakbanik/the-movies-dataset?select=movies_metadata.csv.**

pom.xml

To load the dataset into our database, we need to build a small application. We could just take the CSV file above and use the data loader on the Astra DB dashboard. However, we will need to adjust the data to load it into our tables properly. Therefore, we will create a small batch application to load our data. In our IDE, we will create a new Maven project with the following properties:

- **Group ID: `com.codewithjava21`**
- **Artifact ID: `movieapp`**
- **Name: `moviedataloader`**

Once the project is created, edit the resulting **pom.xml** file and add the following **properties** section:

```
<properties>

    <java.version>21</java.version>

    <maven.compiler.source>21</maven.compiler.source>

    <maven.compiler.target>21</maven.compiler.target>

    <cassandra.driver.version>4.17.0</cassandra.driver.version>

</properties>
```

Next, add the following **dependencies** section:

```
<dependencies>

    <dependency>

        <groupId>com.datastax.oss</groupId>

        <artifactId>java-driver-core</artifactId>

        <version>${cassandra.driver.version}</version>

    </dependency>

</dependencies>
```

CassandraConnection class

As our data loader will not use Spring Data Cassandra, we will need to create our ses to manage our connections to Cassandra. Create a new class named **CassandraConnection** inside the **com.codewithjava21.movieapp.cassandraconnect** package. It will have imports for Java's **InetSocketAddress**, **Paths**, and **Lists** classes, as well as the **CqlSession** class from the **DataStax driver** library:

```
package com.codewithjava21.movieapp.cassandraconnect;

import java.net.InetSocketAddress;

import java.nio.file.Paths;

import java.util.List;

import com.datastax.oss.driver.api.core.CqlSession;
```

In the class definition, we will define a property for the **CqlSession**, and our first constructor will accept the necessary parameters to connect to an Apache Cassandra cluster:

```
public class CassandraConnection {

    private CqlSession cqlSession;

    public CassandraConnection(String username, String pwd,
            List<InetSocketAddress> endpointList, String keyspace,
            String datacenter) {
        try {
            cqlSession = CqlSession.builder()
                .addContactPoints(endpointList)
                .withAuthCredentials(username, pwd)
                .withKeyspace(keyspace)
                .withLocalDatacenter(datacenter)
                .build();

            System.out.println("[OK] Success");
            System.out.printf("[OK] Welcome to Apache Cassandra! Connected
```

```
        to Keyspace %s\n", cqlSession.getKeyspace().get());

    } catch (Exception ex) {

        System.out.println(ex.getMessage());

    }

}
```

Inside the constructor, we will initialize the **cqlSession** property with **CqlSession**'s **builder()** method. We will use the builder's **with** methods to define our credentials, keyspace, and local datacenter, finishing by calling the **build()** method. This should be done inside of a **try/catch**, so that we can trap for and display an exception message that comes along.

Next, we will build a second constructor. This will accept the parameters necessary to connect to an Astra DB cluster:

```
public CassandraConnection(String username, String pwd,

    String secureBundleLocation, String keyspace) {

    try {

        cqlSession = CqlSession.builder()

            .withCloudSecureConnectBundle(

                    Paths.get(secureBundleLocation))

            .withAuthCredentials(username, pwd)

            .withKeyspace(keyspace)

            .build();

        System.out.println("[OK] Success");

        System.out.printf("[OK] Welcome to Astra DB! Connected to
        Keyspace %s\n", cqlSession.getKeyspace().get());

    } catch (Exception ex) {

        System.out.println(ex.getMessage());

    }

}
```

With the exception of using the secure bundle instead of the endpoints and local data center name, this constructor will be largely similar to the first.

Next, we will need a **public** getter method to expose our **cqlSession** property:

```
public CqlSession getCqlSession() {

    return cqlSession;

}
```

Finally, we will add a **finalize** method (called when the object is **destroyed**) to announce our shutdown and simply make sure that the session is closed:

```
protected void finalize() {

    System.out.println("[shutdown_driver] Closing connection");

    System.out.println();

    cqlSession.close();

}
```

AstraConnection class

Next, we will build a class to abstract the **CassandraConnection** class so that we can build a constructor for connecting to Astra DB. Let us create a new class named **AstraConnection** inside of the **com.codewithjava21.movieapp.cassandraconnect** package. It will extend the **CassandraConnection** class and have an **import** for the **CqlSession** class from the **DataStax driver** library:

```
package com.codewithjava21.movieapp.cassandraconnect;


import com.datastax.oss.driver.api.core.CqlSession;


public class AstraConnection extends CassandraConnection {

    static final String ASTRA_ZIP_FILE =
            System.getenv("ASTRA_DB_SECURE_BUNDLE_PATH");

    static final String ASTRA_PASSWORD =
            System.getenv("ASTRA_DB_APP_TOKEN");

    static final String ASTRA_KEYSPACE =
            System.getenv("ASTRA_DB_KEYSPACE");
```

Our class will also define three **static**, constant (**final**) **String** properties for our secure connect **BUNDLE**, **PASSWORD**, and **KEYSPACE**. These properties will automatically be pulled from their corresponding OS environment variables when the class is instantiated.

We will have one constructor, and it will invoke the **CassandraConnection**'s constructor that we built for connecting to Astra DB. As we are using our Astra DB token as our password, we can hard-code the username of **token** to avoid confusion:

```
public AstraConnection() {

    super("token", ASTRA_PASSWORD, ASTRA_ZIP_FILE,

        ASTRA_KEYSPACE);

}
```

Similar to what we did with the **CassandraConnection** class, we will expose the **CqlSession** object, and provide a **finalize()** method as well. Both of these will invoke their **super** counterparts on the **CassandraConnection** class:

```
public CqlSession getCqlSession() {

    return super.getCqlSession();

}


public void finalize() {

    super.finalize();

}
```

Movie class

Create a new class named **Movie** inside of the **com.codewithjava21.movieapp. batchloader** package. It will have imports for Java's **LocalDate** and **Map** classes, as well as the **CqlVector** class from the **DataStax driver** library:

```
package com.codewithjava21.movieapp.batchloader;


import java.time.LocalDate;

import java.util.Map;

import com.datastax.oss.driver.api.core.data.CqlVector;
```

The **Movie** class should have properties that match up with our **movies** table:

```
public class Movie {
```

```
private Integer movieId;

private String imdbId;

private String title;

private String description;

private Float runtime;

private String originalLanguage;

private Map<Integer,String> genres;

private String website;

private LocalDate releaseDate;

private Long budget;

private Long revenue;

private Integer year;

private CqlVector<Float> vector;
```

We will also need **public** getter and setter methods for each property.

> Note: We are using the wrapper classes for the properties of primitive types such as Float, Integer, and Long. This makes this easier when we bring these properties into our view later.

MovieDataLoader class

Create a new Java class named **MovieDataLoader** inside of the **com.codewithjava21. movieapp.batchloader** package. Make sure that it has a **main** method. This class will also require several imports, including four from the **DataStax driver** library and ten from the standard Java libraries:

```
package com.codewithjava21.movieapp.batchloader;


import com.codewithjava21.movieapp.cassandraconnect.AstraConnection;


import com.datastax.oss.driver.api.core.CqlSession;

import com.datastax.oss.driver.api.core.cql.BoundStatement;

import com.datastax.oss.driver.api.core.cql.PreparedStatement;

import com.datastax.oss.driver.api.core.data.CqlVector;
```

```
import java.io.BufferedReader;

import java.io.FileReader;

import java.io.IOException;

import java.time.LocalDate;

import java.util.ArrayList;

import java.util.HashMap;

import java.util.List;

import java.util.Map;

import java.util.Set;


public class MovieDataLoader {
```

Our **MovieDataLoader** class is going to have seven privately-scoped properties, with four of those dedicated to building our prepared statements for our database writes:

```
private static CqlSession session;

private static PreparedStatement INSERTStatement;

private static PreparedStatement INSERTByTitleStatement;


private final static String strCQLINSERT = "INSERT INTO movies "

"(movie_id,imdb_id,original_language,genres,"

"Website,title,description,release_date,year,budget,"

"revenue,runtime,movie_vector) "

"VALUES (?,?,?,?,?,?,?,?,?,?,?,?,?)";

private final static String strCQLINSERTByTitle =

"INSERT INTO movies_by_title (title, movie_id)"

"VALUES (?,?)";


private static Map<String,Integer> genreIDMainMap = new HashMap<>();

private static Map<Integer,Integer> collectionIDMainMap =

        new HashMap<>();
```

Our **main()** method will begin by connecting to our Cassandra cluster on Astra DB and preparing two **CQLINSERT** statements:

```
public static void main(String[] args) {

    AstraConnection conn = new AstraConnection();

    session = conn.getCqlSession();


    INSERTStatement = session.prepare(strCQLINSERT);

    INSERTByTitleStatement = session.prepare(strCQLINSERTByTitle);
```

Next, we will begin our **try**/**catch** statement, open our data file, read the first line, and build a variable to see if the file's header has been read. We will also initialize a variable to keep a count of how many movies have been processed:

```
    try {

        BufferedReader reader = new BufferedReader(

                new FileReader("data/movies_metadata.csv"));

        String movieLine = reader.readLine();

        boolean headerRead = false;

        int movieCount = 0;
```

Next, we will build a **while** loop to process the fields in each line as long as the header has been read. As **comma separated values (CSV)** files are obviously comma-delimited, can split the data fields on a comma. However, some of the descriptions and other text may have commas inside of double-quotes. To solve this problem, we will need to use a regular expression:

```
        while (movieLine !=  null) {

            if (headerRead) {

                String[] movieColumns = movieLine

                    .split(",(?=(?:[^\"]*\"[^\"]*\")*[^\"]*$)", -1);
```

Essentially, the regular expression allows us to split on a comma (*Baeldung 2023*) using positive lookahead. Ensure that the comma is not enclosed within a pair of double-quotes or that there is an even number of double quotes ahead of it.

Next, we will create a **new** **Movie** object named **movie**, and assign properties from the **movieColumns String** array:

```
                Movie movie = new Movie();
```

```
String collections = movieColumns[1];

movie.setBudget(Long.parseLong(movieColumns[2]));

String genres = movieColumns[3];

movie.setWebsite(movieColumns[4]);

movie.setMovieId(Integer.parseInt(movieColumns[5]));

movie.setImdbId(movieColumns[6]);

movie.setOriginalLanguage(movieColumns[7]);

movie.setDescription(movieColumns[9]);

float popularity = Float.parseFloat(movieColumns[10]);
```

During test runs, it was noticed that release dates and running time properties were frequently empty, so we will check and respond appropriately:

```
if (!movieColumns[14].isEmpty()) {

    movie.setReleaseDate(

            LocalDate.parse(movieColumns[14]));

    movie.setYear(movie.getReleaseDate().getYear());

}


movie.setRevenue(Long.parseLong(movieColumns[15]));


if (!movieColumns[16].isEmpty()) {

    movie.setRuntime(

            Float.parseFloat(movieColumns[16]));

} else {

    movie.setRuntime(0F);

}
```

In addition to setting the **title** property, we have a few more local variables which need to be set to help us compute our **vector** embedding:

```
movie.setTitle(movieColumns[20]);

float voteAverage = Float.parseFloat(
```

```
                movieColumns[22]);

        int voteCount = Integer.parseInt(movieColumns[23]);

        int collectionId = getCollectionId(collections);


        // process genres

        Map<Integer,String> genreMap = buildGenreMap(genres);

        movie.setGenres(genreMap);

        Integer[] genre = getGenreIds(movie

            .getGenres().keySet());
```

Finally, we call our **generateVector()** method to build our **vector** embedding, and set the **vector** property on the **movie** object. With that complete, we then write our data to Cassandra, process our check for the **headerRead boolean**, and then read the next line in the file before continuing on with the **while** loop:

```
        CqlVector<Float> vector = CqlVector.newInstance(

            generateVector(collectionId, genre, popularity,

            voteAverage, voteCount));


        movie.setVector(vector);

        System.out.println(movie.getTitle());

        writeToCassandra(movie);

        movieCount++;

    } else {

        headerRead = true;

    }

    // read the next line

    movieLine = reader.readLine();

}
```

With the loop complete, we close our file reader, display our total **movieCount**, **catch** our exception, and close the method:

```
    reader.close();
```

```
        System.out.printf("%d movies written\n", movieCount);

    } catch (IOException readerEx) {

        System.out.println("Error occurred while reading:");

        readerEx.printStackTrace();

    }

}
```

Now we can proceed to the **private** methods for specific functions. Start by creating a new, **private** method named **writeToCassandra**. It will accept a **Movie** object, and ensure that its data is written to our two tables:

```
private static void writeToCassandra(Movie movie) {


    // write movie data

    BoundStatement movieInsert = INSERTStatement.bind(
            movie.getMovieId(), movie.getImdbId(),

            movie.getOriginalLanguage(), movie.getGenres(),

            movie.getWebsite(), movie.getTitle(),

            movie.getDescription(), movie.getReleaseDate(),

            movie.getYear(), movie.getBudget(),

            movie.getRevenue(), movie.getRuntime(),movie.getVector());

    session.execute(movieInsert);


    // write to movies_by_title

    BoundStatement movieByTitleInsert = INSERTByTitleStatement.bind(
            movie.getTitle().toLowerCase(), movie.getMovieId());

    session.execute(movieByTitleInsert);

}
```

Notice that for the **movies_by_title** table, we are forcing the title to be lowercase. As Cassandra requires an exact match on case when querying, forcing lowercase helps us to eliminate the problems with movies that have mixed cases in the title. We will also force the user queries to lowercase, thus improving the chances of a match by removing case as a query condition.

Next, we need a **private** method that accepts a string and parses it to return a **collectionId**. Collection IDs are ways in which movies with one or more sequels are grouped together. Since movies with the same collection ID are related to each other, we will use it for our **vector** embedding parameters. We will name this method **getCollectionId** and it will return an **Integer** while accepting a string. The string we pass to it contains a list of key/ value pairs. Essentially, we will split the **collection**'s **String** parameter by a comma, iterate through the array to find the **id** key, and return its value as an integer.

However, we also want to normalize these collection IDs, as they will be used as parameters in our vector search. If there is too much variance between certain IDs, our recommendation results could be skewed. Therefore, we will store the original **collectionId** in our **collectionIDMainMap** class property and give each collection a number that is auto-incremented:

```java
private static int getCollectionId(String collections) {

    int collectionId = 0;

    boolean idFound = false;

    String[] collArray = collections.split(",");


    for (String collection : collArray) {

        String[] kv = collection.split(":");


        if (kv[0].contains("'id'")) {

            idFound = true;

            int originalCollectionId = Integer.parseInt(kv[1].trim());


            if (collectionIDMainMap
                    .containsKey(originalCollectionId)) {
                collectionId = collectionIDMainMap
                        .get(originalCollectionId);
            } else {
                collectionId = collectionIDMainMap.size() + 1;

                collectionIDMainMap.put(originalCollectionId,
                        collectionId);
            }
        }
```

```
        break;

    }

  }


  if (!idFound) {

    collectionId = 999;

  }


  return collectionId;

}
```

If we do not find a **collectionId** (movie is not part of a collection), then we will give it a numeric value of **999**. This helps to ensure that it does not create a situation where not belonging to a collection has the same effect as belonging to a large collection. In vector terms, **999** should be far enough away from the legitimate collection IDs so as not to influence the results.

Next, we will need a method to build a map of our movie's genres. All movies are tagged into categories like action, science fiction, drama, and so on. However, the number of genres that each movie is a part of can vary wildly. Some may be a part of four or five, while some only belong to one or two. Therefore, a map is a good data structure to store them.

We will create a new **private** method that returns a map of **Integer** and **String** types named **buildGenreMap**. It will parse a comma separated list of **id**/**name** pairs. We will ignore the ID (similar to what we did above with collection IDs) and create a normalized genre ID instead. The **genre** string parameter is also likely to have a few extra characters in the name, so we will run a few **String replace()** methods to eliminate them:

```
private static Map<Integer,String> buildGenreMap(String genres) {

    Map<Integer,String> returnVal = new HashMap<>();

    String[] genreArray = genres.split(",");


    Integer id = 0;

    String name = "";
```

```java
for (String genre : genreArray) {

    String[] genreKV = genre.split(":");

    if (genreKV[0].contains("'name'")) {
        name = genreKV[1]
                .replaceAll("'","")
                .replaceAll("\"","")
                .replaceAll("}","")
                .replaceAll("]","");

        // is name is genreIDMainMap?
        if (genreIDMainMap.containsKey(name)) {
            id = genreIDMainMap.get(name);
        } else {
            id = genreIDMainMap.size() + 1;
            genreIDMainMap.put(name, id);
        }
        returnVal.put(id, name.trim());

    }

}


    return returnVal;

}
```

As we build out our search vector, we will also use the first three genres for each movie. Given the variance of genres per movie, three is a nice median value. Now, we could just get the IDs of the map we generated above as a **Set** and run a **toArray()** on it, but that could leave us with less than three. So, we will write a method to handle this for us, initializing a genre ID array with three zeros and updating them as needed:

```java
private static int[] getGenreIds(Set<Integer> genreIds) {

    int[] genre = {0, 0, 0};
```

```
    int counter = 0;

    for (Integer id : genreIds) {
        if (counter >= genre.length) {
            break;
        }

        genre[counter] = id;
        counter++;
    }

    return genre;
}
```

Last, we need a method to generate our vector. As previously mentioned, our **movie_vector** column is a seven-dimensional float, which we will build as a list using the **Float** wrapper type. Essentially, each movie is going to have a **vector** made up of the following properties in order:

- Collection ID
- Genre 1
- Genre 2
- Genre 3
- Popularity score
- Average vote rating
- Total votes for the above average rating

To properly process each of these properties into a vector embedding, we will use the following code:

```
private static List<Float> generateVector(Integer collectionId,
        Integer[] genre, float popularity, float voteAverage,
        Integer voteCount) {
// movie_vector <float,7>

List<Float> returnVal = new ArrayList<>();
```

```
returnVal.add(Float.parseFloat(collectionId.toString()));

returnVal.add(Float.parseFloat(genre[0].toString()));

returnVal.add(Float.parseFloat(genre[1].toString()));

returnVal.add(Float.parseFloat(genre[2].toString()));

returnVal.add(popularity);

returnVal.add(voteAverage);

returnVal.add(Float.parseFloat(voteCount.toString()));


return returnVal;
}
```

Before running the data loader, add the environment variables to the run configuration. Our data loader requires the following environment variables to be set:

- **ASTRA_DB_SECURE_BUNDLE_PATH**
- **ASTRA_DB_APP_TOKEN**
- **ASTRA_KEYSPACE**

With our code complete and the environment variables set, we should now be able to run our data loader. If everything worked, we should see the names of movies scrolling past as they are loaded from the file. When complete, we should see that a count of **1005 movies** were loaded:

```
The Empire Strikes Back

Return of the Jedi

Back to the Future

Aliens

Alien

1005 movies written
```

Querying the data

Now that the data has been loaded, we can check it by testing out some of the queries we will support in the application. In a browser, go back to the Astra DB dashboard, select the **bpbMovies** database, and then the **CQL Console** tab.

The first thing that we will need to do is use our keyspace:

```
use movieapp;
```

Now, we can try querying by **title**. Remember to pass movie titles as lowercase values only. As we only have **1005 movies** in our database, we do not have the entire dataset from Kaggle. So, feel free to pick one from the output displayed when the loader was run:

```
SELECT * FROM movies_by_title
WHERE 'star wars';
```

```
 title     | movie_id
-----------+----------
 star wars |       11
```

(1 rows)

From that query, we have a **movie_id** to work with. So, now we can query the **movies** table:

```
SELECT movie_id, title, release_date FROM movies
WHERE movie_id=11;
```

```
 movie_id | title     | release_date
----------+-----------+--------------
       11 | Star Wars |   1977-05-25
```

(1 rows)

As this table has a lot of columns, we were judicious about the ones selected above to preserve space. But now, let us rerun that query with a different column on the end:

```
SELECT movie_id, title, movie_vector FROM movies
WHERE movie_id=11;
```

```
 movie_id | title     | movie_vector
----------+-----------+-----------------------------------
       11 | Star Wars | [37, 4, 8, 13, 42.1497, 8.1, 6778]
```

(1 rows)

Now that we have the **movie_vector** column, we can try a vector search. The query syntax here will be a little different. In this case we are not going to use a **WHERE** clause. But instead, we will use an **ORDER BY** with CQL's **ANN OF** clause:

```
SELECT title FROM movies

ORDER BY movie_vector ANN OF [37, 4, 8, 13, 42.1497, 8.1, 6778]

LIMIT 6;
```

```
 title                   | movie_vector
-------------------------+------------------------------------------
           Star Wars |  [37, 4, 8, 13, 42.1497, 8.1, 6778]
 The Empire Strikes Back |  [37, 4, 8, 13, 19.47096, 8.2, 5998]
    Return of the Jedi |  [37, 4, 8, 13, 14.58609, 7.9, 4763]
       The Lion King |   [49, 1, 3, 7, 21.60576, 8, 5520]
          Pocahontas |  [10, 1, 3, 4, 13.28007, 6.7, 1509]
            Batman |   [18, 5, 8, 0, 19.10673, 7, 2145]
```

(6 rows)

As shown above, a vector search based on the **movie_vector** that we created for the title **Star Wars** has returned similar movies. The first two results (after itself) are two other **Star Wars** movies, as evidenced by the value of **37** in the collection ID position of the **vector**.

Whether or not the bottom three movies are considered to be similar is subjective. Results would certainly improve with more data, and as indicated above, we are only using a fraction of the original **movies_metadata.csv** file.

If we wanted to understand a little about the order that the movies are coming back in, we could add the CQL **similarity_cosine()** function to our query. It accepts a **vector** column and a **vector** as parameters:

```
SELECT title, similarity_cosine(movie_vector,

    [37, 4, 8, 13, 42.1497, 8.1, 6778]) as similarity

FROM movies

ORDER BY movie_vector ANN OF [37, 4, 8, 13, 42.1497, 8.1, 6778]
```

```
LIMIT 6;
```

```
title                    | similarity | movie_vector

-------------------------+-------------------------------------------------

           Star Wars |          1 |  [37, 4, 8, 13, 42.1497, 8.1, 6778]

The Empire Strikes Back |   0.999998 | [37, 4, 8, 13, 19.47096, 8.2, 5998]

     Return of the Jedi |   0.999996 | [37, 4, 8, 13, 14.58609, 7.9, 4763]

        The Lion King |   0.999995 |   [49, 1, 3, 7, 21.60576, 8, 5520]

           Pocahontas |   0.999995 |  [10, 1, 3, 4, 13.28007, 6.7, 1509]

              Batman |   0.999992 |   [18, 5, 8, 0, 19.10673, 7, 2145]
```

(6 rows)

> **Note:** Usually, vector searching is used with vector embeddings created from the output of a LLM using Word2Vec or some other natural language processing (NLP) method. While relative values of the collection IDs are meaningless to each other, vector search is a quick and easy way to provide recommendations to users.

Creating the movie application project

With the data in-place, we can move on to building the movie application. As we will use Spring Boot and Spring Data to make things easier for us, open a browser and go to the **Spring Initializr** at **https://https://start.spring.io/**.

Ensure that the following options are selected:

- **Project: Maven**
- **Spring Boot: 3.1.2**
- **Group: com.codewithjava21**
- **Artifact: movieapp**
- **Name: movieapp**
- **Description: Movie application for the Code with Java 21 book.**
- **Package name: com.codewithjava21.movieapp**
- **Packaging: Jar**
- **Java: 21** (or the highest available)
- **Dependencies: Spring Web, Spring Data for Apache Cassandra**, and **Vaadin**

Refer to the following *Figure 10.3*:

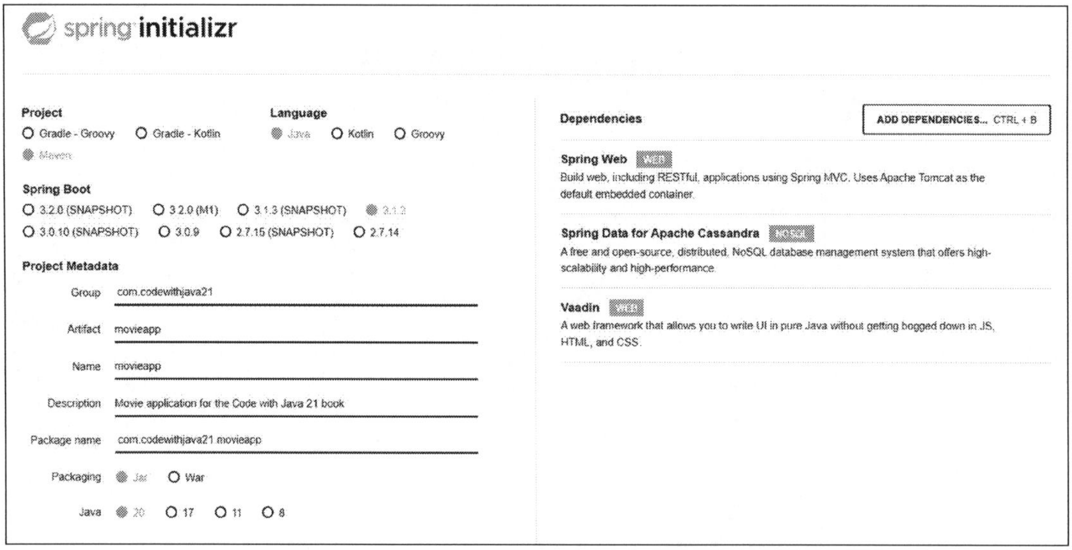

Figure 10.3: *The Spring Initializr showing the required parameters for the movie application.*

With that complete, click on the **Generate** button to start the download. We will then move the downloaded zip file to our IDE's workspace directory and unzip it. Then we will proceed to our IDE and import it as a new Maven project.

Images directory

This application will require the creation of a directory (**folder**) to store the movie images. Inside the project folder (at the same level as the **pom.xml** file), be sure to create a new directory named **images**.

pom.xml

With the project imported, there are some adjustments that we need to make to the **pom. xml** file. First of all, if we had to select something other than Java 21 (Java 20 shown in *Figure 10.3*), we should make that change in the **properties** section. Additionally, we should add a property for the Cassandra driver version so that it uses the **4.17.0** version:

```
<properties>

    <java.version>21</java.version>

    <cassandra.driver.version>4.17.0</cassandra.driver.version>

    <vaadin.version>24.1.2</vaadin.version>

</properties>
```

Next, we need to add dependencies for the Astra Spring Boot Starter and for the Cassandra driver. The Astra Spring Boot Starter will see that our Astra environment variables are properly wired-up. The Cassandra driver dependency will allow us to override Spring Data's version of the Cassandra driver, allowing us to use the Vector Search functionality:

```
<dependency>

    <groupId>com.datastax.astra</groupId>

    <artifactId>astra-spring-boot-3x-starter</artifactId>

    <version>0.6.4</version>

</dependency>

<dependency>

    <groupId>com.datastax.oss</groupId>

    <artifactId>java-driver-core</artifactId>

    <version>${cassandra.driver.oss.version}</version>

</dependency>
```

application.yml

Spring Boot should automatically generate an **application.properties** file. We will rename this file to **application.yml** and edit it to contain the following:

```
server:

  port: 8080

  error:

    include-stacktrace: always


spring:

  application:

    name: MovieApp

  profiles:

    active: default

  data:

    cassandra:
```

```
      schema-action: NONE

astra:
  api:
    application-token: ${ASTRA_DB_APP_TOKEN}

    database-id: ${ASTRA_DB_ID}

    database-region: ${ASTRA_DB_REGION}

    cross-region-failback: false

  cql:
    enabled: true

    download-scb:
      enabled: true

    driver-config:
      basic:
        session-keyspace: ${ASTRA_DB_KEYSPACE}

        request:
          timeout: 8s

          consistency: LOCAL_QUORUM

          page-size: 5000

      advanced:
        connection:
          init-query-timeout: 10s

          set-keyspace-timeout: 10s

        control-connection:
          timeout: 10s
```

Model

With the preliminaries for the project created, we can finally move on to the application itself. We will start with the model, as that is the foundation upon which the application is built.

Movie class

First, we will start with our **Movie** class. Create a new Java class named **Movie** with a package named **com.codewithjava21.movieapp.service**. The class will require six imports, including the **CqlVector** class from the **DataStax** library; the **Column**, **PrimaryKey**, and **Table** classes from Spring Data; and the Local/Date and **Map** Java classes:

```
package com.codewithjava21.movieapp.service;


import java.time.LocalDate;

import java.util.Map;


import org.springframework.data.cassandra.core.mapping.Column;

import org.springframework.data.cassandra.core.mapping.PrimaryKey;

import org.springframework.data.cassandra.core.mapping.Table;


import com.datastax.oss.driver.api.core.data.CqlVector;
```

The class definition will require Spring Data's **@Table** annotation, specifying the name of the **movies** table:

```
@Table("movies")

public class Movie {
```

We can then create properties for each column in the movies table. As the **movieId** property is our primary key on the table, we will use Spring Data's **@PrimaryKey** annotation:

```
    @PrimaryKey("movie_id")

    private Integer movieId;
```

We can then begin specifying the remaining properties:

```
    private String title;

    private String description;

    private float runtime;

    private String image;

    private Map<Integer,String> genres;

    private String website;

    private Long budget;
```

```
private Long revenue;

private Integer year;
```

However, some of our property names will not match up with the column names on the table. We can use Spring Data's **@Column** annotation to help with this:

```
@Column("imdb_id")

private String imdbId;

@Column("original_language")

private String originalLanguage;

@Column("release_date")

private LocalDate releaseDate;

@Column("movie_vector")

private CqlVector<Float> vector;
```

These properties should all have appropriate getters and setters created. This will not be shown here for brevity.

MovieRepository interface

Create a new Java interface inside the **com.codewithjava21.movieapp.service** package named **MovieRepository**. It will extend the **CassandraRepository** class from the **Spring Data** library. The **CassandraRepository** should be typed with the **Movie** class and an **Integer** which matches the type of the primary key. The interface definition should also be annotated with the Spring Data **@Repository** annotation:

```
package com.codewithjava21.movieapp.service;


import org.springframework.data.cassandra.repository.CassandraRepository;

import org.springframework.stereotype.Repository;


@Repository

public interface MovieByRepository extends

        CassandraRepository<Movie,Integer> {


    @Query("SELECT * FROM movies ORDER BY movie_vector ANN OF ?0 LIMIT 6")

    List<Movie> findMoviesByVector(CqlVector<Float> vector);
```

}

Inside the interface, we will define a custom query using the **@Query** annotation. Here, we will specify our vector search query. The parameters are denoted by a question mark and ordinal pair. As our query accepts a single parameter, we will use **?0** to bind the first parameter. Below the annotation, we will name the query **findMoviesByVector** and have it return a **List** of type **Movie**. It will accept a **CqlVector** of type **Float** as its lone parameter.

MovieByTitle class

Create a new Java class inside the **com.codewithjava21.movieapp.service** package named **MovieByTitle**. The **MovieByTitle** class will use the same Spring Data imports that the **Movie** class did. The properties should match the two columns in the **movies_by_title** table as closely as possible, using the Spring Data annotations as required:

```java
package com.codewithjava21.movieapp.service;


import org.springframework.data.cassandra.core.mapping.Column;

import org.springframework.data.cassandra.core.mapping.PrimaryKey;

import org.springframework.data.cassandra.core.mapping.Table;


@Table("movies_by_title")
public class MovieByTitle {

    @PrimaryKey("title")
    private String title;

    @Column("movie_id")
    private int movieId;

    public int getMovieId() {
        return movieId;
    }

    public void setMovieId(int movieId) {
        this.movieId = movieId;
```

```
    }

    public String getTitle() {

        return title;

    }

    public void setTitle(String title) {

        this.title = title;

    }

}
```

MovieByTitleRepository interface

Create a new Java interface inside the **com.codewithjava21.movieapp.service** package named **MovieByTitleRepository**. It will extend the **CassandraRepository** class from the **Spring Data** library. The **CassandraRepository** should be typed with the **MovieByTitle** class and a **String** which matches the type of the primary key. The interface definition should also be annotated with the Spring Data **@Repository** annotation:

```
package com.codewithjava21.movieapp.service;


import org.springframework.data.cassandra.repository.CassandraRepository;

import org.springframework.stereotype.Repository;


@Repository

public interface MovieByTitleRepository  extends
CassandraRepository<MovieByTitle,String> {


}
```

Controller

Our controller will require only a single class. We will name it the **MovieAppController**.

MovieAppController class

Create a new Java class inside the **com.codewithjava21.movieapp.service** package named **MovieAppController**. The **MovieAppController** class will require imports for Spring's **ResponseEntity**, **GetMapping**, **PathVariable**, and **RestController** classes. It will also require standard Java imports for the **ArrayList**, **List**, and **Optional** classes:

```
package com.codewithjava21.movieapp.service;


import java.util.ArrayList;

import java.util.List;

import java.util.Optional;


import org.springframework.http.ResponseEntity;

import org.springframework.web.bind.annotation.GetMapping;

import org.springframework.web.bind.annotation.PathVariable;

import org.springframework.web.bind.annotation.RequestMapping;

import org.springframework.web.bind.annotation.RestController;


@RequestMapping("/movieapp")

@RestController

public class MovieAppController {


    private MovieRepository movieRepo;

    private MovieByTitleRepository movieTitleRepo;
```

The **MovieAppController** class will need both the **@RequestMapping** and **@RestController** annotations. The **@RequestMapping** annotation should also specify a relative URL for the service. We will specify it as **/movieapp**. The class will also require two privately-scoped properties; one for each **Repository** interface.

The class will require one constructor, which accepts parameters for each of the repositories, and sets the **private** properties:

```
public MovieAppController(MovieRepository movieRepo,

        MovieByTitleRepository movieTitleRepo) {

    this.movieRepo = movieRepo;
```

```
    this.movieTitleRepo = movieTitleRepo;

}
```

Our controller will expose three endpoints, one for each required query. We will start with the simplest endpoint method, which will return a single movie by its ID (inside of the **ResponseEntity** class). It will require the **@GetMapping** annotation to specify an additional piece of the relative URL for the movie's ID:

```
@GetMapping("/movies/{id}")

public ResponseEntity<Optional<Movie>>

        getMovieByMovieId(@PathVariable(value="id") int movieId) {

    Optional<Movie> returnVal = movieRepo.findById(movieId);

    if (returnVal.isPresent()) {

        return ResponseEntity.ok(returnVal);

    }


    return ResponseEntity.ok(Optional.ofNullable(null));

}
```

The method uses the **Optional** type, which is helpful when working with data requests that may return null values. Essentially, if the call to **movieRepo's findById()** method returns null, we can handle that appropriately.

Next, we will build an endpoint method to return a single movie by its title. This method will work on the same premise as the last, except we need to make two queries to get a movie. Additionally, we can have a third query to happen, as we will query the **movies_by_title** table a second time while prefacing the title with **"the"**. Between that and querying the titles by lower case, we have hopefully loosen-up our search criteria enough to be helpful:

```
@GetMapping("/movies/{title}")

public ResponseEntity<Optional<Movie>> getMovieByTitle(@
PathVariable(value="title") String movieTitle) {

    Optional<Movie> returnVal = Optional.ofNullable(new Movie());

    Optional<MovieByTitle> movieByTitle =
```

```
        movieTitleRepo.findById(movieTitle.toLowerCase());


    if (movieByTitle.isEmpty()) {

        // try one more time with "the " on the front"

        movieByTitle = movieTitleRepo.findById("the "

                + movieTitle.toLowerCase());

    }


    if (movieByTitle.isPresent()) {

        int movieId = movieByTitle.get().getMovieId();

        returnVal = movieRepo.findById(movieId);


        return ResponseEntity.ok(returnVal);

    }


    return ResponseEntity.ok(Optional.ofNullable(null));

}
```

The final method on the controller will be for our **recommendations** endpoint. It will use the **@GetMapping** to define the endpoint URL, which will accept a movie ID as its lone parameter. This method performs two queries, first returning a movie by its ID, so that it can access the movie's vector. The second query is the actual vector search, using the returned vector as its parameter:

```
@GetMapping("/recommendations/movie/{id}")

public ResponseEntity<List<Movie>> getMovieRecommendationsById(

        @PathVariable(value="id") int movieId) {


    List<Movie> returnVal = new ArrayList<>();

    Optional<Movie> origMovie = movieRepo.findById(movieId);


    // get list of movies by original movie's vector

    returnVal = movieRepo.findMoviesByVector(

            origMovie.get().getVector());
```

```
    // The 1st item in the list will be the original movie, so REMOVE

    returnVal.remove(0);


    return ResponseEntity.ok(returnVal);

}
```

If we recall from the CQL queries that we ran earlier in the chapter, the original movie is always the first entry in the result set. Therefore, we can safely remove that movie from our **List** before returning it.

Querying the service

With this complete, we should be able to run our Spring Boot application and query our service endpoints using either the **curl** command (from a terminal session) or a web browser.

Movies by ID

To retrieve data for a movie by ID, run the following **curl** command:

```
curl -XGET http://localhost:8080/movieapp/movies/id/1891
```

```
{"movieId":1891,"title":"The Empire Strikes Back","description":"\"The epic
saga continues as Luke Skywalker, in hopes of defeating the evil Galactic Em-
pire, learns the ways of the Jedi from aging master Yoda. But Darth Vader is
more determined than ever to capture Luke. Meanwhile, rebel leader Princess
Leia, cocky Han Solo, Chewbacca, and droids C-3PO and R2-D2 are thrown into
various stages of capture, betrayal and despair.\"","runtime":124.0,"im-
age":null,"genres":{"4":"Adventure","8":"Action","13":"Science        Fic-
tion"},"website":"http://www.starwars.com/films/star-wars-episode-v-the-em-
pire-strikes-back","budget":18000000,"revenue":538400000,"year":1980,"imd-
bId":"tt0080684","originalLanguage":"en","releaseDate":"1980-05-17","vec-
tor":{"empty":false}}
```

Movies by title

To retrieve data for a movie by title, run the following **curl** command:

```
curl -XGET http://localhost:8080/movieapp/movies/title/aliens
```

{"movieId":679,"title":"Aliens","description":"\"When Ripley's lifepod is found by a salvage crew over 50 years later, she finds that terra-formers are on the very planet they found the alien species. When the company sends a family of colonists out to investigate her story, all contact is lost with the planet and colonists. They enlist Ripley and the colonial marines to return and search for answers.\"","runtime":137.0,"image":null,"genres":{"8":"Action","10":"Thriller","11":"Horror","13":"Science Fiction"},"website":"","budget":18500000,"revenue":183316455,"year":1986,"imdbId":"tt0090605","originalLanguage":"en","releaseDate":"1986-07-18","vector":{"empty":false}}

Movie recommendations

To retrieve recommendation data for a movie by ID, run the following **curl** command:

```
curl -XGET http://localhost:8080/movieapp/recommendations/movie/id/1891
```

```
[{"movieId":1892,"title":"Return of the Jedi",...

 {"movieId":8587,"title":"The Lion King",...

 {"movieId":862,"title":"Toy Story",...

 {"movieId":10530,"title":"Pocahontas",...
```

View

Like the controller, the view layer of our application will consist of a single class. The **MovieApMainView** class will implement many of **Vaadin**'s classes and components, and will act as the **main** interface for our users.

MovieAppMainView class

The final part of our application is the view. Create a new Java class named **MovieAppMainView** in the **com.codewithjava21.movieapp** package. It should extend the **VerticalLayout** class from the **Vaadin** library. This class will require many imports, so we will not list them here. They can be found in the code resources for this book.

> **Note: The IDE may recommend or require that a new serialVersionID be defined. This is ok, and one may be generated without concern.**

The class definition will require Vaadin's **@Route** annotation. Different routes can be defined for different **Vaadin** classes (web pages). But for our purposes an empty URL should put our application on the **root**:

```
@Route("")

public class MovieAppMainView extends VerticalLayout {

    private TextField queryField = new TextField();

    private RadioButtonGroup<String> queryBy =

            new RadioButtonGroup<>();

    private Button queryButton;

    private Button upButton;
```

We will also define many **Vaadin** components and properties as privately-scoped on the class itself. This is necessary because the dynamic nature of our application will require us to access and modify **Vaadin** components that have already been placed as visible on the page. We will define our query components (**Field**, **RadioButton**, and **queryButton**), as well as our upload button.

Next, we can define our six image properties. The first is named **image**, and will be used as the main **image** for each movie. The remaining images are for the recommendations, and they are numbered one through five:

```
    private Image image = new Image();

    private Image recImage1 = new Image();

    private Image recImage2 = new Image();

    private Image recImage3 = new Image();

    private Image recImage4 = new Image();

    private Image recImage5 = new Image();
```

We will also use Vaadin's **Span** component to build **tags** or **badges** for each of the movie's genres:

```
    private Span genre1 = new Span();

    private Span genre2 = new Span();

    private Span genre3 = new Span();
```

Additionally, we will need several **TextField** components:

```
    private TextField movieId = new TextField("ID");

    private TextField releaseDate = new TextField("release date");

    private TextField website = new TextField("website");
```

```
private TextField imdbWebsite = new TextField("IMDB website");

private TextField imdb = new TextField("IMDB");

private TextField language = new TextField("original language");

private TextField budget = new TextField("budget");

private TextField revenue = new TextField("revenue");

private TextField voteRating = new TextField("rating");

private TextField votes = new TextField("total votes");
```

The **Paragraph** components will be used to show pieces of the movie data, for which we do not want a text well or border around:

```
private Paragraph description = new Paragraph();

private Paragraph title = new Paragraph();

private Paragraph recommendation1 = new Paragraph();

private Paragraph recommendation2 = new Paragraph();

private Paragraph recommendation3 = new Paragraph();

private Paragraph recommendation4 = new Paragraph();

private Paragraph recommendation5 = new Paragraph();

private Paragraph year = new Paragraph();
```

There are some additional components and properties that we need to define. We will need a locale defined to format currency amounts for revenue and budget. A regular expression Pattern will be used to determine if a value is a number. We will need a memory buffer, stream resource, and **Upload** component to allow us to **upload** our images for each movie:

```
private Locale enUS = Locale.US;

private Pattern numericPattern =
        Pattern.compile("-?\\d+(\\.\\d+)?");

private MemoryBuffer buffer;

private Upload upload;

private StreamResource noImgFileStream;

private String noImageFile = "images/noImage.png";

private Map<Integer,String> mapGenres = new HashMap<>();

private MovieAppController controller;
```

Additionally, we will define properties for a local implementation of a movie's **genre map**, as well as one to provide easier access to the controller.

The constructor will accept parameters for each repository to allow us to define our controller. These parameters will be injected by Spring Boot at runtime. We will also use Vaadin Layout's **add()** method to build out the individual parts of our page vertically. We have not created the methods specified in the calls to **add()**, so we will do this next:

```
public MovieAppMainView(MovieRepository mRepo,

        MovieByTitleRepository mtRepo) {


    controller = new MovieAppController(mRepo, mtRepo);


    add(buildQueryBar());

    add(buildTitle());

    add(buildImageUpdateControls());

    add(buildImageData(), description);

    add(buildGenreData());


    add(buildMovieMetaData());

    add(buildFinancialData());

    add(buildRatingData());

    add(buildWebsiteData());

    add(new Paragraph("You may also enjoy these similar titles:"));

    add(buildRecommendations());

}
```

First, we will construct our **QueryBar**. This will be the main way in which users will find movies. Our **build** methods will begin by defining a **layout** object of the **HorizontalLayout** class. In this method, we will define our **queryButton**, add a **magnifying glass** icon to our **queryField**, and then call an additional **build** method to assemble a **radio** button:

```
private Component buildQueryBar() {

    HorizontalLayout layout = new HorizontalLayout();


    queryButton = new Button("Query");
```

```
queryButton.addThemeVariants(ButtonVariant.LUMO_PRIMARY);

Icon search = new Icon(VaadinIcon.SEARCH);

queryField.setPrefixComponent(search);


layout.add(queryField, queryButton, buildQueryRadio());


queryButton.addClickListener(click -> {

    refreshData();

});


    return layout;

}
```

Additionally, we will add a listener to **queryButton**. This will simply call a method named **refreshData** when it is clicked.

The **buildQueryRadio()** method will build a radio button for us. This will let the user select whether to perform a query by **ID** or a query by **Title**. We will set a default value of **ID**. Take a look at the following code:

```
private Component buildQueryRadio() {

    HorizontalLayout layout = new HorizontalLayout();


    queryBy.setLabel("Query by:");

    queryBy.setItems("ID", "Title");

    queryBy.setValue("ID");


    layout.add(queryBy);


    return layout;

}
```

Our **buildTitle()** method is very simple. We use it to configure the underlying **cascading style sheet** (**CSS**) parameters for the movie's title text. In this case, we want the title to be bolded and of an extra-large font size:

```
private Component buildTitle() {
```

```
HorizontalLayout layout = new HorizontalLayout();

title.getStyle()
    .set("font-weight", "bold")
    .set("font-size", "x-large");

layout.add(title, year);

return layout;
}
```

Our **buildGenreData()** method will initialize our **genre** (**Span**) components. We are adjusting the theme for the **Span** to be of a **badge**, and we are setting each **genre** to be invisible initially. This way, if a movie only has one or two genres, we do not have to display an **empty** badge:

```
private Component buildGenreData() {

    HorizontalLayout layout = new HorizontalLayout();

    genre1.getElement().getThemeList().add("badge");
    genre1.setVisible(false);

    genre2.getElement().getThemeList().add("badge");
    genre2.setVisible(false);

    genre3.getElement().getThemeList().add("badge");
    genre3.setVisible(false);

    layout.add(genre1, genre2, genre3);

    return layout;
}
```

One of the issues that we have with our application is that the movie data is free, public domain. However, the images associated with those movies are the intellectual property of the movie studios, so we cannot provide them. But what we can do is build a mechanism that allows users to upload an image for each movie themselves. Our **buildImageUpdateControls()** method will provide this functionality.

First, we will build our upload button. Then, we will define our memory buffer to load the **image** files and use it to instantiate our **Upload** component. We can add our **upload** button to the component and configure it to accept only **JPG** or **PNG** images. On the **Upload** component, we will also add a listener that is triggered upon the successful uploading of an image file (either by file picker or drag-and-drop):

```java
private Component buildImageUpdateControls() {

    HorizontalLayout layout = new HorizontalLayout();


    upButton = new Button("Upload JPG or PNG");

    upButton.addThemeVariants(ButtonVariant.LUMO_PRIMARY);

    buffer = new MemoryBuffer();

    upload = new Upload(buffer);

    upload.setUploadButton(upButton);

    upload.setAcceptedFileTypes("image/png", "image/jpg",
            "image/jpeg");

    upload.addSucceededListener(event -> {
        // generate filename
        int movieID = Integer.parseInt(movieId.getValue());

        StringBuilder filename = new StringBuilder("images/");

        String mimeType = event.getMIMEType();


        filename.append("movie_");

        filename.append(movieId.getValue());


        if (mimeType.equals("image/jpg") ||
                mimeType.equals("image/jpeg")) {
            filename.append(".jpg");
        } else {
```

```java
        // we only accept jpegs or pngs, so it must be a png
        filename.append(".png");
    }

    InputStream inStream = buffer.getInputStream();
    try {
        // get file from memory
        byte[] byteBuffer = new byte[inStream.available()];
        inStream.read(byteBuffer);

        // write to disk
        File destination = new File(filename.toString());
        Files.write(byteBuffer, destination);
        //inStream.close();
    } catch (IOException e) {
        e.printStackTrace();
    }

    // display new image
    getImage(movieID);
    upload.clearFileList();
});

layout.add(upload);

return layout;
}
```

The success listener will first generate a **filename** for the newly-uploaded image, while providing the appropriate extension (**.jpg** or **.png**) based on the image's type. From there, we will pull the image data from the buffer's input stream and write it to disk. The last task that the listener shall perform, will be to display the image and clear the **filename** from the **upload** component.

Next, we are going to write a method to build the main image data. The **buildImageData()** method will set the default image to be our no image **image**. We will also adjust the image's height via CSS to be that of 300 pixels:

```java
private Component buildImageData() {

    HorizontalLayout layout = new HorizontalLayout();

    try {

        FileInputStream fileStream = new FileInputStream(
                new File(noImageFile));

        noImgFileStream = new StreamResource("image",() -> {

            return fileStream;

        });

        image.setSrc(noImgFileStream);

    } catch (Exception e) {

        e.printStackTrace();

    }

    getImage(-1);

    image.setHeight("300px");

    layout.add(image);

    return layout;

}
```

Next, we will build the **getImage()** method. This method will abstract away the details behind loading an image. This will allow it to be used for either the **main** image or the recommended movie images:

```java
private void getImage(int movieID) {

    StreamResource src = getImageStream(movieID);

    image.setSrc(src);
```

```
}
```

The **getImageStream()** method will handle loading the requested image from the local disk. It will build the **filename**, and attempt to load the image as a **jpg** first. If that fails, it will then attempt to load the image as a **png**. If the image file is valid and the image can be loaded, its file stream is then returned:

```java
private StreamResource getImageStream(int movieID) {

    StringBuilder filename = new StringBuilder("images/");

    if (movieID >= 0) {

        filename.append("movie_");

        filename.append(movieID);

        filename.append(".jpg");

        // try jpg first

        if (!new File(filename.toString()).exists()) {

            // try png next

            filename = new StringBuilder("images/");

            filename.append("movie_");

            filename.append(movieID);

            filename.append(".png");

        }

        try {

            FileInputStream imgFileStream = new FileInputStream(
                    new File(filename.toString()));

            StreamResource src = new StreamResource("image",() -> {

                return imgFileStream;

            });

            return src;

        } catch (FileNotFoundException ex) {
```

```
            // file not found; set to "No Image" file stream

            return noImgFileStream;

        } catch (Exception ex) {

            ex.printStackTrace();

        }

    }


    return noImgFileStream;

}
```

Next, we will build a method to assemble much of the remaining uncategorized data. This includes the **movieId**, the movie's ID on **imdb.com**, and the movie's original language. As these data points will be assigned to **TextField** components, they will be set as **ReadOnly**:

```
private Component buildMovieMetaData() {

    HorizontalLayout layout = new HorizontalLayout();

    movieId.setReadOnly(true);

    imdb.setReadOnly(true);

    language.setReadOnly(true);

    layout.add(movieId, imdb, language);

    return layout;

}
```

Following that, we will assemble the financial data concerning the movie. This includes the movie's **budget**, **revenue**, and **releaseDate**. We also want to ensure that their respective **TextFields** are set to be **ReadOnly**:

```
private Component buildFinancialData() {

    HorizontalLayout layout = new HorizontalLayout();

    releaseDate.setReadOnly(true);

    budget.setReadOnly(true);
```

```
    revenue.setReadOnly(true);


    layout.add(releaseDate, budget, revenue);


    return layout;

}
```

Next, we will build a method to assemble the movie's rating data. There are only two data points here, including the average vote on a rating scale of **1** to **10**, and the total number of votes. We will also use the **buildRatingData()** method to add a **gold star** (icon) to the **voteRating TextField**:

```
private Component buildRatingData() {

    HorizontalLayout layout = new HorizontalLayout();


    voteRating.setReadOnly(true);

    votes.setReadOnly(true);


    Icon star = new Icon(VaadinIcon.STAR);

    star.setColor("gold");

    voteRating.setPrefixComponent(star);


    layout.add(voteRating, votes);


    return layout;

}
```

The next method will be to assemble the external website data. We will write the **buildWebstieData()** method to assemble and appropriately display the data for the movie's official website, and for its entry on **imdb.com**:

```
private Component buildWebsiteData() {

    HorizontalLayout layout = new HorizontalLayout();


    website.setReadOnly(true);

    website.setWidth("400px");
```

```
imdbWebsite.setReadOnly(true);

imdbWebsite.setWidth("400px");


layout.add(website, imdbWebsite);


return layout;
```

}

The next method will be complicated. We will be creating the display areas for the five movie recommendations that come back for each movie. Each recommendation will be its own vertical layout with a height of 100 pixels. It will also have a listener allowing the user to click on it and display that movie. Additionally, the text of the recommendation will be set to extra-small via CSS:

```
private Component buildRecommendations() {

    HorizontalLayout layout = new HorizontalLayout();


    VerticalLayout vLayout1 = new VerticalLayout();

    recImage1.setHeight("100px");

    recImage1.addClickListener( event -> {

        String[] movieText = recommendation1.getText().split(" - ");

        queryField.setValue(movieText[0]);

        queryBy.setValue("ID");

        refreshData();

    });

    recommendation1.getStyle()

        .set("font-size", "x-small");

    vLayout1.add(recImage1,recommendation1);


    VerticalLayout vLayout2 = new VerticalLayout();

    recImage2.setHeight("100px");

    recImage2.addClickListener( event -> {

        String[] movieText = recommendation2.getText().split(" - ");
```

```java
        queryField.setValue(movieText[0]);

        queryBy.setValue("ID");

        refreshData();

    });

    recommendation2.getStyle()

        .set("font-size", "x-small");

    vLayout2.add(recImage2,recommendation2);
```

Above are the code blocks to build the displays for the first two recommendations. Unfortunately, as they are pre-added to the main layout as components, we can address only one at a time. The following code repeats the logic for the three remaining recommendations:

```java
    VerticalLayout vLayout3 = new VerticalLayout();

    recImage3.setHeight("100px");

    recImage3.addClickListener( event -> {

        String[] movieText = recommendation3.getText().split(" - ");

        queryField.setValue(movieText[0]);

        queryBy.setValue("ID");

        refreshData();

    });

    recommendation3.getStyle()

        .set("font-size", "x-small");

    vLayout3.add(recImage3,recommendation3);


    VerticalLayout vLayout4 = new VerticalLayout();

    recImage4.setHeight("100px");

    recImage4.addClickListener( event -> {

        String[] movieText = recommendation4.getText().split(" - ");

        queryField.setValue(movieText[0]);

        queryBy.setValue("ID");
```

```
        refreshData();

    });

    recommendation4.getStyle()

        .set("font-size", "x-small");

    vLayout4.add(recImage4,recommendation4);


    VerticalLayout vLayout5 = new VerticalLayout();

    recImage5.setHeight("100px");

    recImage5.addClickListener( event -> {

        String[] movieText = recommendation5.getText().split(" - ");

        queryField.setValue(movieText[0]);

        queryBy.setValue("ID");

        refreshData();

    });

    recommendation5.getStyle()

        .set("font-size", "x-small");

    vLayout5.add(recImage5,recommendation5);


    layout.add(vLayout1,vLayout2,vLayout3,vLayout4,vLayout5);


    return layout;

}
```

As we display the movie's revenue and budget data, we will also want to format that money appropriately. Our **formatMoney()** method will handle that using the **enUS** property we defined earlier for the English-US locale:

```
private String formatMoney(Long money) {

    NumberFormat numFormat = NumberFormat.getCurrencyInstance(enUS);

    return numFormat.format(Double.parseDouble(money.toString()));

}
```

Additionally, we will also need a method to check whether or not a string is a number. This will be done with a **regular** expression, using the **numericPattern** we defined earlier. Take a look at the following code:

```java
private boolean isNumeric(String value) {

    if (value == null) {

        return false;

    }


    return numericPattern.matcher(value).matches();

}
```

The **refreshData()** method has a lot of moving parts, but it also drives the logic behind how things are displayed for each movie. As this method is largely driven by the user's interactions with the query bar, we will begin by determining if the user is querying by ID or by the movie's title. Based on that, we determine how to retrieve the movie (either by ID or title) and pull its data back from the database:

```java
private void refreshData() {

    Optional<Movie> optionalMovie;

    if (queryBy.getValue().equals("ID")) {
        if (isNumeric(queryField.getValue())) {
            optionalMovie = controller.getMovieByMovieId(
                    Integer.parseInt(queryField.getValue()))
                .getBody();
        } else {
            optionalMovie = Optional.ofNullable(null);
        }
    } else {
        // name
        optionalMovie = controller.getMovieByTitle(
                queryField.getValue()).getBody();
```

```
    }
```

Once we have a movie, we can begin assigning the data to the class properties:

```java
    if (optionalMovie != null && optionalMovie.isPresent()) {

        Movie movie = optionalMovie.get();

        String strTitle = movie.getTitle();

        String strDescription = movie.getDescription();

        LocalDate ldReleaseDate = movie.getReleaseDate();

        Integer intYear = movie.getYear();

        mapGenres = movie.getGenres();

        String strWebsiteUrl = movie.getWebsite();

        String strImdbId = movie.getImdbId();

        String strLanguage = movie.getOriginalLanguage();

        title.setText(strTitle);

        description.setText(strDescription);

        if (movie.getMovieId() != null) {
            movieId.setValue(movie.getMovieId().toString());
            // once we have the ID, get the image
            getImage(movie.getMovieId());
        }

        if (movie.getReleaseDate() != null) {
            releaseDate.setValue(ldReleaseDate.toString());
        }

        if (intYear != null) {
            year.setText(intYear.toString());
```

```
}
```

Here, we will process the **genre badges**. We begin by setting them all invisible. Next, we iterate through **mapGenres**, setting the **genre** text to the **badges** in an ordinal fashion:

```java
// process genre "badges"

int genreCounter = 0;

genre1.setVisible(false);

genre2.setVisible(false);

genre3.setVisible(false);


for (String genre : mapGenres.values()) {

    switch (genreCounter) {
    case 0:

        genre1.setText(genre);;

        genre1.setVisible(true);

        break;
    case 1:

        genre2.setText(genre);

        genre2.setVisible(true);

        break;
    case 2:

        genre3.setText(genre);

        genre3.setVisible(true);

        break;
    default:

        Break;
    }

    genreCounter++;

}
```

Next, we will set the website and language data, along with the **budget** and **revenue**. The **budget** and **revenue** also make calls to our **formatMoney()** method. We will also set the vote data from their respective places in the movie's vector:

```
website.setValue(strWebsiteUrl);

imdbWebsite.setValue("https://www.imdb.com/title/"
+ strImdbId);

imdb.setValue(strImdbId);

language.setValue(strLanguage);

if (movie.getBudget() != null) {

    budget.setValue(formatMoney(movie.getBudget()));

}

if (movie.getRevenue() != null) {

    revenue.setValue(formatMoney(movie.getRevenue()));

}

if (movie.getVector() != null) {

    voteRating.setValue(movie.getVector().get(5).toString());

    votes.setValue(movie.getVector().get(6).toString());

}
```

Next, we will build out the data for each of the movie's recommendations:

```
if (movieId.getValue().length() > 0) {

    Integer movieID = Integer.parseInt(movieId.getValue());

    List<Movie> recommendedMovies =
            controller.getMovieRecommendationsById(movieID)
        .getBody();

    int movieCounter = 0;
    for (Movie recMovie : recommendedMovies) {
```

```
StreamResource resource =

        getImageStream(recMovie.getMovieId());

StringBuilder titleText = new StringBuilder(

        recMovie.getMovieId().toString());

titleText.append(" - ");

titleText.append(recMovie.getTitle());


switch (movieCounter) {

case 0:

    recImage1.setSrc(resource);

    recommendation1.setText(titleText.toString());

    break;

case 1:

    recImage2.setSrc(resource);

    recommendation2.setText(titleText.toString());

    Break;

case 2:

    recImage3.setSrc(resource);

    recommendation3.setText(titleText.toString());

    break;

case 3:

    recImage4.setSrc(resource);

    recommendation4.setText(titleText.toString());

    break;

default:

    recImage5.setSrc(resource);

    recommendation5.setText(titleText.toString());

}
```

```
        movieCounter++;

        if (movieCounter > 4) {

            break;

        }

    }

}

} else {

    Notification.show("No movie found for those query parameters."

        ,5000, Position.TOP_CENTER);

}

}
```

Finally, in the event that a movie cannot be found given the user's query input, we will use Vaadin's **Notification** class to display a message for five seconds at the top of the page.

With the view complete, we can now run our application. Go to a browser and navigate to **http://127.0.0.1:8080/**. The application should be similar to *Figure 10.4*:

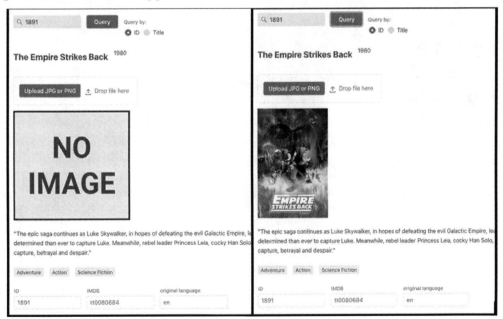

Figure 10.4: *A screenshot for "The Empire Strikes Back," before and after a downloaded image was dragged on to the upload component*

Once we navigate to a particular movie page we can see more of its data by scrolling down. This is shown in *Figure 10.5*:

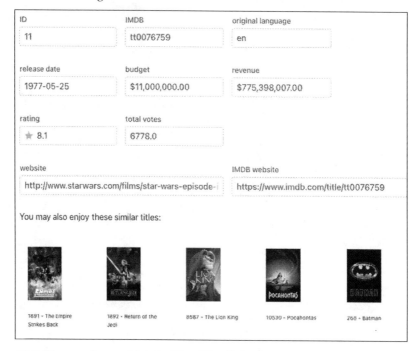

Figure 10.5: *The second page of data for "Star Wars," showing its recommendations at the bottom*

Conclusion

In this chapter, we applied much of what we learned in the preceding chapters and created a fairly complex application. We also learned about `Optional` type and `vector` search.

One of the more complex parts of this project was having to create a special application to process the data. This is, unfortunately, a harsh reality of data processing. Simply importing the data or doing a drag-and-drop of a CSV file into the database is rarely sufficient on its own. Data must often be subjected to various levels of preprocessing before being considered usable. Even the `movies_metadata.csv` file downloaded as-is from `Kaggle` was not usable, as several of the entries contained extra line breaks in the description which tripped-up the ingest process.

While functional, this application is not complete. There are several things that a developer could do to extend its functionality further. A feature could be written to allow the user to edit a movie's data, or even to enter a new movie using the user interface. We could also allow users to rate each movie and then recalculate the rating data and vector embedding. Additionally, an LLM could be used to create a `vector` embedding based on the `movie` titles, and then a similarity method could run a `vector` search based on that. Like stars in the sky, the possibilities are endless.

Points to remember

- Cassandra databases created through Astra require a special kind of instance to be **vector** enabled.
- Secondary index queries on a distributed database are meant for convenience and not for performance.
- A CQL **ANN vector** search query does not have to use a **WHERE** clause, but requires an **ORDER BY** and **LIMIT** clauses.
- The **Optional** type in Java is a great way to prevent **NullPointerExceptions** when querying a database.
- **Vaadin** uses the **getStyle()** method to expose the underlying CSS of its components. This allows precise visual adjustments and configurations to be done.

Join our book's Discord space

Join the book's Discord Workspace for Latest updates, Offers, Tech happenings around the world, New Release and Sessions with the Authors:

https://discord.bpbonline.com

APPENDIX A:
References

Baeldung (2022). *Java Preview Features*. Retrieved on 2023-04-12 from: **https://www.baeldung.com/java-preview-features**.

Baeldung (2022b). *A Guide to Java Regular Expressions API*. Retrieved on 2023-05-06 from: **https://www.baeldung.com/regular-expressions-java**.

Baeldung (2023). *Ignoring Commas in Quotes When Splitting a Comma-separated String*. Retrieved on 2023-08-18 from: **https://www.baeldung.com/java-split-string-commas**.

Brewer E., Fox A. (1999). *Harvest, Yield, and Scalable Tolerant Systems*. Proceedings of the Seventh Workshop on Hot Topics in Operating Systems, Rio Rico, AZ, USA. Pages 174-178.

Darcy J. (2021). *Floating-Point Arithmetic: What Every Java Programmer Should Know!* Retrieved via the @Java YouTube channel on 2023-06-02 from: **https://www.youtube.com/watch?v=ajaHQ9S4uTA**.

Gillis A., Lewis S. (2021). *Object Oriented Programming (OOP)*. TechTarget. Retrieved on 2023-04-01 from: **https://www.techtarget.com/searchapparchitecture/definition/object-oriented-programming-OOP**.

Hanson B. (2015). *How Steve Wozniak's Breakout Defined Apple's Future*. Game Informer. Retrieved on 2023-09-30 from:

https://www.gameinformer.com/b/features/archive/2015/10/09/how-steve-wozniak-s-breakout-defined-apple-s-future.aspx.

IBM (2022). *Big Decimal (BigDecimal) Support for Real Numbers*. IBM Sterling B2B Integrator documentation. Retrieved on 2023-06-03 from: **https://www.ibm.com/docs/en/b2b-integrator/5.2?topic=fdif-big-decimal-bigdecimal-support-real-numbers-2**.

IMDB (2023). *IMDB.com: Overview | LinkedIn*. Retrieved on 2023-08-06 from: **https://www.linkedin.com/company/imdb-com/**.

JavaTPoint (2021). *Red-black tree in Data Structure*. JavaTPoint. Retrieved on 2023-05-21 from: **https://www.javatpoint.com/red-black-tree**.

Oracle (2004). *Introduction to Oracle SQL - History of SQL*. Oracle Database SQL Reference. Oracle Corporation. Retrieved on 2023-06-19 from: **https://docs.oracle.com/cd/B13789_01/server.101/b10759/intro.htm**.

Oracle (2023). *Java Hotspot VM Options* Oracle Corporation. Retrieved on 2023-09-14 from: **https://www.oracle.com/java/technologies/javase/vmoptions-jsp.html**.

Parlog N. (2023). *New (Sequenced) Collections in Java 21 - Inside Java Newscast #45*. Retrieved on 2023-04-08 from: **https://nipafx.dev/inside-java-newscast-45/**.

Posa R. (2022). *Java LinkedList - LinkedList in Java*. Digital Ocean. Retrieved on 2023-05-19 from: **https://www.digitalocean.com/community/tutorials/java-linkedlist-linkedlist-java**.

Tyson M. (2022). *Intro to virtual threads: A new approach to Java concurrency*. InfoWorld. Retrieved on 2023-04-07 from: **https://www.infoworld.com/article/3678148/intro-to-virtual-threads-a-new-approach-to-java-concurrency.html**.

Wiffin E. (2017). *Floating Point Math*. Retrieved on 2023-06-03 from: **https://0.30000000000000004.com/**.

Join our book's Discord space

Join the book's Discord Workspace for Latest updates, Offers, Tech happenings around the world, New Release and Sessions with the Authors:

https://discord.bpbonline.com

APPENDIX B:
UTF Conversion Chart

In this appendix, we will look at the following UTF conversion chart:

Dec	Oct	Hex	UTF	Binary	Dec	Oct	Hex	UTF	Binary
0	0	0	NULL	00000000	128	200	80		10000000
1	1	1	SOH	00000001	129	201	81		10000001
2	2	2	STX	00000010	130	202	82		10000010
3	3	3	ETX	00000011	131	203	83		10000011
4	4	4	EOT	00000100	132	204	84		10000100
5	5	5	ENQ	00000101	133	205	85		10000101
6	6	6	ACK	00000110	134	206	86		10000110
7	7	7	BELL	00000111	135	207	87		10000111
8	10	8	BSP	00001000	136	210	88		10001000
9	11	9	TAB	00001001	137	211	89		10001001
10	12	A	LF	00001010	138	212	8A		10001010
11	13	B	VTAB	00001011	139	213	8B		10001011

Dec	Oct	Hex	UTF	Binary	Dec	Oct	Hex	UTF	Binary
12	14	C	FF	00001100	140	214	8C		10001100
13	15	D	CR	00001101	141	215	8D		10001101
14	16	E		00001110	142	216	8E		10001110
15	17	F		00001111	143	217	8F		10001111
16	20	10		00010000	144	220	90		10010000
17	21	11		00010001	145	221	91		10010001
18	22	12		00010010	146	222	92		10010010
19	23	13		00010011	147	223	93		10010011
20	24	14		00010100	148	224	94		10010100
21	25	15		00010101	149	225	95		10010101
22	26	16		00010110	150	226	96		10010110
23	27	17		00010111	151	227	97		10010111
24	30	18		00011000	152	230	98		10011000
25	31	19		00011001	153	231	99		10011001
26	32	1A		00011010	154	232	9A		10011010
27	33	1B		00011011	155	233	9B		10011011
28	34	1C		00011100	156	234	9C		10011100
29	35	1D		00011101	157	235	9D		10011101
30	36	1E		00011110	158	236	9E		10011110
31	37	1F		00011111	159	237	9F		10011111
32	40	20	SPACE	00100000	160	240	A0		10100000
33	41	21	!	00100001	161	241	A1	¡	10100001
34	42	22	"	00100010	162	242	A2	¢	10100010
35	43	23	#	00100011	163	243	A3	£	10100011
36	44	24	$	00100100	164	244	A4	¤	10100100
37	45	25	%	00100101	165	245	A5	¥	10100101
38	46	26	&	00100110	166	246	A6	¦	10100110

Dec	Oct	Hex	UTF	Binary	Dec	Oct	Hex	UTF	Binary
39	47	27	'	00100111	167	247	A7	§	10100111
40	50	28	(	00101000	168	250	A8	¨	10101000
41	51	29	)	00101001	169	251	A9	©	10101001
42	52	2A	*	00101010	170	252	AA	ª	10101010
43	53	2B	+	00101011	171	253	AB	«	10101011
44	54	2C	,	00101100	172	254	AC	¬	10101100
45	55	2D	-	00101101	173	255	AD		10101101
46	56	2E	.	00101110	174	256	AE	®	10101110
47	57	2F	/	00101111	175	257	AF	¯	10101111
48	60	30	0	00110000	176	260	B0	°	10110000
49	61	31	1	00110001	177	261	B1	±	10110001
50	62	32	2	00110010	178	262	B2	²	10110010
51	63	33	3	00110011	179	263	B3	³	10110011
52	64	34	4	00110100	180	264	B4	´	10110100
53	65	35	5	00110101	181	265	B5	μ	10110101
54	66	36	6	00110110	182	266	B6	¶	10110110
55	67	37	7	00110111	183	267	B7	·	10110111
56	70	38	8	00111000	184	270	B8	¸	10111000
57	71	39	9	00111001	185	271	B9	¹	10111001
58	72	3A	:	00111010	186	272	BA	º	10111010
59	73	3B	;	00111011	187	273	BB	»	10111011
60	74	3C	<	00111100	188	274	BC	¼	10111100
61	75	3D	=	00111101	189	275	BD	½	10111101
62	76	3E	>	00111110	190	276	BE	¾	10111110
63	77	3F	?	00111111	191	277	BF	¿	10111111
64	100	40	@	01000000	192	300	C0	À	11000000
65	101	41	A	01000001	193	301	C1	Á	11000001

Dec	Oct	Hex	UTF	Binary	Dec	Oct	Hex	UTF	Binary
66	102	42	B	01000010	194	302	C2	Â	11000010
67	103	43	C	01000011	195	303	C3	Ã	11000011
68	104	44	D	01000100	196	304	C4	Ä	11000100
69	105	45	E	01000101	197	305	C5	Å	11000101
70	106	46	F	01000110	198	306	C6	Æ	11000110
71	107	47	G	01000111	199	307	C7	Ç	11000111
72	110	48	H	01001000	200	310	C8	È	11001000
73	111	49	I	01001001	201	311	C9	É	11001001
74	112	4A	J	01001010	202	312	CA	Ê	11001010
75	113	4B	K	01001011	203	313	CB	Ë	11001011
76	114	4C	L	01001100	204	314	CC	Ì	11001100
77	115	4D	M	01001101	205	315	CD	Í	11001101
78	116	4E	N	01001110	206	316	CE	Î	11001110
79	117	4F	O	01001111	207	317	CF	Ï	11001111
80	120	50	P	01010000	208	320	D0	Ð	11010000
81	121	51	Q	01010001	209	321	D1	Ñ	11010001
82	122	52	R	01010010	210	322	D2	Ò	11010010
83	123	53	S	01010011	211	323	D3	Ó	11010011
84	124	54	T	01010100	212	324	D4	Ô	11010100
85	125	55	U	01010101	213	325	D5	Õ	11010101
86	126	56	V	01010110	214	326	D6	Ö	11010110
87	127	57	W	01010111	215	327	D7	×	11010111
88	130	58	X	01011000	216	330	D8	Ø	11011000
89	131	59	Y	01011001	217	331	D9	Ù	11011001
90	132	5A	Z	01011010	218	332	DA	Ú	11011010
91	133	5B	[	01011011	219	333	DB	Û	11011011
92	134	5C	\	01011100	220	334	DC	Ü	11011100

Dec	Oct	Hex	UTF	Binary	Dec	Oct	Hex	UTF	Binary
93	135	5D	]	01011101	221	335	DD	Ý	11011101
94	136	5E	^	01011110	222	336	DE	Þ	11011110
95	137	5F	_	01011111	223	337	DF	ß	11011111
96	140	60	`	01100000	224	340	E0	à	11100000
97	141	61	a	01100001	225	341	E1	á	11100001
98	142	62	b	01100010	226	342	E2	â	11100010
99	143	63	c	01100011	227	343	E3	ã	11100011
100	144	64	d	01100100	228	344	E4	ä	11100100
101	145	65	e	01100101	229	345	E5	å	11100101
102	146	66	f	01100110	230	346	E6	æ	11100110
103	147	67	g	01100111	231	347	E7	ç	11100111
104	150	68	h	01101000	232	350	E8	è	11101000
105	151	69	i	01101001	233	351	E9	é	11101001
106	152	6A	j	01101010	234	352	EA	ê	11101010
107	153	6B	k	01101011	235	353	EB	ë	11101011
108	154	6C	l	01101100	236	354	EC	ì	11101100
109	155	6D	m	01101101	237	355	ED	í	11101101
110	156	6E	n	01101110	238	356	EE	î	11101110
111	157	6F	o	01101111	239	357	EF	ï	11101111
112	160	70	p	01110000	240	360	F0	ð	11110000
113	161	71	q	01110001	241	361	F1	ñ	11110001
114	162	72	r	01110010	242	362	F2	ò	11110010
115	163	73	s	01110011	243	363	F3	ó	11110011
116	164	74	t	01110100	244	364	F4	ô	11110100
117	165	75	u	01110101	245	365	F5	õ	11110101
118	166	76	v	01110110	246	366	F6	ö	11110110
119	167	77	w	01110111	247	367	F7	÷	11110111

Dec	Oct	Hex	UTF	Binary	Dec	Oct	Hex	UTF	Binary
120	170	78	x	01111000	248	370	F8	ø	11111000
121	171	79	y	01111001	249	371	F9	ù	11111001
122	172	7A	z	01111010	250	372	FA	ú	11111010
123	173	7B	{	01111011	251	373	FB	û	11111011
124	174	7C	|	01111100	252	374	FC	ü	11111100
125	175	7D	}	01111101	253	375	FD	ý	11111101
126	176	7E	~	01111110	254	376	FE	þ	11111110
127	177	7F		01111111	255	377	FF	ÿ	11111111

Skipping to ASCII Art codes used in *Chapter 3, Strings, Characters, and Regular Expressions*. Removed the octal conversion for brevity:

Dec	Hex	UTF	Binary	Dec	Hex	UTF	Binary
9472	2500	─	10010100000000	9600	2580	■	10010110000000
9473	2501	━	10010100000001	9601	2581	▁	10010110000001
9474	2502	│	10010100000010	9602	2582	▂	10010110000010
9475	2503	┃	10010100000011	9603	2583	▃	10010110000011
9476	2504	┄	10010100000100	9604	2584	▄	10010110000100
9477	2505	┅	10010100000101	9605	2585	▅	10010110000101
9478	2506	┆	10010100000110	9606	2586	▆	10010110000110
9479	2507	┇	10010100000111	9607	2587	▇	10010110000111
9480	2508	┈	10010100001000	9608	2588	█	10010110001000
9481	2509	┉	10010100001001	9609	2589	▉	10010110001001
9482	250A	┊	10010100001010	9610	258A	▊	10010110001010
9483	250B	┋	10010100001011	9611	258B	▋	10010110001011
9484	250C	┌	10010100001100	9612	258C	▌	10010110001100
9485	250D	┍	10010100001101	9613	258D	▍	10010110001101
9486	250E	┎	10010100001110	9614	258E	▎	10010110001110
9487	250F	┏	10010100001111	9615	258F	▏	10010110001111

Dec	Hex	UTF	Binary	Dec	Hex	UTF	Binary
9488	2510	┐	10010100010000	9616	2590	▐	10010110010000
9489	2511	┐	10010100010001	9617	2591	░	10010110010001
9490	2512	┐	10010100010010	9618	2592	▒	10010110010010
9491	2513	┓	10010100010011	9619	2593	▓	10010110010011
9492	2514	└	10010100010100	9620	2594	▔	10010110010100
9493	2515	└	10010100010101	9621	2595	▕	10010110010101
9494	2516	└	10010100010110	9622	2596	▖	10010110010110
9495	2517	┗	10010100010111	9623	2597	▗	10010110010111
9496	2518	┘	10010100011000	9624	2598	▘	10010110011000
9497	2519	┘	10010100011001	9625	2599	▙	10010110011001
9498	251A	┘	10010100011010	9626	259A	▚	10010110011010
9499	251B	┛	10010100011011	9627	259B	▛	10010110011011
9500	251C	├	10010100011100	9628	259C	▜	10010110011100
9501	251D	├	10010100011101	9629	259D	▝	10010110011101
9502	251E	├	10010100011110	9630	259E	▞	10010110011110
9503	251F	├	10010100011111	9631	259F	▟	10010110011111
9504	2520	├	10010100100000	9632	25A0	■	10010110100000
9505	2521	├	10010100100001	9633	25A1	□	10010110100001
9506	2522	├	10010100100010	9634	25A2	▢	10010110100010
9507	2523	┣	10010100100011	9635	25A3	▣	10010110100011
9508	2524	┤	10010100100100	9636	25A4	▤	10010110100100
9509	2525	┤	10010100100101	9637	25A5	▥	10010110100101
9510	2526	┤	10010100100110	9638	25A6	▦	10010110100110
9511	2527	┤	10010100100111	9639	25A7	▧	10010110100111
9512	2528	┤	10010100101000	9640	25A8	▨	10010110101000
9513	2529	┤	10010100101001	9641	25A9	▩	10010110101001
9514	252A	┤	10010100101010	9642	25AA	▪	10010110101010

Dec	Hex	UTF	Binary	Dec	Hex	UTF	Binary
9515	252B	┤	10010100101011	9643	25AB	▫	10010110101011
9516	252C	┬	10010100101100	9644	25AC	▬	10010110101100
9517	252D	┬	10010100101101	9645	25AD	▭	10010110101101
9518	252E	┬	10010100101110	9646	25AE	■	10010110101110
9519	252F	┬	10010100101111	9647	25AF	▯	10010110101111
9520	2530	┳	10010100110000	9648	25B0	▰	10010110110000
9521	2531	┱	10010100110001	9649	25B1	▱	10010110110001
9522	2532	┲	10010100110010	9650	25B2	▲	10010110110010
9523	2533	┳	10010100110011	9651	25B3	△	10010110110011
9524	2534	┴	10010100110100	9652	25B4	▴	10010110110100
9525	2535	┴	10010100110101	9653	25B5	▵	10010110110101
9526	2536	┴	10010100110110	9654	25B6	▶	10010110110110
9527	2537	┴	10010100110111	9655	25B7	▷	10010110110111
9528	2538	┴	10010100111000	9656	25B8	▸	10010110111000
9529	2539	┴	10010100111001	9657	25B9	▹	10010110111001
9530	253A	┴	10010100111010	9658	25BA	►	10010110111010
9531	253B	┻	10010100111011	9659	25BB	▻	10010110111011
9532	253C	┼	10010100111100	9660	25BC	▼	10010110111100
9533	253D	┽	10010100111101	9661	25BD	▽	10010110111101
9534	253E	┾	10010100111110	9662	25BE	▾	10010110111110
9535	253F	┿	10010100111111	9663	25BF	▿	10010110111111
9536	2540	╀	10010101000000	9664	25C0	◀	10010111000000
9537	2541	╁	10010101000001	9665	25C1	◁	10010111000001
9538	2542	╂	10010101000010	9666	25C2	◂	10010111000010
9539	2543	╃	10010101000011	9667	25C3	◃	10010111000011
9540	2544	╄	10010101000100	9668	25C4	◄	10010111000100
9541	2545	╅	10010101000101	9669	25C5	◅	10010111000101

Dec	Hex	UTF	Binary	Dec	Hex	UTF	Binary
9542	2546	┆	10010101000110	9670	25C6	◆	10010111000110
9543	2547	┼	10010101000111	9671	25C7	◇	10010111000111
9544	2548	┬	10010101001000	9672	25C8	◈	10010111001000
9545	2549	┤	10010101001001	9673	25C9	◉	10010111001001
9546	254A	┝	10010101001010	9674	25CA	◊	10010111001010
9547	254B	┿	10010101001011	9675	25CB	○	10010111001011
9548	254C	--	10010101001100	9676	25CC	◌	10010111001100
9549	254D	--	10010101001101	9677	25CD	◍	10010111001101
9550	254E	┊	10010101001110	9678	25CE	◎	10010111001110
9551	254F	┋	10010101001111	9679	25CF	●	10010111001111
9552	2550	═	10010101010000	9680	25D0	◐	10010111010000
9553	2551	║	10010101010001	9681	25D1	◑	10010111010001
9554	2552	╒	10010101010010	9682	25D2	◒	10010111010010
9555	2553	╓	10010101010011	9683	25D3	◓	10010111010011
9556	2554	╔	10010101010100	9684	25D4	◔	10010111010100
9557	2555	╕	10010101010101	9685	25D5	◕	10010111010101
9558	2556	╖	10010101010110	9686	25D6	◖	10010111010110
9559	2557	╗	10010101010111	9687	25D7	◗	10010111010111
9560	2558	╘	10010101011000	9688	25D8	◘	10010111011000
9561	2559	╙	10010101011001	9689	25D9	◙	10010111011001
9562	255A	╚	10010101011010	9690	25DA	◚	10010111011010
9563	255B	╛	10010101011011	9691	25DB	◛	10010111011011
9564	255C	╜	10010101011100	9692	25DC	◜	10010111011100
9565	255D	╝	10010101011101	9693	25DD	◝	10010111011101
9566	255E	╞	10010101011110	9694	25DE	◞	10010111011110
9567	255F	╟	10010101011111	9695	25DF	◟	10010111011111
9568	2560	╠	10010101100000	9696	25E0	◠	10010111100000

Dec	Hex	UTF	Binary	Dec	Hex	UTF	Binary
9569	2561	╡	10010101100001	9697	25E1	◡	10010111100001
9570	2562	╢	10010101100010	9698	25E2	◢	10010111100010
9571	2563	╣	10010101100011	9699	25E3	◣	10010111100011
9572	2564	╤	10010101100100	9700	25E4	◤	10010111100100
9573	2565	╥	10010101100101	9701	25E5	◥	10010111100101
9574	2566	╦	10010101100110	9702	25E6	∘	10010111100110
9575	2567	╧	10010101100111	9703	25E7	◧	10010111100111
9576	2568	╨	10010101101000	9704	25E8	◨	10010111101000
9577	2569	╩	10010101101001	9705	25E9	◩	10010111101001
9578	256A	╪	10010101101010	9706	25EA	◪	10010111101010
9579	256B	╫	10010101101011	9707	25EB	◫	10010111101011
9580	256C	╬	10010101101100	9708	25EC	△	10010111101100
9581	256D	╭	10010101101101	9709	25ED	◭	10010111101101
9582	256E	╮	10010101101110	9710	25EE	◮	10010111101110
9583	256F	╯	10010101101111	9711	25EF	◯	10010111101111
9584	2570	╰	10010101110000	9712	25F0	◰	10010111110000
9585	2571	╱	10010101110001	9713	25F1	◱	10010111110001
9586	2572	╲	10010101110010	9714	25F2	◲	10010111110010
9587	2573	╳	10010101110011	9715	25F3	◳	10010111110011
9588	2574	╴	10010101110100	9716	25F4	◴	10010111110100
9589	2575	╵	10010101110101	9717	25F5	◵	10010111110101
9590	2576	╶	10010101110110	9718	25F6	◶	10010111110110
9591	2577	╷	10010101110111	9719	25F7	◷	10010111110111
9592	2578	╸	10010101111000	9720	25F8	◸	10010111111000
9593	2579	╹	10010101111001	9721	25F9	◹	10010111111001
9594	257A	╺	10010101111010	9722	25FA	◺	10010111111010
9595	257B	╻	10010101111011	9723	25FB	◻	10010111111011

Dec	Hex	UTF	Binary	Dec	Hex	UTF	Binary
9596	257C	⊸	10010101111100	9724	25FC	■	10010111111100
9597	257D	╎	10010101111101	9725	25FD	▫	10010111111101
9598	257E	⊸	10010101111110	9726	25FE	◾	10010111111110
9599	257F	╎	10010101111111	9727	25FF	◿	10010111111111

Join our book's Discord space

Join the book's Discord Workspace for Latest updates, Offers, Tech happenings around the world, New Release and Sessions with the Authors:

https://discord.bpbonline.com

Appendix C:
Database Command
Reference

This appendix will provide a short description of common database commands used in SQL, CQL, and their variants. Adherence to the official SQL standard syntax varies by database, so check the vendor's official documentation.

Note: Optional syntax is denoted in brackets [] below.

SELECT

The **SELECT** statement is used to return data from a database table. It can specify a list of columns to return from a table (specified with the **FROM** clause). The rows returned are governed by the **WHERE** clause.

Syntax:

```
SELECT * | [column1_name [AS alias],column2_name,columnN_name]

FROM [database_name|keyspace_name.]table_name

[[INNER|LEFT|RIGHT] JOIN join_table_name ON column_name[operator]value]

[WHERE column_name[operator]value [[AND|OR] column_name[operator]value]]

[LIMIT N];
```

A **WHERE** clause can contain several filtering conditions based on relational algebra. Its conditions are a range of equality operators, including equals (=), not equals (!= or <>), and greater or less than (<, >). Conditions are separated by the logical operators of **AND** and **OR**.

> Note: Only some NoSQL SELECT syntax allows the use of the OR operator, which often initiates a multi-partition scan. However, all relational databases allow the use of OR.

It is important to note that **SELECT** query performance is largely controlled by the contents of the **WHERE** clause. Unbound queries (**SELECTs** without a **WHERE** clause) will result in a full-table scan to ensure all rows are returned.

INSERT

The **INSERT** statement allows new data to be written into a table. With this statement, the column values to be written must be listed in parens, followed by a **VALUES** clause with the respective column values enclosed in parens.

Syntax:

```
INSERT INTO [database_name|keyspace_name.]table_name
(column1[,column2,columnN])

VALUES (value1[,value2,valueN]);
```

Relational databases will likely throw an error when a user attempts to insert a row that already exists. NoSQL databases (like Cassandra) will likely allow the operation, overwriting any non-key values for the row.

UPDATE

The **UPDATE** statement is designed to adjust existing column values. It requires a **SET** clause to indicate which column/value pairs should be set. There is also a **WHERE** clause on the **UPDATE** statement, which instructs the database on which rows should be updated.

Syntax:

```
UPDATE [database_name|keyspace_name.]table_name

SET column1=value1[,column2=value2,columnN=valueN]

[WHERE column_name[operator]value [[AND|OR] column_name_N[operator]
value_N]];
```

Relational databases will likely throw an error when a user attempts to update a row that does not exist. NoSQL databases (like Cassandra) are likely to allow the operation, effectively inserting a new row into the table.

Care should be taken with the **WHERE** clause. With CQL, it must contain the partition key and may contain additional clustering key columns. However, in SQL, it is optional. This means that an **UPDATE** without a **WHERE** clause will apply the writes in the **SET** clause to *every row in the table.*

DELETE

The **DELETE** statement is designed to remove existing row(**s**) that matches its criteria in the **WHERE** clause.

Syntax:

```
DELETE [column_name]

FROM [database_name|keyspace_name.]table_name

[WHERE column_name[operator]value [[AND|OR] column_name_N[operator]
value_N]];
```

> Note: Running a DELETE without a WHERE clause will remove data for every specified column in the table. If no columns are specified, then all rows in the table will be deleted, so use caution with this statement.

CREATE TABLE

The **CREATE TABLE** syntax creates a new table for data rows to be stored in.

Syntax:

```
CREATE TABLE [IF NOT EXISTS] [database_name|keyspace_name.]table_name (

    column1_name data_type [PRIMARY KEY],

    [column2_name data_type,

    columnN_name data_type,]

    [PRIMARY KEY(key1,key2)]

);
```

Some databases will allow the absence of a defined primary key at creation time, while others will not.

CREATE INDEX

This command creates an index on the specified table and column combination.

Syntax:

```
CREATE INDEX [index_name] ON [table]([column]);
```

The effects and requirements behind additional *secondary* indexes will vary by database type. For most relational database tables, columns that support regular **WHERE** clause filtering conditions should contain an index. Usually, the addition of an index will improve query performance.

However, for NoSQL databases, secondary indexes tend to be counter-productive to query performance. NoSQL databases (for example, Apache Cassandra) are engineered to distribute data in specific ways. Secondary indexes, while convenient, violate their original data flow designs and intentions. Therefore, secondary indexes should be created sparingly with NoSQL databases and used infrequently.

One common effect between indexes on all types of databases is that they increase the resources required to perform a write operation. This is because writes will not only have to update the data in the table but also any related indexes.

Join our book's Discord space

Join the book's Discord Workspace for Latest updates, Offers, Tech happenings around the world, New Release and Sessions with the Authors:

https://discord.bpbonline.com

APPENDIX D:

Common HTTP Response Codes

This section will provide a list of common HTTP response codes. There are other HTTP codes; however, the following table is useful for deciphering common response codes while troubleshooting a problem:

HTTP Response Code	Description
200	Ok
301	Redirect
302	Temporary redirect
304	Not modified
400	Bad request
401	Unauthorized
403	Forbidden
404	Resource not found
405	Method not allowed
500	Server error
502	Bad gateway
503	Service unavailable

Table Appendix D.1: *A listing of common HTTP response codes*

Join our book's Discord space

Join the book's Discord Workspace for Latest updates, Offers, Tech happenings around the world, New Release and Sessions with the Authors:

https://discord.bpbonline.com

APPENDIX E:
Common Color Codes

This appendix will provide a short list of commonly used colors, along with their **red, green, blue (RGB)**, and hexadecimal codes. These codes are standard across most web and GUI frameworks:

Color	Codes			
	Red	Green	Blue	Hex
Black	0	0	0	000000
Dark Blue	0	0	139	00008B
Blue	0	0	255	0000FF
Dark Green	0	128	0	008000
Green	0	255	0	00FF00
Cyan	0	255	255	00FFFF
Maroon	128	0	0	800000
Purple	128	0	128	800080
Dark Purple	128	0	192	8000C0
Gray	128	128	128	808080
Brown	165	42	42	A52A2A

Color	Codes			
	Red	**Green**	**Blue**	**Hex**
Silver	192	192	192	C0C0C0
Red	255	0	0	FF0000
Magenta	255	0	255	FF00FF
Orange	255	165	0	FFA500
Yellow	255	255	0	FFFF00
White	255	255	255	FFFFFF

Table Appendix E.1: *A listing of common colors and their codes.*

Join our book's Discord space

Join the book's Discord Workspace for Latest updates, Offers, Tech happenings around the world, New Release and Sessions with the Authors:

https://discord.bpbonline.com

APPENDIX F:

Garbage Collection

Garbage collection is a necessary function of the JVM. While lower-level languages like C require the developer to manage their memory usage, Java uses garbage collection to remove out-of-scope objects from memory. Different versions of Java will default to different methods to achieve this. This is a short list of the different Java garbage collectors:

Name	Java versions	Relevant settings	Notes
Concurrent Mark and Sweep (CMS)	5-8	`-XX:+UseConcMarkSweepGC`	Proper CMS configuration requires many different parameters. See the OpenJDK documentation for more information.
Garbage First Collector (G1GC)	7-	`-XX:+UseG1GC` `-XX:MaxGCPauseMillis`	Default GC as of Java 9.
Z Garbage Collector (ZGC)	15-	`-XX:+UseZGC`	
Shenandoah Garbage Collector	17-	`-XX:+UseShenandoahGC`	

Table Appendix F.1: *A list of Java garbage collectors and common parameters.*

Note: The versions listed for each garbage collector represent the versions where the collector is considered *production-ready* and not in a status of *deprecated*.

It is recommended to set the parameters concerning the size of the Java heap rather than rely on a default calculation. Some collectors (like G1GC) recommend only setting a subset of these parameters (for example, **-Xmn** should not be used with G1GC). Here are the JVM size parameters:

Parameter	Description
-Xmx	Maximum size of the JVM memory heap.
-Xms	Initial size of the JVM memory heap.
-Xmn	Size of the **new generation** space in the JVM memory heap.

Table Appendix F.2: A list of the heap sizing parameters for Java.

More information on Java heap and garbage collection parameters can be found in the Oracle documentation on *Java Hotspot VM Options*: **https://www.oracle.com/java/technologies/javase/vmoptions-jsp.html**.

Join our book's Discord space

Join the book's Discord Workspace for Latest updates, Offers, Tech happenings around the world, New Release and Sessions with the Authors:

https://discord.bpbonline.com

Index

Made in United States
Orlando, FL
20 January 2024

42722401R00237